Books by Deborah Aubrey-Peyron

Miraculous Interventions™ Series:

MI- I *Miraculous Interventions™*

MI-II *Modern Day Priests, Prophets, Pastors &
Everyday Visionaries*

MI-III *2012 The Miraculous Year*

MI-IV *The Gathering Season*

MI-V *The Small, Still Voice*

MI-VI *The Warning*

MI-VII *The Saving of America*

MI-VIII *Extraordinary Miracles*

Best of Miraculous Interventions™ [these are books 1-4]

Best of Miraculous Interventions™ Books V - VIII

Sampler Miraculous Interventions™ Book

Christmas Chaos!

Christmas Chaos! Coloring book

An Old Man's Christmas by Ronald J. Aubrey and
Deborah Aubrey-Peyron

*Deb's Christmas Cookbook, Four Generations
of Family Recipes*

Let's Take a Walk, Dave, The David Becker Story

You are My Sunshine Co-written with Lisa Wisdom

My Story, Richard Riddell Mosely

*My Faith Journey, Dennis Murphy,
Miracles I Have Experienced*

#20?

Best of

Miraculous Interventions™
Books V - VIII

by *Deborah Aubrey-Peyron*

with bonus previews of
Deb's Christmas Cookbook,
Four Generations of Family Recipes
and "**Five Generations,** *Stories from My Father*" by Ronald J. Aubrey edited by Deborah Aubrey-Peyron

Home Crafted Artistry & Printing
New Albany, IN 47150

ISBN: 978-1-7323437-9-5

"Miraculous Interventions™ V, The Small, Still Voice" copyright © 2017 by Deborah Aubrey-Peyron. All rights reserved. Published by Home Crafted Artistry & Printing 2017 with permission. ISBN-13: 978-0-9974347-4-3

"Miraculous Interventions™ VI: The Warning" copyright 2017 by Deborah Aubrey-Peyron. All rights reserved. Published by Home Crafted Artistry & Printing 2017 with permission. ISBN 13: 978-0-9974347-6-7

"Miraculous Interventions™ VII: The Saving of America" copyright 2018 by Deborah Aubrey-Peyron. All rights reserved. Published by Home Crafted Artistry & Printing in 2018 with permission. ISBN 13: 978-0-9974347-7-4

"Miraculous Interventions™ VIII: Extraordinary Miracles" copyright 2019 by Deborah Aubrey-Peyron. All rights reserved. Published by Home Crafted Artistry & Printing in 2019 with permission. ISBN 13: 978-1-7323437-7-1

"Deb's Christmas Cookbook, Four Generations of Family Recipes Released 2016 by Deborah Aubrey-Peyron. All Rights reserved. Published by Home Crafted Artistry & Printing in 2016 with permission. ISBN 13: 978-0-9974347-2-9

"Five Generations, Stories from My Father" copyright 2015 Ronald J. Aubrey. All rights reserved. Published by Home Crafted Artistry & Printing in 2015 with permission. ISBN 13: 978-0-9964089-1-2

Home Crafted Artistry & Printing
2404 Scenic Drive NE, #6, Lanesville IN 47136
Contact information:
e-mail: HomeCraftedArtistry@yahoo.com
e-mail: peyronsinjesus@yahoo.com
Cover design by Mary Dow Bibb Smith   Photographs are author's family photos

"...whatsoever ye do,

do all to the glory of God."

I Cor. 10:31b KJV

TABLE OF CONTENTS

Miraculous Interventions™ VII

The Saving of America

Miraculous Interventions™ VIII

Extraordinary Miracles

**Deb's Christmas Cookbook, Four Generations
of Family Recipes…and Stories** 286

Five Generations, Stories from My Father

Miraculous Interventions V

Small Still Voice
An Intimate Walk with God

"Be still and know that I am God"
Psalm 46:10 KJV

DOWNLOADS

(January, 2016)

I was sick with a mild stomach flu; crummy still. I was on my way to yet another bathroom visit. "Sorry" was my companion. I spoke with the Lord. I heard the word, *"beset."* I believed it.

"Lord, I don't know if I can handle an *end of the world* thingy while I'm sick. I'm not that strong. When Jesus makes his appearance, I'm not keen on being here during a nuclear war. Rapture, please? I know you can't tell me when it is, but maybe You could tell me the season it belongs to?"

I really didn't expect an answer...but there it was. God was right there with me in the midst of my misery.

"Count six months and three years."
"September 2019?"
"Yes."

"Lord, I have read Your book, Revelations. I know in there, before a (nuclear) holocaust, there is a treaty signed. I know of no treaty that has been signed for peace."

"Your president (Mr. Obama) **signed a treaty in November** (2015) **with Iran, hoping it would bring peace."**
"Oh my. Oh my. Yes, Sir. Yes Sir."

I thought back to a conversation I'd had with a female pastor several years back. She felt that Jesus would come back during the Jewish fall festivals. She just wasn't sure of the year.

10

So what could have changed the original timeline? What could have happened in the world that could put off—even for a season—the three-and-a-half years the Lord God mentioned?

A non-politician—politician. A patriotic billionaire from New York showed up on the scene just in the nick of time.

(June 1)

"It is the time of good versus evil. You will receive a second chance depending on who you elect. It will change history. If you elect her, it will be dark, and the last year. If you elect Trump, he represents light and you will have an extended time."

I later understood Mr. Trump had an anointing like the Persian king, Cyrus from the Old Testament. Daniel, I think.

I heard in the fall of 2016, ***"If they will elect him, I won't let the other side steal it."***

(November 9th)

Donald J. Trump became the 45th President of the United States and Mike Pence became Vice-President.

"You have a reprieve. Make good use of it."

I was overjoyed.

GOD'S HEART
(Early March 2016)

I was preparing our bed for nighttime when I found myself smack into the middle of a very serious conversation.

"Imagine if you had a child and they acted like your enemy. Wouldn't it break your heart?"

"Oh, yes Sir! Yes Sir!"

"It does MINE too, every time MY children act like MY adversary."

"Who is that, Lord?" (I should've asked, "What is that, Lord?" Because that is what He answered.)

"Sin. When people sin on purpose it is as though they deny MY existence. They ignore ME. They don't act like they are MY children."

I felt truly sorry for God with this revelation. I felt He was sharing His heart with me. It broke my heart for Him.

I replied, "I am sorry Lord when I have done this to You. Please forgive me."

I cried myself to sleep.

Chink
(Early March 5)

As I was praying the next morning, the conversation continued. I heard, **"Cursing or swearing is a chink in the armor of a Christian. Do not conform to this world but be transformed through Jesus Christ into one new man."**

Holy with a Small "h"
(April 6)

Mark and I were having an evening by ourselves. We were headed downstairs to watch a couple of episodes of "AD" when I heard the word **"holy."**

I laughed and replied, "Surely you mean with a small h if You are talking to me. But I accept that word. Thank You."

Mark and I watched the television show until 11:30 p.m. We walked upstairs to get ready for bed. By midnight, Mark was asleep, and I wasn't.

"What is it, Lord?"

"Get paper."

"Yes, Sir. Writing paper."

"Drawing paper."

"Huh? Uh, what?" I stammered. I had no drawing paper and hadn't had any for years. That was when I woke my husband.

"Mark, you got any drawing paper?"

"Yes," he replied sleepily. "They are in the office under my desk. Why? What are you drawing?"

"I'm not sure," I replied. "You can see it when I am finished."

Mark was asleep before I finished my sentence.

I retrieved his pad of paper and the only two pencils I could find in the house—very little lead and barely an eraser between them. The poorest of the poor, meager at best.

I came back to bed and sat up with my pillows behind my back. I sat next to Mark. So as not to wake him, I conversed with the Lord in thought.

"What would You like me to draw?"

"Me."

At least I knew I was talking to the Son of the Living God. I chuckled. "Well, Sir, there are several versions of what You look like down here. I'm not sure which one is accurate."

"I'll help you."

"Thanks!" I was elated. "Where would You like me to start?"

"I have two eyes."

At 12:30 at night, the King of Kings decided to be funny. I scolded myself. "Do not fuss at the Savior of the world! Do not call Him a stinker! Do not even think it!"

I said to Him, "Okay, funny man, two eyes it is."

What people need to know about me, and what Jesus already knew when He asked to take this project on, was I am what Daffy Duck lovingly calls a "slop artist." If I can see it, or it is drawn first, I can draw it second. I have successfully, to the line, drawn DaVinci's *Man*, twice. But he had to draw it first. This was no small undertaking the Lord was asking me to do and He knew it.

I started with His eyes. Immediately, I was corrected.

"No. You have it wrong. I lived in an arid desert with lots of sun and wind. My eyes were squinted with lines around them. They were smaller, not rounded."

"Okay. Got it." I drew for a while. Finally, I said, "Better?"

"Yes."

Then I started to draw His nose. And a noble nose it was—straight line. After all, He is the King of Kings. Again, He spoke.

"Uh, no. No. I was born into a Jewish family. A Levite back ground. I had a bigger nose."

"Okay." I erased and started again.

"No. You are being too timid."

I erased once again and drew it again. "Better?" I asked.

"No! I'm a Jew and I look like one!"

By then it was almost one o'clock in the morning. My tired and grumpy me were coming forth.

"Okay! Okay!"

I erased again.

Exasperated I cried out, "Show me!"

That time, as I drew, it took shape and form.

He said, **"Better."**

As I drew more, I saw in my head, visions of Jesus playing as a child on the streets of Nazareth. I saw Mary and Joseph walking behind him. He spoke of the small village where He was raised, His parent's home, and of His earthly background. In my mind, I could see him playing in the streets; laughing with the other children. It was an ordinary start to an extraordinary life that changed the world.

I drew the rest of His face.

"Better. Better."

Jesus had one more comment I thought worthy to write down. Gently, as if speaking to a young child, He said, **"I don't want to upset you, but I'm not white."**

I sat my pencil down at 2:30 a.m. and the Lord stopped speaking. I sat the picture up on Mark's dresser and snuggled next to him.

"Let me know what you think of it when you get up to go to the bathroom."

Of course, Mark had to get up and see it right away. Even in the dark, I could see him smiling. He said one word, "Wow."

The next morning I texted my sister-in-Christ, Katie Yocum.

"I drew Jesus."

Thirty seconds later, I received a reply.

"We'll be right over!"

Katie and her son, Nick—who is an excellent artist—came over that afternoon. I took them back to meet Yeshi.

Katie said, "Wow Deb. It's good."

Then Nick went up to examine the picture with a critical eye. After a few moments of evaluation, he said, "It is a good likeness, a good start."

I was crushed.

"I'm not done?!"

"No," he sighed. "Now, we will give Him dimension and depth."

"You'll instruct me?" I asked.

"Sure!" Nick brightened up like a light bulb!

"Wheee!" I cried.

After all, Jesus equips His saints. I couldn't have finished it without Nick Yocum.

For the next two days, the Yocums came over in the afternoons, (I was typing in the mornings, books you know.) Nick showed me the intricacy of eyes, pulling them forward, shading and hair structure.

Nick gifted me with a fine set of grafting pencils and a great eraser named "Dave."

I hadn't had that much fun drawing since five years before when Ben asked Mark and me to draw and paint with him. Hmmmm. I guess we have another artist in the family.

Obscure
(April 12)
(7:30 a.m.)

"Go to the picture in your Bible."
"Okay, Lord."

It was right after Amos 9:15 in Obadiah. There were only two lines underlined in the two pages of the book of Obadiah. It is an obscure chapter and verses 15a and 17a.

15) "For the day of Adonai is near for all nations..."
17) "But on Mt. Tziyon* there will be a holy remnant who will escape... my sheep know me."

Do you know Him?
I am still trying...

* Mt. Tziyon is the spelling in CJB. More commonly known as Mt. Zion in English.

Closed-Eyes Vision
(April 13)

I had gotten up to go to the bathroom at 4:30 that morning and went back to our comfy bed. I closed my eyes expecting to go right back to sleep. Instead of seeing darkness, in the dark, clouds began to form.

First, I saw the Eye of God. I saw that He saw all.

Second, I saw the face of Jesus.

Third, His face turned into a lamb. And out of that Lamb, He spit lambs out of His mouth onto the Earth.

Fourth, I saw the Earth. At first it was pretty.

Fifth, then I saw a huge nuclear explosion cloud. It was horrible and scary.

Sixth, it all went to nothingness. It was done.

After the day be fore's word in the Bible, it all had an ominous feeling to it.

Interpretation

When Jesus became the Lamb, out of His mouth lambs started popping out. They were His apostles and believers. The lambs of God were sent from the Lamb of God. I heard Scripture, **"Peter, feed my sheep."**

David's Turn to Tell a Story
(May 8th, 2016, 8:58 p.m.)
By David Merk

On Mother's Day 2016, Thomas Andrew, our youngest son, decided to take his wife and his mommah out to a five-star restaurant to celebrate. I had celebrated the day before with oldest son Ben and his wife, Amanda with gifts and special time together. Although I wasn't able to spend time with my middle son David, he called that evening and we had a nice chat.

After our talk, I kept getting the feeling I needed to check Facebook. I thought in my head, "Oh, Lord, there will be lots of nice Mother's Day wishes on it. I have already seen Ben and Amanda on Thursday and Friday. And saw Andy and Sam on Friday and today. I heard from David, what else could there be?"

The feeling persisted, and as I got ready for bed, I turned my phone on once more, looking for what, I did not know. And there it was. The third post down on my page, a long letter from my son, David Merk. Evidently, it was his turn to tell a story. Ben is right. David really is the best writer of us all...

David's Story

Growing up in Lanesville, with two brothers and being raised by a single mom, I had no idea how poor we were.

All of our school supplies were donated.

Our groceries were donated.

20

Christmas was donated.

But every Sunday my brothers and I would go to church and when they were passing the basket, mom would give us, maybe a dollar or a couple of dimes to donate.

I remember one Sunday, she gave my brothers' quarters and me a nickel. I asked her if I too could have a quarter to put in the collection and I'll never forget her reply.

"Honey, that's all the money we have in the world."

Every Sunday she would give everything we had, however much or little it was, so the church could help families like ours.

We wound up moving to the Charlestown projects. She told my brothers and I to draw pictures of what we thought it would look like. Even though it was smaller and government-subsidized, she made it sound like a castle. She knew we had lost our home. She knew how poor we were, and she still gave everything she had.

Deborah Aubrey-Peyron, you are the strongest person I know. And even though I don't like it when you tag me in things or comment on my wall, I am so grateful that you were so strong for us when it would have been much easier to sell Paul or Thomas to the gypsies.

You taught me how to give with all of my heart, and because of everything you've been through I know I can make it through anything life throws at me.

You are the world's best mom. Happy Mother's Day!

Well, after I was through crying while reading his post the first time, I replied to him on Facebook, "David Merk, you really noticed. Thank you son. You and your brothers (the ones I didn't sell to the gypsies) have made me very proud. I love you, Momma."

David replied shortly after that with, "I forgot to say this up there but I love you too, Momma."

Insight in an Instant
(May 15)

God was waiting for me...information was downloaded to me as I awoke.

"Mark, you heard the things he said to me and did nothing." I was perturbed. I shook my husband awake from his deep sleep. It was the wrong way to wake someone up on a Sunday morning.

It was in that instant, God revealed the real Mark to me.

"He's Peter the apostle...."

I was startled. "What?" I stammered.

Knowledge downloaded. Peter did not always come to the aid of Christ. But he did love Him and grew His church.

"He (Mark) may not always protect you, but I will always protect you. Cling to ME."

Mark came back from the bathroom and joined the unheard conversation. "I believe you have been special from the get-go. God saved your life and your mother dedicated you back to the Lord. You have been special ever since."

It was as if he had been in on the whole conversation the whole time. I started shouting.

"Mark Peyron, it is not mere man that showed you this! Thank you for believing and understanding. Do you want to know what the Lord calls you?"

Mark looked at me quizzically.

I laughed and said, "God calls you Peter.... and I am not Jesus by any means! But God has revealed things to you, too. I love you with all my heart!" I fairly jumped into his arms.

Then I was shown my family member that had made the ruckus.

He speaks curses out of his mouth. Curses walk with him. Rebuke them when they come. This is why gifts come from his wife, not him. She picks out Holy books for you, and knew the video you wanted for Christmas last year. She has a spiritual connection with God. Look at her church.

Then I was shown the Bible. In my heart I heard the scripture of Phillip and the eunuch. How the eunuch had been searching for God, and Phillip taught him and baptized him that very day.

Then I heard God's voice, **"Do I love the eunuch any less?"**

"No, Sir!"

I realized then that it was God that had sent her to the House of Ecclesia. [church name]

Then I was shown other family members. I saw them in relation to Saul and David and Jonathan. One was a Jonathan. I saw the other family member as Saul. Saul for no reason went mad with hatred for David—who was also younger than Saul, and who walked with God—and wanted to kill him, too. It was Jon that loved David and warned him. Even though Saul and Jonathan were from the same household, they had not the same spirit. Just like in my family. The Saul figure had been given over to a reprobate mind. How sad.

I heard over and over:

"Nothing is new under the sun. These are all the same spirits, good and evil. Be grateful for the side you are on."

Then I heard myself say, "*As for me and my house, we shall serve the Lord.*"

6:32 a.m.

I was shown France. Their statue of Liberty. Diane and Linda were shown a bomb would hit Florida. Well, on a map, France and Florida look alike. We checked France on Israel News Now with Steven Ben Nun. There was a great upheaval going on.

I asked the Lord, "Where would you like me to go?"

He replied, **"Jeremiah 51:29."**

"The earth quakes and writhes as Adonai designs against Bavel [Babylon] are fulfilled, to make the land of Bavel a ruin, with no one living there."

The dire proposal caused pain in my stomach for the earth. I asked another question.

"What should we be doing?!"

It was as if He was right there with me in my prayers.

"51:27"

"Yes, Sir!"

"Raise up a banner in the land, blow the shofar among the nations."

"Remember, a remnant was saved."

7:30 a.m.

Again, a signal came. (Still awake.)

"Jeremiah 50:31"

"Got it!"

"I am against you, arrogant (nation), says Adonai ELOHEIM-Tzav'ot. For your day has come,

the time for you to be punished. The arrogant (nation) will stumble and fall, and no one will lift him up again. I will set his cities on fire, and it will devour everything around him."

This was the very prophesy of David Wilkerson. ["The Cross and the Switchblade" was his autobiography.]

On and on came scripture to us; me or Mark, or whoever had come by to pray over the two days.

If those who are called by My name, repent of their sins, turn from their wicked ways, I will heal their land and restore their nation.

"1ˢᵗ Thes 5:4-11"

"But you brothers, are not in the dark, so that the day shall take you by surprise like a thief; for you are all people that belong to the light, who belong to the day. We don't belong to the night or to darkness, so let's not be asleep, like the rest are; on the contrary, let us stay alert and sober. People who sleep, sleep at night; and people who get drunk, get drunk at night. But since we belong to the day, let us stay sober, putting on trust and love as a breastplate and the hope of being delivered as a helmet. For God has not intended that we should experience His fury, but that we should gain deliverance through our Lord Yeshua the Messiah, who died on our behalf so that whether we are alive or dead, we may live along with Him. Therefore, encourage each other and build each other up—just as you are doing."

We are living this right now.

And this is why we are watchers of the times we are in now, and the times shortly to come.

All Power and Glory

(Nov. 2)

This is a right now story!

A powerful dream while at Andy and Sam's.

The word of God was a weapon to use against the devil. We were in a fight against evil. Every time we used the words from the Bible, they turned into rocks and we hurled them at the devil. He and his minions ducked and ran.

Interpretation: Victory is coming! Evil is on the run! Keep praying and using the word of God.

Loving Completely
(Dec. 30)
(4:30 a.m.)

Have you ever felt, with or without cause, that everything you did in life turned out well for everyone but yourself? Well, that was where I was that early morning. I turned to my best friend and told Him I was sorry.

"I'm sorry I have failed you."

"You haven't failed. How could you have failed when you have loved all that I gave you?"

With tears and sniffles, I still wasn't getting the real message.

"Because I couldn't do enough. I never had enough to do with."

Wisdom fell in to my heart and ears as Jesus spoke ever so softly to me, **"You can never do enough when you love completely. There is never enough in this life to match love, because you never run out of love to give. That is the ache of loving completely. You give away everything until there is nothing left to give but yourself. That is what I did. I gave myself completely."**

"You sure did. You sure did."

Lo! I Come Quickly!

(Jan. 30)

I was doing dishes in the early morning. Thinking of nothing, really. All of a sudden, my thoughts were not my own. I could see clearly, why Jesus had to come back quickly, lest there be no faith found on Earth. And it was not what you would think, or even what we've been taught.

It is not because of Christians becoming unbelievers. It's because of the rise of Islam. Three countries in the Middle East and east, used to be Coptic Christian, Hindu and Buddhist. But over the last 100 years, they have been overcome by Muslims with the sword. Now, the same is happening over in Europe. At the rate of things going on over there, with all the unrest and civil disobedience by the arrival of the new Syrians, Germany won't last another 20 years. Sweden is in trouble, as is Canada, and France is all but gone.

Maranatha, Yeshua.

The Same Dream
(Feb. 10)

Katie Yocum and I had the same dream on the same night at almost the same hour.

We both saw hail and brimstones falling out of the sky. I started crying out in my dream, "It's now! It's happening now!"

Second Dream
(Remember this!)

I saw two sides battling each other. I knew one was called the New World Order and the other was the Freedom Fighters. They were free in Christ Jesus.

Then I heard a loud voice from out of the sky. **"The Old lion stood first for freedom."** I knew immediately it was England and Brexit. Brexit is the exiting of England out of the European Union. British + exit = Brexit.

"The Young lion followed suit." That was America with the election of Donald Trump.

Britain First

America First

Then I heard a loud voice cry out, **"This is the prophecy I have been telling you!"**

It was repeated four times.

Two nights later, I saw fighting again. This time it was other worldly. I had to use discernment, and gifts to figure out who was who. And in an instant, I went from the dream, *to a vision:*

I stood in front of a large, two-story building. It had four white columns on the front porch. The sky was light, not a trace of blue in it, just simply

31

lit up. It was the light of God that shone all around. Peace and serenity lived there.

The outside of the building was made with smooth white Bedford stone. I sighed a deep sigh.

I looked toward the angel and asked with mounting excitement, "Is this my home?"

We walked toward the building, and went inside. It opened into a large foyer. On the other side of the foyer, was the living room, divided by a double doorway leading in. Along the living room wall, was a beautiful marble wall table. Everything was simple elegance. I did not see any furniture in the living room.

I asked again, "Is this mine?!"

Down the hall to my left, I saw doors leading to other rooms. To the right was an open area for a dining room. As we walked past another wall with an opening, I felt it was a cooking area, or a kitchen of a sort. At the end of the house was a large doorway that led to an outside covered porch. I could see alabaster and jeweled patio furniture. It had much of a Greek feel to it. An open area for visiting.

I asked the angel who was with me, "Are you showing me this for here in Heaven, or a representation of what is still to come on earth?"

Before he could answer, I was back in my body in our bedroom. I still ponder what it all meant.

Don't Forget
(Mid-Feb.)

Do you wonder if you are really making a difference for the Kingdom of God? Watch your enemies....that'll tell you.

Around the middle of February, Mark and I were shopping at a national store in New Albany. I was looking in a bin, (possibly towels as I remember) when another lady walked up and looked in the bin too. She was very ordinary looking. Short dark hair, dressed casually, middle-class. I thought she was fine until she opened her mouth and started to speak.

She said quietly, "So when is the exact date that Jesus is coming back?"

Before I could form a thought, I spoke clearly out of my spirit, "I would be a liar if I told you I knew the exact date Jesus was coming back!"

Immediately my armor was on. My face was set and my eyes were sharp. I was not friendly.

She looked from side to side with her eyes rolled upward in a sly motion. Curtly once, she nodded her head, and put down what she was looking at. She left quickly. The unwelcome visitor went in one direction and I went in the other. I headed straight for my husband!

What does this tell us?

The devil knows that time is short.

And he can tell who is walking close with the Lord and watching the times we are living in.

I wondered, could he see the light of God and the Blood of Jesus on me?

After all, I am a scribe. Now, not only for miracles, signs and wonders, but as a watcher for the times we are living in.

Everyone – look for Jesus, point to Jesus.

He is coming back.

Out of My Body
(Mid-Feb.)

It had been almost 20 years since I had been taken out of my body and seen from space the happenings on the Earth. I thought that time was over in my life. After all, it had been so long...

I was once again taken out in space. I had no fear, no gasping. It was very ordinary to me. I was sure I was with my angel.

I turned and looked toward the Earth. I saw our planet, and not far off from it, I saw a red, larger planet heading straight for the earth. I knew it meant sudden destruction.

I started screaming for all I was worth, "Stay Your hand, Lord! Stay Your hand!" As the planet moved closer and closer, I continued to yell, "Lord, please, stay Your hand!!"

I had sheer panic for the inhabitants of the Earth.

It ended as quickly as it came.

And Then There Weren't Ten
(April 3)

"I know it's a scary thought. But if this world is going the way we think it is, you've got to get your teeth taken care of. We can't have you dying from a tooth infection." As melodramatic as it sounded, I was perfectly serious.

Katie sighed. "You're right. And my tax money will just about pay for it all." She stopped for a moment, then continued. "Will you come with me and hold my hand?"

"I'll do better than that," I replied with a smile. "Ten teeth out at once is a big deal. You and Nick can come and stay with us while you recuperate. Let me wait on you."

"Hmmm, almost worth it!" Katie exclaimed.

"Dr. Cook is an excellent dentist. He has helped me and Ben. And you've been to him once before. We will all take very good care of you." I smiled back.

As the day drew near, in my thoughts, I wondered what I had talked Katie into. I knew she would be healthier in the long run, but in the short run, she might want to kick me a time or two!

The Sunday before her appointment, Katie's church, Kay's Chapel prayed for her at morning and evening service. They prayed a speedy recovery. And they had seen miracles; they knew how to call them down. Mark and I prayed for a

"Fr. Bernie-faster-than-normal" healing. That way we would know God was all over that mix!

Mark and I spoke to Katie and Nick on Sunday evening.

Katie started the conversation, "Oh, I'm so nervous! What if I oversleep?"

With bravado I replied, "Nobody is oversleeping! All will be well! See you before 8 in the morning!" Well, weren't those famous last words....

Sleepily, I rolled over and peeked one eye open. Daylight... daylight!

"Waaaaaaaaa!!" My discord resounded throughout the house.

"Mark! What time is it? Didn't you set the alarm?!"

Mark looked at the clock. He moaned as I threw covers everywhere.

"I'm sorry, hon. I forgot to turn it on!"

I was already in flight mode.

"They will be here any minute!" I cried.

Zoom to the bathroom! Potty, check. Brush teeth, check. Brush hair, (well, sort a) check! Zoom to the bedroom! Clothes!! Matching does not apply. On went anything. Check! I was still hopping into one shoe when Katie and Nick arrived. Mark went out to greet them and help carry things in for their three-day stay.

Katie came in smiling. She could barely contain herself. By the look on her face, my husband—the rat—had told.

Katie said with a smile, "Well, you look like you've been up for hours!"

Now, I am telling you honestly, I don't remember my response. Whether for your benefit or mine, I guess it didn't bear repeating.

Don't worry, the story gets better from here....

We arrived at Dr. Cook's office. Katie took the elevator and I took the stairs. I thought I'd be cute and try to beat the elevator up to the fourth floor. Was not and still is not a good idea. I was so out of breath, I thought I might pass out. So this is what went through my head...

"Come on! Really?! Get it together!"

Katie and I walked down the hall to Dr. Cook's office. I was still trying to do a controlled breathe. My heart was pounding.

As Katie was checking in, I was still having a conversation with my body.

"Look. If I pass out, I can't do what I'm here to do; help Katie. The doctor won't let me drive her home. You have to cooperate. I won't race the elevator anymore, I promise!"

Finally, everything came into line. I knew, somewhere in me, something was amiss. But I had no time to worry about it then.

After a half-hour or so, they called Katie's name. We both stood up, I hugged her and she went back.

The nurse at the front desk said she should be out in an hour. I waited. I had brought two books to read. Of course, that was when people started texting on both of our phones.

"Is Katie in with the doctor yet?"

"How's Katie doing?"

"Is it over?"

I replied to each one. I don't think I had a chance to read two paragraphs. Then, in walked a neighbor, named Money, who had driven another lady to get her dental work done. I had a wonderful time catching up with her. Before I knew it, the nurse called me to go back. Katie was done.

I walked around the corner and Katie was sleeping soundly.

"She did great!" The nurse replied cheerily.

"Wonderful!"

"You can wake her."

"Katie? Hi! They said it went great! Just like we prayed!"

Katie opened her eyes and smiled. Even with a mouthful of cotton, she was already trying to speak. "Mmmffflllluummpp."

"No speaking! If you want something, hold up fingers. One for yes, two for no."

Well, she was so groggy, the instructions didn't take. The doctor came in and spoke with us. He handed out instructions and prescriptions. He shook my hand and off he went to another patient.

I was instructed to go get my car and pull up to the patient loading area. I pulled up just in time to see them wheeling Katie outside in a wheelchair.

"Katie, I've got your instructions and your prescriptions, and your purse. Is there anywhere else you need to go? Hold up one finger for yes, and two for no."

The dear lady held up two fingers, then one finger, then shook her head. She was still trying to talk. I laughed.

39

"Okay. I won't ask you anything else till your medicine wears off."

It was a quiet ride home. Katie slept off and on.

We were home before Nick went to work. He was downstairs asleep. I shouted down the stairs. "Nick! We're home! Your mom's back!"

"Oh! I'm on my way up!"

I already had Katie's bed ready, and an extra soft blanket for her to use. I changed the cotton in her mouth, and Nick and I discussed who would pick up her medication. It was decided he would take it in and I would pick it up. Katie fell asleep on the couch with her jacket still on.

Our mutual friend, Deb Grimes was already calling to be of help. But she sounded awful herself!

"What's wrong with you?" I asked.

"Oh Deb I have been so sick! My allergies turned into something else. I feel like death warmed over. I went to the doctor in between taking Brian to the hospital. His pain is back." How could so much happen to one family in a week?

"I'm so sorry, Deb. Listen, I think we have everything under control here. We won't need your help. You take care of yourself. See you Saturday."

Nick got ready for work, and Katie was asleep on the couch. I took that time to pull out of our cupboard anything I thought she could eat. And she had brought plenty of back up food too. If she was up to it, we planned on two family movie nights in a row.

Nick took the prescriptions and dropped them off. Fifteen minutes later I ran and picked them up. I came back and woke Katie. It was time for some broth soup and medicine. Her bleeding had let up enough to be able to get something down.

Katie looked at me with her sad, big brown eyes and said, "This is hard."

"I know," I replied. "But every day will be better. I just have a feeling."

While having lunch, Mark called to see how Katie was doing. I put him on speaker. I knew if anyone could make her smile, it would be him.

Well, she was already in true-Katie form!

Mark said in his loud, booming voice, "Well, Katie, how are you?!"

Without missing a beat, she replied, "Oh, Mark! She's making me scrub the floors!"

I rolled my eyes. How had I not seen it coming?

Mark laughed a hearty laugh. "Oh no!"

Katie's smile was back. And it had not even been two hours post op. Health and healing were already on their way. During the course of her recovery, she only had to take two pain pills twice. And after twelve hours, none at all. Just simple Tylenol for her headache. Her bleeding stopped by four the same afternoon. Wow. Good job.

The evenings were spent with fun meals for the guys and anything I could puree for Katie. Abbott and Costello were the order for each evening. The second night, Nick and I went and got ice-creams for everyone, our treat!

As our time together came to a close, Katie and I recapped what an amazing recovery she'd had. By her third day, I couldn't hold her down. She helped with dinner. When we rinsed her gums, they were already looking healthy, back to pink, in just three days!

All I could think to say was, "Wow."

God had truly shown up "large and in charge" of her healing. You could practically feel His presence everywhere we were.

Katie and Nick went home Wednesday evening after a series of thunder storms had passed us by. All had gone well for her. I couldn't have been happier. It looked like she would be getting her new teeth sooner than everyone anticipated.

Remember how I had been out of breath four days earlier? And I wondered what was up?

By the end of that same week, I went to the doctor with a light touch of Bronchitis and an upper respiratory infection diagnosis.

There was no time for sickness...we had a gathering planned for that Saturday. And I was in no shape to cook.

Care to guess who came over to help me so I could rest?

Katie Kost Yocum.

You see, God allows the good that goes around to come around....

Never Too Late
(May 15)

It was 5 in the morning when my stomach began to hurt. I was nervous because I was going to give a speech later that day. And God knew my heart. Immediately in my head, I heard, **"Go to facebook."**

I rolled over and checked my home page. I scrolled down to the 4th post when I saw a song video put out by *Voices of Lee*, by Lee University in Cleveland TN.

I knew it was for me. But I dared not open it with a sleeping husband lying beside me. I saved it on my feed for later. I got up and took medicine for a sour stomach and went back to sleep.

At 9 a.m. that morning while in the kitchen, my heart was pressed to go back in and look for it. I did. And as usual, God was spot on and on time. The song was about being a child of God and knowing the power therein. It was mingled with the song, "There is power in the name of Jesus to break every chain."

Before I knew it, I was on the floor weeping. The verses spoke of a child called to God's duty while in their mother's womb—just like me. At the end of the video, I got up off the floor without any more pain or anxiety.

I was even given two words on what to speak about that night and how it should go.

"There is never too young an age to set a goal."

*"And there is never too old an age to see
it achieved."*

That night I started with the two quotes. I
followed with examples in my life of how the
quotes applied:

"At four years old, I used to make make-
believe books. I would color pictures and scribble
down below them. My wonderful momma would
staple them together for me. I stacked them up.

"At 6 years old I started first grade. The
nuns taught me how to read and write. I could
finally put together pictures and words. I started
bringing them home. Seeing these, my momma
threw away my old books. I cried and cried.

"'Momma, why, oh why did you throw away
my books before I knew words?'

The wise old sage replied, 'Because now
you will write books that people can read.'"

I paused, for effect, looking at the audience.

"50 long years later, I was honored with
Pope Benedict XVI's apostolic blessing and my
first two books, *Miraculous Interventions,* and
*Miraculous Interventions II, Modern Day Priests,
Prophets, Pastors and Everyday Visionaries,* were
placed in the Vatican Library in Rome, Italy.

Never give up!"

I received two rounds of applause that night.

Divine Appointment
at a Funeral Home
(June 4, 1 p.m.)

(It was not my intention to end book V in this way. But in the last week before publishing, this all came about at once. I felt it very important, and not to be left out.)

For well over a month, Debbie Grimes was insistent about us going to a meeting together in Louisville, Kentucky. She wanted me to meet John and Carol Leary who had been ordered by God to make a refuge out of their home and land. Of course they obeyed. She thought it was important; a God thingy.

I finally consented...and boy am I glad I did!

John and Carol Leary are Catholic ministers for the Lord. John has heard locutions for 24 years. Almost every day when John is at a devotional place, at a mass after communion, or at adoration on most nights, he hears and writes what the Lord God tells him. Wow. What a calling.

Now, by trade, he was a Chemist, retired after 29 years at Kodak in Rochester, New York. And you can tell he was by the way he explains details in his teachings. He is one sharp cookie.

His wife, Carol is equally as sharp. After all, she has to keep up with him! And she's a fantastic story teller to boot! I reckon we share something in common.

They are both small in stature; not a one of us is over five-feet-three inches. And they are my elders by almost 15 years. Yet they appear ageless, with energy and joy abounding!

But I am getting ahead of the story! After all, I haven't even arrived in the building they were speaking at yet...

Deb and Dave Grimes pulled up to our driveway to pick me up. I was ready on time. Deb knocked on our door and away we went. We all shared small talk on our way. Deb spoke about a little of the information we were going to hear during the scheduled three-hour talk. It sounded right up my alley.

Dave drove us to downtown Louisville's west end. I won't say it looked deserted, but there was not a lot of activity going on that we could see. We even passed up the funeral home it was being held in. Dave drove around the block and the second time through, we found the right driveway.

As we were walking up to the entrance of the building, Dave noticed a man lying in the street. The man was moving, and speaking loudly to a couple of men on the other sidewalk.

Since I was originally from Louisville, I knew at that end of town, you had to take precautions. I did not feel anything in my spirit to go check things out.

We knocked on the door and a man appeared from the hallway. He pointed to another door around the corner.

I said, "Come on Deb. He wants us to come in the other door."

Dave was fixed on what was going on in the street. He said, "Why do you suppose there is a man lying in the street? He wasn't there a minute ago?" I could feel Dave's concern.

Deb even asked if we should go over and give assistance. I shook my head no and motioned her along with me to the other doorway.

I replied, "He's talking with the other two men, maybe he knows them and they will take care of him. Maybe he's fallen, or has been drinking. We don't live around here and don't know what's up."

Dave followed us inside a few minutes later. He gave explanation of what had happened.

"The man in the street was just walking along when another man attacked him with a hammer. The other men he was talking to went over and called the police and an ambulance for him."

"I'm so sorry he was hurt," I said. "I hope the ambulance comes soon."

Deb, always the helpful one, said to me again, "Deb, do you think you should go over and offer assistance?"

I looked at her with a blank expression and asked, "With what, Deb? I have no medical triage equipment with me. The best we can do from here is pray for the man." One of the first things they teach you in nursing school is never go into an area that hasn't been cleared of danger—especially if you are alone. And it sounded like a pretty good rule to me to keep at the time.

Deb led us in a short prayer for the unknown assailed, and we walked into the meeting room.

The back two rows were filled with people who came to hear the Leary's speak. Deb, on the other hand, wanted to be right up front where we wouldn't miss a thing! I myself longed for the back.

So up front we went!

You see, I had promised the Lord in my heart, I would sit quietly in the back and take notes. Not tell a bit of my story. After all, the day was about the Leary's. No questions were in my heart. But from the moment Deb plunked herself down in her seat, all smiles and talking, I knew the day I had thought I was there to have, was not at all in the plans...live and learn.

Since the primary speakers had not arrived yet, Deb stood and introduced herself to the people in the back rows. In turn, they introduced themselves and how they ended up at the meeting. As others were coming in, Deb told about Fr. Bernie, his ministry and his candles— of which she had brought a few. And then I told of my book that had Fr. Bernie stories in it. As we finished our conversation, John and Carol walked in the room with all of their books with them. The meeting soon came to order.

Since several of us were new faces to the Leary's, John went over their background. He spoke on receiving current messages on Pentecost. He said he felt much like the apostles in the Upper Room, inspired by the Holy Spirit to write and speak. It comes to him as inner Locutions. The Spirit of God rests on him. John called it the Spirit of Love. That ever since the tongues of fire appeared over the apostles and Mary-the 120 in the room, and they received gifts of the Holy Spirit, it is our duty to pass these gifts down to our families too.

Here is a paraphrase of some of John's conversation.

"Many people in today's society, have little gods. People have made sports their god that are played on Sundays. This is especially serious because the children are not attending Mass. Big homes and positions can also become gods to people. Anything that you place of importance over God is a sin. The first commandment is to love God will all your heart, mind and strength. We have to keep this! In our life review, God will show us this. Things cannot have precedence over God or Jesus. The only way we can come to heaven is through Jesus."

John paused for a moment and then went on.

"Jesus loves all of us. He was God, visiting us in person. He is the only power that can overcome the demons."

The audience nodded their heads with approval.

John said, "At the end of Jesus' time here on earth, he was walking with Peter. He asked Peter three times if he loved Him. Have you ever wondered why Jesus asked him three times?"

Truthfully, I had to say I hadn't wondered, but since John brought it up, I thought it was a great question!

"Jesus asked Peter three times because he denied Jesus three times. Peter repented and he was led to life by the Holy Spirit."

John let that sink in.

"And Judas didn't repent and he was led by satan to his death."

"Jesus told Peter to feed His sheep. What he would bind, would be bound, and what he would release, would be released. That is why Catholics should go to confession once a month.

Forgiveness is essential. No soul should go to God with a mortal sin on it. Guard your soul. God wants friendship, and relationship with you."

John stopped for a moment and gathered his notes from around him. He went on.

"Well I guess I need to give an overview, the message of the big picture. There is an urgency in the messages I have been getting lately. I saw a large football stadium. There came a great wind. I saw it meant life reviews with a warning attached. The Warning is the first of the major events. It will happen during a time of chaos in the world. There will appear to be two suns in the sky on that day. Everyone in the world at the same time will be drawn out of their bodies, and outside of time. Each will experience their own life review from conception to that moment. You will see yourself as God and others see you. You will experience a mini-judgment and what it would be like in the place of heaven, hell or purgatory. The Antichrist is coming, and he will have a short reign during the tribulation. There is a man in Europe who will be leading the charge against Christians. During this time, we will all receive our mini life review. It will be done outside of time. A mini judgement and then go back to our bodies. We will have an opportunity for the next six weeks to repent and confess how we have offended God."

It was a lot of information to take in. John went on.

"There are four types of forgiveness. The first one is confession of your sin. The next one is to ask forgiveness from the people you've offended. The next type is to forgive the ones who have harmed us. And lastly, we have to forgive ourselves. That is important too. And remember, to pray for everyone even those that could be lost."

John switched topics.

"Our friend Marino Restrepo, was captured by the rebels in Columbia and put in a cave. The Lord revealed to him the "economy of the soul." Just as we have the balance of nature in the physical world, there is the balance in the spiritual world. An amount of grace is given to save every family. In Scripture it says, he who has much, more will be given and he who has little, it will be taken away. All the graces rejected by the fallen away ones, are given to the prayer warriors to save them."

"Wow!" In my head, John's explanation of grace being given to one family member because the others did not want it, fairly shouted to me. It in part, explained my life, my children's lives and the blessings Mark and I have seen.

John went on to speak on a sort of timeline. There would be a Warning, and six weeks to repent and make reparation. It would be a time to gather your family, get rid of computers and electrical devices, and for some, to get to refuges in your area. (Safety in numbers.) We would all be guarded by angels. First, Jesus will alert us with an inner locution that it is time to leave for the refuge. We must leave quickly. Our guardian angels will lead us with a small flame and invisible shield to the nearest refuge. The angels have already marked the faithful with the crosses on their foreheads. After the Warning, those who convert will be marked also. This is like in Ezekiel 9:4 *"And the Lord said unto him, "Go through the midst of the city, through the midst of Jerusalem, and set a mark upon the foreheads of the men that sigh and that cry for all the abominations that be done in the midst thereof."* Those with God will recognize each other. John felt there would be invisible crosses on each person's forehead.

Now, before anyone thinks it's a far-fetched concept, Mark and I have been making the sign of the cross on each other's foreheads morning and evening for the past three years. And say blessings over each other. Mark said he felt the Lord tell him it was time to do it. Confirmation.

John said many people will convert after the warning comes. At that time, we have to be ready to spread the Gospel really fast. People will make a choice for God or the devil. God's people will come to us, and the devil's people will come after us. And that is why the saved need refuges at that time. This is a modern-day Exodus.

John mentioned several new inventions that are here now that are not of service to mankind. And some about the political world. He said there was a world-wide implanted chip coming. This is foretold in Revelations 14:9-*10 "And the third angel followed them, saying with a loud voice, "If any man worship the beast and his image, and receive his mark in his forehead, or in his hand, the same shall drink of the wine of the wrath of God, which is poured out without mixture into the cup of his indignation; and he shall be tormented with fire and brimstone in the presence of the holy angels, and in the presence of the Lamb:"* Do not take it! The One World Order will try to take over with it.

There is a large machine called HAARP that controls weather patterns. There are five of them that he knows of. It can cause an earthquake as well as change wind patterns. He believes it has already caused the earthquake in Japan that has caused the nuclear catastrophe to the people and waters abroad. It has caused droughts, Hurricane Sandy, and controls in the jet stream. It is a 60 million dollar project.

These are some of the things that John Leary said would happen:

There is an implantable chip coming. It will have control over you and you will give up your will. Demons are attached to the addictions of sex, drugs, smoking, etc., which is why it is so difficult to break them.

A world famine is coming.

The dropping of a huge bomb could trigger a major war. And the small war could expand to a WWIII. (This was spoken of in Fatima 100 years ago – that nations would be annihilated, and that it would be nuclear. John does not believe it will be a major power that will achieve this but a rogue nation such as North Korea or Iran. Pray this doesn't happen because millions will die.

Martial law is coming.

There will be a division in the Roman Catholic Church.

After each person's life review, and warning, there will be six weeks to get yourself and your family together. You will have to get rid of all of your electrical items.

As the antichrist takes over, Christians will have to go to refuges for safety. He will reign less than 3 ½ years.

At the end of the tribulation, the comet will be seen in the sky, much of the earth's inhabitants will suffer and die. It will hit in the Atlantic Ocean.

The three days of darkness will happen.

Before the comet hits the earth, all believers will be lifted up.

The evil ones will be cast into hell.

And the new face of the earth, Eden will begin again. The Era of Peace will start. Healing will come upon mankind.

I am reporting what he is reporting. I have always believed in a pre-tribulation rapture. That is my hope. But we are brothers in Christ and as I have said many times, I am a tribulation rapture person. I don't care if its pre, mid, or post. I just want to go, with my preference as a pre-trib person. In John and Carol's opinion, they believe in a post-tribulation to be purified as gold is tested in the fire.

Allow me to bring out one point here. For many of our Coptic Christian brothers and sisters that have given their lives for their faith over the last four to five years, the pre-trib has already passed by. For them, we are already in the tribulation days. To them, we are in the zero – seven and countdown. And I can't tell you with a full heart, that they are wrong...

John addressed the political aspect of what is going on and what he called the New World Order. He spoke of the European Union, and how they want to make a North American Union out of Canada, the United States and Mexico. This new One World Order, with those at the top openly worshipping satan, with evidence of their death culture of wars, abortions and euthanasia. John mentioned the chemtrails and what is in them and why it is dangerous for people and what it causes. Jesus has asked them many times to take hawthorn tea or capsules as a way of protecting them against the chemtrails.

John also spoke on the Georgia Guide Stones. They are outside of Atlanta. They believe it was built in 1980. Some call it the "American Stone Henge." There are eight large slabs with writing in the languages of Arabic, Chinese, Cuneiform, Greek, Hindi, Swahili, Hebrew and I believe English.

John said that as long as you follow the Apostles' teachings, you will be fine.

John said to prepare for the end times, for it will happen in our lifetime – those in their 60s and 70s years.

Pray for peace with all you have in you.

John said Mary the Mother of Jesus has a peace plan to follow for the Catholics. Consecrate daily, pray, wear your brown scapular, pray for 15 minutes every day for peace, go to confession and communion.

John did quote several scriptures that were dear to his heart and that Jesus gave him. John 14:1-6. To paraphrase, it speaks of Jesus and heaven. That there are many mansions, and where He goes, He prepares a place for us. And if He prepares a place for us, He will come back and gather us to Himself. Jesus is the Way, the Truth, and the Life. He is the Gatekeeper.

For the Catholics, if you love Jesus, repent of your sins, and are a faithful, pure soul, you will minimize your time in purgatory.

I myself, believe scripture that states, "to be absent from the body is to be present with the Lord." Yet I know Protestants that fight among themselves over this.

John said that now is the time to pray and commend all your children to the Lord. Place your mantle of protection and caring over them. It is yours to pass down to your generations. And stay faithful even through problems. Trust God anyway. Even during our trials in life, God will work things out. Give God thanks and praise.

John has seen the hammer and the sickle take down North Korea, Venezuela, Cuba and many others. John called it the Progressive Left, the Godless Socialism that is trying to destroy families and churches. Once again, please pray for peace that it does not fully spread here in America. It is an annihilator.

John has seen hell. The real hell. There were lots of souls like molten coals and demons. Many people in their soul bodies were suffering. The soul body was burned but not consumed. It never stopped. It is a place that is outside of time, prepared only for the fallen angels. Archangel Michael, Prince of the angels, told John that hell is eternal and real! A soul body in hell is black and ugly. It recoils from pain much like a baby in the uterus of a mother that is having an abortion. All that go to hell, <u>choose</u> hell over God and heaven.

John has also seen glimpses of heaven. He said there is a treasure box that is attached to every soul. All of our tears, happy and sad, prayers and good deeds are stored there. Graces and rewards are stored there. The list of good deeds is kept there to offset our sins. Our soul is the most valuable of all. This is just like Nathan from Israel said in 2015 when he died and went to heaven. [I found his interview on-line.]

John has seen within the past month of May, a tall steeple of a church crumbling to the ground. It had been persecuted, closed and destroyed. That the people of the church had to go to refuges to find safe haven. This would be the sign of the beginning of the tribulation.

These refuges would be small, interim homes to start. People would move up to larger places, hundreds of acres prepared for them to come to. The larger refuges are shrines, places of Our Lady's Apparition, monasteries and convents that have stayed faithful, and some caves. The large refuges will have a luminous cross over them. When you look upon it you will be healed.

The smaller interim refuges will be places to stop along the way. People there will be healed by holy water or a miraculous spring. The angels will also help to multiply the space. If they don't have a priest present, the angels will also bring them Holy Communion. John said the Shekinah flame would be over them. They would be protected by the angels. John mentioned some of the things people would need to store up on. Such as; bedding, soap to wash with, heat, fuel, kerosene, wood, a Coleman stove, batteries, water, heirloom seeds, etc. Jesus will multiply what you have, especially food, water, fuel and some necessities.

John also said to pray for priests and pastors during this time. They will be sorely needed. Jesus is sending out prophets right now to prepare the people.

God and John have discussed how long we expect our Heavenly Father to put up with all these mortal sins going on. God named a few of them as: abortion, homosexuality, fornication, sterilization, euthanasia, transgenderism, and the unjust Supreme Court rulings. The punishment for these things if we don't turn from our wicked ways will be wars, terrorist attacks, and natural disasters. This would be the door to World War III.

In the midst of all this, John did speak about love. See the love of God, the love of God with your family. For God is love. If you can, be married in the church, that way God is a third partner. He mentioned that only 1/3 of modern day families are still together. Living together in fornication is not good for souls. It is hard on the children. They end up with problems in education and finding a meaningful job. The Lord God said they have to seek Him. Where there is a great need, invite the Lord in to help and prosper a marriage.

Atheists' teachings are trying to break down families. They are causing mortal sin.

John said time is running out until the major events start to occur. We are living in dangerous times; very close to a nuclear war strike. When Donald Trump was elected, the Lord was in on it. It was a miracle from the Lord.

Just as I (Debbie) was shown months ago, Americans had a choice to make. And if they would make a vote for Mr. Trump, vote for life, then God would not allow the devil to steal the election. I believe that is exactly what happened.

John feels that a large earthquake is coming to California and the New Madrid Fault. He does not know the time frame.

During the intermission break, I walked up and spoke with John and then over to Carol. I gave the five minute version of my early birth, my mother's prayer and dedication back to God, and then the fruit that started showing up at seven years old. I told Carol that many of the things that her husband had experienced, I had experienced too. He said it was good that my mom dedicated me back to the Lord. I told Carol that the blessings extended down to my children. One can see when good is about to happen to people. And another can see when to be wary.

Toward the end of John's talk, he gave the floor to his wife, Carol to speak about her father's deathbed conversion. Wow. What a story. He should have died several times while in the hospital but survived long enough to be seen by a priest, given absolution, and given the last rights.

To top her story off, which was incredible enough, she spoke of how John can see the dead while in their transitional state. He can usually see the person at their funeral Mass looking younger and standing at the head of his/her casket. Everyone is present for their own funeral. He heard her father speak while at his funeral. He was at the head of his casket. He asked forgiveness from his family for not taking them to church like he should have. And that he will be watching them from heaven because of their prayers while he was alive. Her father still comes if they have a Mass offered for him on the anniversary of his birth or death. In January of 2017, he said the angels in heaven were preparing now for the battle.

Then both John and Carol chimed in on how we should listen to the Lord when He gives us something to do. And do it right away! God is constantly nudging us. That is how I ended up writing books.

Does that beat all? Many times, that is exactly the way He comes to me. I can be awake, or asleep, it always comes when there is a need somewhere.

They ended with a last few points and two stories.

First, get our lives in order. Prepare!

Be close to the Lord. Have a relationship with Him.

We must love God and our neighbor.

Don't wait until the last minute.

Soon, there is a battle coming for the tribulation. We have only been given a short reprieve for the time being.

The One World government has changed their plans and started a resistance. They are threatening our new president. First they will try to impeach him. (Which I do not think will work.) And then they may try to kill him.

They do not like that President Trump was a pro-life candidate. And they will likely try to ruin our economy.

In their first story, they spoke about a man, Louis, who had been robbed of an invention. He was so mad, that he wanted to go over and kill the person that stole it. When he was walking out of his house and down the street with his gun, he passed a woman in white.

She said to him, "Just have faith in my Son, Jesus."

He went back inside his home and decided to sue him and his company. Which he did against strong odds. Fr. Paul Bergeron told Louis to put blessed salt in all the drinking water of those in the courtroom. Each person who went on the witness stand to lie against the inventor, ended up breaking out in bumps and boils. Even the one who stole the invention broke out in boils.

Louis prayed during the time the judge was making his decision. He prayed to Archangel Michael. "Would you let an innocent person be stolen from?"

When the judge came back in the courtroom, he sat at his desk and said to everyone in the room, "Can I sit here and let an innocent man be stolen from?"

He was awarded $25 million dollars.

The very last story they told was about a French Canadian priest, Fr. Rodrigue, who also happened to be an exorcist.

At three years old, he started hearing from God the Father. He was the youngest of 23 children. Their family home was haunted. Finally, at the age of eleven, they burned their home down to get rid of the infestation. Once the area was cleared, miracles started to happen.

Carol was healed of breast cancer under his prayers. They heard how a woman at a 2012 Christmas mass, died. Four doctors tried to revive her, and couldn't. The priest in frustration shouted out, "Lord, You came to give us life and not death! In the name of Jesus, get up!" And she did. They told several more of his stories.

While Carol was telling Fr. Rodrigue's stories, John looked at me and said, "Good enough to write a book about?"

I replied, "It sure would!"

"You writing a book?"

"I just might." I smiled.

Then John said something that took my breath. "I can read your mind."

I smiled at the Godly man and said, "Keep it up! You're doing a great job!"

After the meeting was over, John offered to pray for the people with the oil, which were the tears collected from the statues of Maureen and Clayton Marrolly in Montreal, Quebec, Canada. And with a blessed cross, that has a relic of the true cross that he wore around his neck. There were four people in front of me in line. I waited patiently.

John made the sign of the cross on each person's forehead and said the same prayer to each one. He kept his eyes lowered when praying.

When John got to me, he anointed my forehead, held my hands in prayer and started to pray. Then he stopped. He opened his eyes and looked at me and took a step back.

John said, "Oh, you're special."

I replied, "I humbly receive that word of knowledge. Thank you." At the time, I prayed I could live up to my calling.

John went on to pray for me and my family.

While John was blessing others who were in line, I went over and tried to buy a book with the only money I had. It was enough to buy one book. Carol wouldn't allow me to pay for it. She gave me a book and I gave her one of my books with Fr. Bernie in it. We exchanged phone numbers and information. I promised her I would send her one of my newest books as soon as it was ready. She gave me a second book to read that was an update of what he spoke on that day. It was very timely!

As Deb approached us, I mentioned I wanted to come up and meet Fr. Rodrigue, who was coming in October.

Carol replied, "Well you should pray about that first. Ask the Holy Spirit."

I replied, "Okay, but why?" I was curious about what she was talking about.

Carol said in a whisper, "I know of a lady that has prophesied, there will be a nuclear attack on Chicago and New York City by the end of September or early October."

Immediately I told her about what the Holy Spirit had shown Pastor David Becker two summers ago, that I had been sitting on. He said the bomb would come down through Canada and the St. Lawrence into Chicago.

Carol stopped, and then said the whole route it would take. That was exactly what the lady had prophesied from New York. From a woman in New York, to a pastor in Lexington, Kentucky, prophets were receiving the same message. Then Carol said it would be a rogue nation. And please pray against it!

*I had their full permission to retell this story. John can be reached at his website at - JohnLeary.com, or CarolML@Juno.com.

Forewarned
(June 11, evening)

It was my best friend in the whole world's birthday. And I was making Mary and Mitch Smith dinner. Mark, Matthew, our grandson, and myself took a home cooked meal over that evening to celebrate. Now, as most know, Mary is also my publisher.

We arrived to a very clean home. The inhabitants were just waiting for their yummy supper. Mitch had made a very yummy dessert to go with our meal – a chocolate pie!

Mary greeted us with hugs, and she and I set the table. We said grace and Mark served plates. Matthew sat beside his Pawpaw. I sat across from them. Mary and Mitch sat at the head of the table. We held wonderful conversation, including Matthew. He asked very bright questions and I was so proud of him being with us. He even ate all his meal. After all, chocolate pie was coming!!

Conversation continued through coffee and dessert. We caught up on all children and grandchildren, and a little of what was going on in the religious world.

After dessert, we all settled in to play a game of cards together—one of our favorite past times. Even Matthew wanted to play. We sat the 10 year old next to his Pawpaw and he instructed him on the rules. Well, we had a blast and it was the most gentlemanly game of cards we've ever played together! Matthew laughed and smiled. He even played very well as a beginner!

The time came for Mark to take Matt back to his dad's. While he was gone, I caught Mary and Mitch up with all the latest happenings. I had just finished up when Mark came walking into their home.

All during my talk, Mitch was doodling and writing on a piece of paper. He looked very serious! As Mark sat down, Mitch spoke.

"Debbie, I just had a word of knowledge. Now, I don't get these so I am sure it is very important."

I nodded my head soberly.

He went on.

"Now, I wish I could say that this word is for everyone, the generic "you," but it isn't. It is geared directly toward you."

Now my stomach hurt.

"The devil hates your faith. He absolutely hates it. He is going to attack you through your faith. Be careful what you listen to and hear. He will send people who seem like prophets to confuse you. Be very careful."

"Yes, sir. I sure will."

Down at the bottom of the page he had written my message on, were the words;
Fires of Love
Assent to Truth
Brethren
Kyrie Eleison (Lord have mercy)
I heard softly in my Spirit, *"Unbeatable."*

Prayer to Archangel Michael

(June 11, end of the evening)

This is a prayer given to me by Mitch, before we left for home.

Archangel Michael, defend us in battle, be our safeguard from the devil. May God rebuke him, we humbly pray, and do thou, O Prince of the Heavenly Host, by the Power of God cast into the pit of hell, satan and all evil spirits that roam the world seeking the ruin of souls.

Epilogue
The End.
Really?

Seven years. Seven long years. And for two years before that, I sat and made notes that I told no one about. I never saw it coming, unless you count the vision I had in 2004: the words *Miraculous Interventions,* floating in the air above my head as I woke up. A warning shot to be sure!

Just because it may end on paper does not mean it ends in life.

I continue to seek God, to see Him, wonder at His will, marvel at His works, and rejoice when Yod Hey Vav Hey shows up and everything changes for His glory and my/our, or someone's benefit.

The world has changed in the last 10 years. As I have continued to write about miracles and the Lord, the world has gotten darker. It is as if more spirits have been unleashed from our eternal enemy for the extreme disregard of life, love and light of God. The chasm between good and evil has grown even wider and longer. And as unusual as this may seem, it makes the good, the miraculous, stand out even brighter.

ISIS and ISIL, and all of their counter evil parts, have been on a war path to steal, horrendously kill and destroy everything in their way.

The New World Order screams to take over as a one-world government, a one-world banking system, and with it, a one-world religion. Supposedly named Chryslam. An anti-Christ for sure. And anti-freedom.

I have watched my ponderings turn from being just God's miracle watcher, to also being a watcher of the times we live in. There is a quickening in my Spirit as I watch Bible prophesy come to life in front of me. Incredible.

As I have seen great evil rear its ugly head, I have also see a great light arise. First it was England with Brexit, then America with the election of a new president; not hand-picked by the ruling establishment, but by the people and for the people. Just like I saw in my dream. Freedom fighters, freed in Christ Jesus. *The Old Lion stood first, then the Young Lion followed.*

Then there's that planet from the binary system that has encroached our galaxy. Some call it *Planet X*, or *Nibiru*, and some high up, whisper, *"Wormwood; the Destroyer."*
The moon is not right, (it or our planet is tilted differently) the sun is not right, (great solar flares and holes); earthquakes are up 2,000%; sink holes are on the rise; and there are massive die-offs of animals on all continents, etc.
And some say, we are not alone on this planet. That the war between the fallen angels and our angels is at its highest peak. The crescendo is coming soon.
Jesus is coming back for His people.
To quote a semi-famous Indiana preacher, *"Are you serious? Are you ready? Are you saved?"*

Please tell your family, friends, and work associates. Today is the day of salvation. Give your life to Christ Jesus. Be a watcher of miracles and the times we live in. Keep your lamps lit and plenty of oil with you. We're going to need it.

All my love,

For now,

Deb

Miraculous Interventions VI
Warn Those Who Will Listen

"To whom shall I speak, and give warning, that they may hear? Jeremiah 6:10

Writing a Warning

Over the next two weeks, I wrote letters to our loved ones that were up north far enough that I couldn't physically get to. I wanted Diane and Rusty, Judy and Terry to be warned—have their eyes opened and their Christian senses alert.

Judy Myers, along with a devout group of Catholics, were going to be in Medjugorje the last week of September. She called me to confirm she received my letter, and that she was still going on her trip. I agreed with her it was the right thing to do.

I chuckled my reply, "I pray you don't have any trouble getting back home."

By the last week of June, Mark and I held a small gathering of friends and family to ease the word out gently. Truthfully, there was not much surprise in the room. The Holy Spirit was already putting seeds down.

June 27th, I could put the phone call off no longer, our lives were already intertwined. I called Carol and John in Rochester. She was the one who had confirmed the original prophecy from Pastor Dave. While speaking with her, we shared both John and I had a history of warnings coming to us. And John was given a great warning message from Jesus that went like this:

From Jesus to John:

"I saw an earthquake hit San Francisco. I was told that two days later, another city of great sin on the East Coast will be hit with a nuclear weapon."

John felt these words were a direct confirmation of the elderly lady in New England who'd had a clear word from the Lord that Manhattan would be hit with a nuclear bomb from N. Korea in or around October 13th.

We agreed by the end of our conversation, we needed to meet. And there was a priest Linda wanted me to meet as well. She was sure he would be interested in the whole story. She set up a conference call for two days later. In the meantime, I had a dream.

An Early Morning Hour
(End of June, 2017)

I could see we were still on vacation in Walt Disney World. We were staying in a nice room. We were having tea on the breakfast bar. I looked down on the counter and saw a calendar with the date of September 30 highlighted.

In my dream, I argued with the Lord. I said in my head, "Lord, we aren't going to be in Walt Disney World on September 30th. We are supposed to check out by the 28th."

At that instant, a tall, black lady in a blue-stripe dress came walking in. She had a small package in her hand. She chuckled to herself and said to me, "I brought you a package for your birthday."

She left the room quickly. Mark and I looked at each other and he asked me, "Do you know her?"

I replied, "She looks familiar…"

As soon as she had left our room, a tall, thin black man walked in. He was full of self-importance and haughtiness. He too carried a small package. He walked over and put it on the counter. He also said, "I have a package for your birthday." We stared after him as he left. Mark and I looked at each other with perplexity.

I asked Mark to look and see if they were still outside. I didn't want their packages. Mark went to the living room window and opened the curtains. They were sitting in chairs on the porch. We could hear them talking.

She said, "She's so stupid."

He replied, "I wonder if they recognize it's us, yet?"

By then, boy was I mad! I was shouting as I was putting on my shoes to take them back their packages.

I grabbed the two packages, and started out the front door. As I opened the door and walked out, I heard him laughing.

He said, "I'm not through with America yet..."

Sidebar: Two days later, Sam called me and said she and Andy had been talking. They felt we were supposed to stay in the WDW hotel through the 30th of September. When I told Mark what she said without knowing anything, he replied, "Make it so."

And I did.

Confirmation of My Dream

Two days after I had my dream about the packages, I heard on Facebook, (sure not from national news), N. Korea fired a missile and sent a message to President Trump.

He sent, "I'm sending a package for your birthday." (Meaning July 4th.)

It was almost the exact same words from my dream, a couple nights before. Ominous to be sure. From the first week of July through the middle of August, the North Korean leader, threatened America and her allies with nuclear attacks. This was the backdrop to our whole unfolding story.

Mark and I fasted and prayed for days against the schemes of the enemy.

God help us. Oh, God help us!

Prophecy Alerts

Around the 5th of July, I was contacted by Prophecy watcher and author, Robert Rite to join his group on Facebook. I still have no idea how he received my information to contact me at this crucial time. Robert approved me for his group and I immediately posted what I knew. Incredible discussions were held back and forth confirming to many the clear visions and dreams they too had been having. It was nice to have another author in the group along with them.

In the meantime, I mailed off another batch of letters, including one to Pastor Paul Begley.

By the middle of July, I had made my rounds to several dear friends and family members to continue to warn families. I was no longer surprised when both Larry and Marilynn Crosier and BJ and Tim McCoy were already planning vacations for the exact days in question. One was headed for Gulf Shores and the other was headed not 90 miles from where we were compelled to be. God was already before us, preparing hearts to leave the area. Just like He did in 70 A.D. when the Lord sent his burgeoning Christian Church out of Jerusalem before the slaughter of the Jews and overturning of the Temple.

Carol and Linda
(July 18th)

So much was happening so fast, I contacted Carol and Linda from the northeast to give updates. As usual, they were the ones with the real updates.

Linda gave more details about the warning from the prophet and the Holy Spirit. This prophet had heard before the last retreat in May, by the Holy Spirit, that there would be no retreat the second weekend of October, honoring the 100th anniversary of Fatima and the Miracle of the Sun. This same prophet was told that North Korea would strike Manhattan Island between the last week of September and the first week of October. (In that time-frame area.) The prophet was sorrowful over these events and tried, but couldn't get anyone in the Heavens to listen.

The prophet had also seen a 9.0 earthquake strike that would decimate Italy. And also expected by sometime in October, a Great Warning to be heard. Two men in the same group prophesied that all the events would start after September 29th, the end of Elul, and Yom Kippur.

The PS Incident
(Third week of July, 2017)

On the heels of the prophecy, we were supposed to go to a Pastor's conference in Louisville, Kentucky. Now this was a well-known young man with great words of knowledge and study. We were always pleased to hear him speak.

The first evening Mark and I, Katie and Nick went together. Boy did we have fun! The pulpit was on fire with words from the Lord and singing with the choirs.

The next morning, Katie and I went by ourselves. Mark and Nick had to work. I told Katie while on the way there, I felt compelled to tell the pastor's first-in-command. But at the time, I had no idea how far up the ladder this message would go. And who would eventually bring me revelation my important message reached its destination.

Katie and I arrived just in time for the start of the morning conference. All the seats in the middle were taken. We either had to sit on the left or right. It was a 50/50 choice. We chose the seats on the left.

Before pastor started his opening sentences, he stopped. He walked over to our side of the room, pointed in our direction, and said, "Someone over here has had (or has had) a very important dream. You have to write it down."

Katie and I looked at each other, feeling his words were intended for us. For me.

An hour-and-a-half went quickly by as the morning came to a close. Once more, pastor came back to our side, pointed, and said, "By the way, I'm going to see the president next week."

I dropped my jaw and looked at Katie. The Lord had told me in my Spirit—not a couple of days before—our story would get before the President of the United States. At the time I had practically shouted that I had no idea how that would happen!

We hurriedly got up to find pastor's right-hand man. We asked to speak to him privately. He nodded his head and we went to the church kitchen. I stammered through the first couple of sentences. Katie took up the next part of the story and I took over mid-way. We told him about all the confirmations and my latest dream with the date. We told him about North Korea.

Katie asked at the end of our conversation as he was walking out, if they got warnings from people much.

He turned to face us and said, "Yes, but not like this, with this much detail and not about North Korea. Can you type this up and have it to me by tonight?"

I replied, "Yes, sir. I sure can."

I paused for a second and said, "Listen, I didn't put any stock into Y2K, and I wasn't a bit worried about December 2012."

He questioned me, "and the eclipse?"

I said, "Be serious! It's just an eclipse! I'm being serious!"

He nodded his head, evidently it was the correct answer.

I went on, "But this, from the time I found out about it three years ago, it hasn't left me. And when it was confirmed, well, my tummy aches over it... Please do something."

He nodded his head and went out the door.

The Presidential Letter
(July 20th)

I am a Christian author. I write my own series, "Miraculous Interventions," and stories for other ministers. I usually write about miracles in people's lives, but as of late, I have watched these stories turn to prophesy as well.

Three years ago, while writing Pastor David Becker's book, "Let's Take a Walk, Dave," he spoke of a prophecy that the Holy Spirit had given him. He was told that America was going to be attacked. It would be a nuclear bomb. The rogue nation would bring it by ship from Canadian waters, down the St. Lawrence, through the Michigan Lakes and port in Chicago. It would be offloaded onto land and detonated. He was not given a date. After I got over the shock of what Dave had shared, I put his prophesy into my heart's pocket, and swore never to tell anyone unless I received confirmation. Then when and if I received confirmation, I would tell quietly, all who would listen.

About three years later, I was speaking with a friend about a conference she was going to. Deb Grimes thought there was a God reason she was asking me to go too. That was this summer, mid-June, 2017. There was a couple she wanted me to meet. Their names were John and Carol Leary. Very nice couple. He is a retired chemist, who is devoted to the Lord. He happens to be Roman Catholic. He teaches about how to build a refuge; what all you need to live through the tribulation times from the Book of Revelation. The Roman Catholic Church doesn't teach rapture, they teach living through the tribulation, and then Jesus will return for His church. Definitely post-trib.

Toward the end of the afternoon conference, Carol Leary got up and spoke. She mentioned a friend of hers, a priest from Canada. His name was Fr. Rodrigue. She told amazing stories of his early childhood, his call from the Lord, and several of his miracles. I thought to myself I would love to write his book.

After the conference was over, I went up to speak to Carol and ask her some questions. I asked her if Fr. Rodrigue was coming back to New York. She said he was coming to New York to hold a one-day conference October 7th. I chuckled and asked what day he was landing on. Carol smiled and said he was landing October 6th. I smiled and told her I would see them October 6th.

Carol replied in earnest that I should ask the Holy Spirit before coming up. I was puzzled and asked why. She said there was a prophet up in New England that said there was going to be an attack on America this fall. I asked where and what kind of attack it would be. She said it would be a nuclear attack on Chicago and New York.

My heart sank as I retold Carol Pastor Becker's story about the nuclear attack on Chicago as told to him by the Holy Spirit. The only thing he hadn't received was when it would be. I asked her the fateful question, "When?"

Carol replied, "She said it would be this year between the last week of September and the first week of October. And it will be a rogue nation." We exchanged phone numbers and addresses and agreed to talk again.

Over the next two weeks I spoke to a couple of friends who were retired military. I begged them to get in touch with anyone and warn our country. They said they would pray God send me to the right person to tell who could carry this message forward.

(Side bar: We were also planning a trip in November for our 20th anniversary. I asked the Lord if it was okay to move that up to the last week of September. I received a confirmation in my spirit and called and made reservations for us and friends at a Walt Disney Resort in Florida from the 25th of September to check out on the 29th.)

In the meantime, I was praying very hard and asking Jesus very specific questions. "Please, as I send this information forward, you have to give me a more specific date. Please show me what to do."

July 1st, I had a dream.

I saw Mark and I and one of our friends, Katie in a hotel suite waiting for a late checkout. (1 p.m.) We were still in Disneyworld. We were sitting around the breakfast bar having tea. I looked down on the counter. On it was a calendar. The date was Saturday, September 30.

All of a sudden, a black lady in a dress came in holding a package. She was chuckling to herself. As she put the small package on the counter she said, "I've brought a present (for you) on your birthday." She left the room.

My husband, Mark asked me if I knew her. I shook my head no. As soon as she left the room, a tall, thin black man walked into our room. He was full of self-importance and pride. He too had a small package. He was laughing to himself. Then he spoke, "I've brought a present (for you) on your birthday." He stood there a minute expecting to be exalted, and when we didn't, he left.

Immediately, I asked Mark to see if they were still out on the porch. He opened the drapes and looked out. They were there and we could hear them.

She laughed and said, "She is so stupid."

He smiled and replied, "I wonder how long it will take for them to recognize us?"

By that time I knew who they were. They were the Obama's. I knew the two small gifts were two small nuclear bombs that were intended to detonate on American soil. I was so mad! I grabbed up the packages and went out to the porch. Before I could say a word, he started laughing and said, "I am not through with America yet."

I read on July 2nd, the dictator over North Korea sent a message to President Trump with these words, "I am sending a present to you on your birthday." (He meant a missile on July 4th, but it was stopped over an ocean, I think?)

Over the next two weeks, I was arguing with God over the dates we had arranged to go on vacation and what I had seen in my dream. I told the Lord the dates didn't match up. We would be gone the 29th. We wouldn't even be there on the 30th of September. (Which happens to be my birthday.)

That was when I got a message from our youngest son and his wife who live in Florida. Andy works at Disneyworld. Sam said they had been talking about it and they felt we are supposed to stay at our hotel for a week. From the 24th of September to the 30th. Just like I had dreamed. When I told my husband about the conversation, he said to make it so. To him it was confirmation. I was also told in the spirit to put the trip on our credit card and carry money with us. We might need it.

By the middle of July when I finished my latest book, I called Carol to let her know their part of one of the last stories was finished. I told her the dream I had and asked her to relay it to the prophet up in New England. I felt I had been given a warning date.

Carol said she felt we all needed to talk together and I should tell her friend the prophet the whole story. We spoke that night, July 18th. They called me. I told them the whole story from my side, beginning to end. The ladies sighed.

Linda said they had gone on a retreat back in May (2017). The prophet was very dismayed. They asked the old prophet what was wrong.

"North Korea is going to hit America with a nuclear bomb. It will hit Manhattan Island."

The prophet asked God the Father to allow one more retreat (dated October 13th) before all hell breaks loose. There was no answer. The prophet asked Jesus for one more retreat. Jesus said nothing. Very rattled, the prophet asked the Holy Spirit for one more retreat. The Holy Spirit said nothing.

Finally, asking our Blessed Mother for one final retreat, Mother Mary replied, "Holy obedience." The prophet asked of the Lord to be taken home before all of this starts. The Lord promised the prophet would not have to endure all that is coming.

The ladies spoke with the prophet who have also seen a series of earthquakes that hit the San Andreas and the New Madrid. There will be tsunamis on both coasts. An earthquake registering a 9.0 is coming to Italy and will decimate the country.

It has been prophesied in their church that all the events will start on or after the 29th of September which is Yom Kippur. John Leary, the one who I had gone to see in June, said he has also seen a large earthquake hit San Francisco and that two days later, the Lord told him, "...another city of great sin on the East Coast will be hit with a nuclear weapon." He knew it was New York. He felt it confirmed the prophet's report.

After hearing all of this, I asked the Lord, "What should I do?"

After all, six weeks before 9/11, I had a dream that I was on a plane that was in trouble. Three weeks later, I had another dream. I was on the same plane. This time I looked out the window. I saw the Hudson River. When I looked up, I saw a tall building. The plane was headed right for it. I screamed, "Pull up! Pull up! You are going to hit the building!"

Carol Leary confirmed that her husband also had two dreams. One was three weeks before and the other was one week before 9/11. He saw the buildings tumbling down.

At that time I again asked the Lord what to do. He said 9/11 was unstoppable.

Seven years later I was shown another prophetic dream. I saw a white, box truck traveling under a VI dock headed straight for a tall building in a big city. That time I also asked what to do? The Lord God said pray to stop it. Five days later I saw on the news that exact scenario. It was stopped.

This time, after hearing all of this, when I asked the Lord what I should do, this was the reply that I heard.

"Prayer alone will not work this time. You must act. You have to tell someone."

Feel free to call any of us. We want to help as much as we can.

August 6th – Mark and I went to see the original person who started this journey, Pastor Becker.

After he spoke of miracles and signs for a few minutes, he sat down and smiled. The room became quiet.

I said, "Your prophecy has been verified."

I gave no information nor date.

David replied, "September 30th, America will suffer an event. I see smoke and fire. It will be either a nuclear attack or a volcano will go off. I see great earthquakes around then."

An Unusual Army of Soldiers
(August 2017)

I started with friends and family. I moved on the telling to doctors, local officials, Ft. Knox personnel, pastors with radio programs and YouTube programs. The word was getting out.

In the meantime, North Korea was threatening to start a war right then, by August 15th. It was during that time, I had two unusual, strong dreams.

My dream:
I dreamed we lived in the country. We had just finished breakfast on a Saturday morning. The kids and Mark left the table to go to the den and watch some television while I did dishes.

While I was at the kitchen sink, I thought I heard a plane going over the house. I looked up and saw the tail—but it looked unusual. It wasn't another minute or two when I heard the sound again. I looked up to see a missile going over and past our home! I screamed and ran to my family! They jumped up and met me in the living room. Crying I told them a missile just went by our home and it looked like it was headed for the city!

They all ran to the front door and saw it. We saw it hit a long way off.

"Are You Serious?!"

"Are you ready?" Mark asked.

I replied, "Have we got everything?"

Katie and Nick's van was all packed up for our day-trip up to see Paul and Heidi Begley in West Lafayette, Indiana. I just knew, he would know people in the military and government who could help with this too.

We met the Begley's at a lovely Italian restaurant in their town. We sat down to a very nice meal. We started with pleasantries and prayer. After a minute, Paul said, "You have information, a story for us?"

I gave him the whole story as I had told everyone up until him. About half-way through, he asked for paper. I smiled and asked him if he would like to have a copy of what I now called, the Presidential Letter. Pastor Paul's eyes lit up as he smiled his answer. I handed him his copy.

Paul and Heidi looked it over for understanding.

I said, "The reason we are here telling you, is because you know so many people in the government and military. Surely there is someone who can help with this."

Pastor replied, "We will pray about what to do about this, and who to give it to. I know at least two people in the military who could possibly help stop this situation."

Bringing Good out of Evil

It was once again time to check in with our New York crew. I put in a call to Carol to check on their arrival time at the airport. As usual, I always got more information than I gave.

Carol spoke on many subjects. She spoke on the urgent messages John was receiving lately. He saw the San Andreas Fault line was soon to suffer a large earthquake.

That would be a first signal that bad times were upon us. John felt days after that, there would be a nuclear attack on Chicago or New York City. Then, sometime in the future, there would be an EMP blast. This was not one of our cheerier talks.

Carol also spoke about Fr. Michele and Fr. David. We spoke about their travels to and back to New York. I quietly spoke my opinion that good priests were under persecution in the Roman Catholic Church. Deb Grimes and I had personally seen how Fr. Bernie had been treated by the elect in his own order.

Then Carol spoke on another subject I had never heard of before.

"Deb, have you ever heard of Catherine Emmerich?" Carol asked.

I replied, "No, ma'am. I haven't. Who is she?"

"Catherine lived in the early 1800's. She was a prophetess. Catherine said before Jesus returns, there would be two popes in the Vatican. She said it would be the greatest schism in history. And the priest (because she would not call the second pope, a pope,) would undermine the Roman Catholic Church. And his name would be Francis."

"Woowww."

Carol went on, "Did you know on the day Francis was ordained, twice lightning struck the Vatican."

"I had no idea!"

I felt New Age was trying to infiltrate the church as a whole; and with Francis, they were trying to embrace a one-world religion to make peace with the Muslims.

They were all very ominous signs.

A Nuclear Vision
(August 5th)

It was early in the morning. I am still not sure if this was indeed a vision or a dream; it came out of a mist. I could see Mark and me sleeping in bed together — peacefully sleeping.

Through closed eyes, I saw an instantaneous brilliant flash of light—it was gone in an eighth of a second—like lightning. My heart sank and I cried as I waited for the percussion of the nuclear blast to hit.

In this vision, I turned toward the clock, it was 8:15 a.m.

I realized then, I was actually turned the other way in bed—opposite of the way I saw me in the vision. When I turned over, I saw it was 7:45 a.m. But just like in the vision, I was crying.

Mark and I started praying against nuclear war that very day, especially from the rouge country of North Korea.

To Start a Revolution in Church
(August 20th, 2017)

Almost two weeks went by as I kept busy with yard sales (earning money to buy food for our conference/guests.) And house cleaning.

The third weekend in August was particularly tiring with back-to-back sixteen and eighteen hour days. By Saturday evening I was crying with fatigue and pain. I took medicine that night and went right to sleep with the intention to stay home Sunday morning.

8 a.m.: I woke straight up in bed. It was as if an internal alarm had gone off in my head. And I didn't hurt. I reckoned I was going to church after all. New Albany, Indiana's Revolution church with Pastors Tom and Bridgette McCullum were the first thing on my list to do. I had a story to tell and a letter to give them. They were expecting Apostle Larry to preach that morning. Mark and I had heard him once before. I figured it would be a pleasant sermon. With Mark still sleeping in our bed, I took off for New Albany.

I walked in just in time to hear the song leaders singing praise songs. Worshipping before the Lord went on for almost 45 minutes. I found myself a seat at a table where I could write and made myself comfortable.

After a while, Tom and Larry got up to pray over communion. Now this is an interesting little evangelical church. When the men laid hands on the bread they started praying down the Holy

Spirit to transform the juice and the bread into the body and blood of Jesus Christ. They believe in transubstantiation. The power and the anointing came down heavy. My personal belief is if the church is asking for transubstantiation, and believing with their hearts, I am not going to tell them they're wrong. God bless them for their faith in a God that can do anything!

On the way up to communion, we were to bring an offering up and place it in their basket. I was ashamed to tears. All I had to give was thirty-three cents. I held it in my hand so that no one would see how meager my offering was. I even tried to hide my pennies beneath the other offerings of dollar bills. That was when I saw that other people there were so poor that all they had to put in was change too. I was relieved I was not the only poor person in Tom's church.

After communion, Pastor Tom introduced Apostle Larry. I pulled my notebook out, reached for a pen and sat down to write whatever the saint had to say. I looked forward to his sermon—and it was a nice one. He spoke on the coming of the Great and Terrible Day of the Lord. Larry quoted many scriptures. He also said to despise not small beginnings—keep going. I seem to attach to this scripture quite often. Larry encouraged the fellowship to have a testimony like the apostles. He encouraged us to have a passion for the Lord God.

As Larry began to wind down his sermon, and before he gave words of knowledge to the parishioners, he began to pace quickly back and forth in front of the altar. He had a burden on his heart.

"The Lord showed me this, this morning. I don't know who this is for, but it is for somebody here. You are like Joseph, you have been set in one place like Joseph was in prison. You are just waiting. Don't worry! Just like the butler remembered Joseph to Potipher, you will be remembered too. Your time of sitting on the sideline is over.

You had a message. And a person of influence is going to a person of great influence with your message. They will remember you! When they are elevated, they will remember you! And you will be elevated!" (Two days later, without me telling Katie anything, she also heard the word 'elevated' over me.) Then Larry started to look around and shout.

"Who is this for? Who is this for? I know you are here! This is big!"

I knew deep in my spirit he was talking straight to me. I raised my hand meekly. Larry hollered as he came walking toward me. To me, he looked like John the Baptist in the flesh!

"Hand me my Bible!"

I thought, "Oh, boy. Here he comes!" I stood waiting.

He stopped in front of me and started praying prayers out of the Bible over me. He laid a hand on the top of my head for the blessing to come down. I felt the weight of the Holy Spirit fall directly on me. I went to my chair and then my knees!

After a minute, he went on to pray over others with their concerns. A short half-hour later, services were over. I sat and waited for Tom to come and talk with me for a few minutes before they left for lunch. I had a letter for him in hand.

After a while, Tom came over and pulled up a chair. He started out all smiles.

"What's up, Deb?"

I gave him the whole conversation, beginning to end in ten minutes flat. The further I got in the story, Tom's smile faded. By the time I was telling the verifications of the prophecy, he was shouting, "You're freaking me out! You're freaking me out!"

I shouted back, "Freaking you out!? You should be me!!"

Of course he made a copy of what I was now calling the Presidential Letter.

As our conversation ended, and we went to go our separate ways, Tom turned back toward me and said, "Deb, you have been appointed for this job. You were assigned to do this. Don't stop."

Then Tom turned back around to me and laughed and said, "Boy are you gonna be the conversation over lunch!"

What a confirmation! I now had no doubt that the letter made its destination. It was received. Not to mention that David also said our government was aware of the situation and were working on it.

Thank God. I sure hope I got it right—my part of all of this.

My prayer: That I had told all of the right people...

Epilogue

Text from Diane:

"My soul is in anguish! I heard in my spirit! 40 days! 40 days! 40 days! It is important we spend this time in repentance prayer and fasting from Elul to Yom Kippur. Warning! Chaos and horror! Oh my soul!"

I had not planned this book. I didn't expect it. I have never put a book together in three weeks flat in my career. But it was never so imperative that it get done that quickly. This is important. The title of this book fell out of my mouth, in front of my publisher, no less.

"Warn Those Who Will Listen."

As we started sending out the warning and letting people know of the conference with John and Carol and Fr. David, people were drawn from the north, south, east and west! Could we please save them a seat?

Why sure!

Volunteers to help were showing up as well. While Mark and I wondered where we would get the money to feed all the people, God sent us more landscape work. It seems no matter what the need, we always had work show up to take care of the cost. It seemed, we could always work our way out of any situation. I wondered, how much longer we could keep it up. I guess God doesn't see sixty the way we see sixty years old.

As this book took me by surprise, God willing, the next book is already named.

"Miraculous Interventions VII The Saving of America."

That one will take place in September and October 2017. I sure hope to see all of you on the other side of October 2017.

Please whatever you do, pray now like you never have before. Pray for safety of the world. And that mankind repents.

For the Kingdom of God is at hand.

See you in the air.

Miraculous Interventions VII

The Saving of America

"Be prepared to rapture up!"

Apocalyptic Events
(The **first week** of September, 2017)

1. Deb Grimes called late one evening to tell me North Korea had just sent a message with the exact words to the White House that had been in my warning dream on June 30th.*

Deb said, "North Korea says they are sending gift packages to America September 7th!"

Prayers went up.

2. September 8th, a noted Indiana pastor with an online YouTube church, Paul Begley reported an earthquake of an 8.0 magnitude in San Francisco, Mexico. He wondered, could it have been part of the warning about an earthquake in San Francisco, we assumed was SF California?

3. I had seen in a vision dream, (back in August) what I thought were oriental people from a large land mass (I thought China, still possibly is) having a huge earthquake. I saw the fear on their faces, and their land split like a river ran through it.

---

* In my dream he said, "I brought you a package for your birthday." What was reported that he said was, "I'm sending a package for your birthday." See Miraculous Interventions VI, Warn Those Who Will Listen, *page 132* "An Early Morning Hour"

102

Prayers went up because one never knows...or can one?

I pondered, what did the rest of September, 2017 hold? Would there be an attempted nuclear attack? Did the fires and smoke all across our nation – as Pastor David Becker had seen in a vision – indicate, as he had wondered, that Yellowstone was going to blow? Or could he have pre-seen the fires that started in California and were now so large that the smoke made it all the way to St. Louis, Missouri?

Even the secular public knew something was in the air, no pun intended. Sales of pre-packaged foods, camping equipment, and medical supplies skyrocketed.

Now, if only we could stop it, God permitting...

September of 2017 had not been kind to America, or the world, for that matter.

A whole host of states in the United States were battling fires, to include:
California
Oregon
Washington State
Montana and others

Other countries were battling their own waves of death and destruction as well. British Columbia, Alberta, Canada, Nova Scotia, Greece, Brazil, Portugal, Algeria, Tunisia, Greenland, Siberia and the Sakha Republic of Russia were also being consumed acres at a time by fires, many of unknown origin.

Surely, this was what the prophet David Wilkerson, and our own dear friend and prophet—David Becker saw in visions of their own, set apart by 30 years.

A triple-digit heat wave dubbed "lucifer" (of all names!) swept through the European countries of Italy, France, Spain, Switzerland, Hungary, Poland, Romania, Bosnia, Croatia, and Serbia.

Southern California also fought triple-digit heat that smashed down all-time record highs of 115 degrees. News stories showed people sweltering as they walked to their vehicles.

Before the middle of September, Yellowstone rumbled with a series of earthquakes and tremors (hundreds) that made even the heartiest souls think the East Coast looked like a good move for safety.

Japan, Mexico, and Australia suffered huge earthquakes registering 6.1, 7.2 and 8.1 respectively. The earthquake that hit San Francisco, Mexico receded beach lines by 50 plus meters.

And then, there was the all-time record-breaking Hurricane Harvey versus Houston with over 50 inches of rain. Devastation of a nuclear capacity had hit Texas.

If that wasn't enough, Hurricane Irma took direct aim at the **whole state** of Florida at category five. Not to mention going on at the same time, the largest CME* flare from our sun ever recorded.

At the time, I wondered, if there was such a thing as Mother Nature, had she really gone mad?

*CME = Coronal Mass Ejection.

A Storm on the Horizon of Epic Proportions...

The entire state of Florida, USA

(September 8-11th, 2017)

At the same time Mark and I were putting out (proverbial) fires around us—no deference to the states out west that really were dealing with unprecedented fires on their own—another storm that threatened devastation in its wake was brewing.

NOAH watched the storm system that came off the coast of Africa take an almost purposeful aim at the islands between Cuba and North America. The area they originated from, off the African coastal waters, was known for creating super-storms of "Biblical" proportions. Real land destroyers. As it crossed the ocean, picking up speed and mass, warnings started all over Cuba, the Virgin Islands and the whole Eastern North American coastline.

Hurricane Irma was four times larger than the destructive Hurricane Matthew of 2016. How on earth could that happen?!

I wondered, were our earth weather systems being influenced by HAARP [High Frequency Active Auroral Research Program] – which may have been influenced by the demons of the nether world? [Search this on Youtube for information on this subject.] Or was it truly a warning system? Was God trying to get our world's attention any and every which way He could?

September 4th, Irma strengthened to a category-4 hurricane over the Atlantic – then, upgraded to a category-5 with winds of 185 mph as it approached land. Irma made its first landfall over the Caribbean Island of Barbuda. Every single building was destroyed and all its 1600 inhabitants were left homeless.

Over the next three days, Irma centered west over Anguilla, St. Martin, St. Bart's and both British and US Virgin Islands. The damage was catastrophic. Ninety percent of the buildings on several of the islands were damaged or destroyed. Irma brushed the coast of Puerto Rico and left one million residents without power. Irma then passed just shy of the Dominican Republic and Haiti. It caused widespread flooding before aiming at the Turks and Caicos Islands in the Bahamas. Irma maintained at Category-5 strength for three days—breaking all records in the satellite era.

And it was on a direct collision course with the entire state of Florida. In its first wake was Cuba. Irma hit Cuba with 160 mph winds at landfall on Camaguey Archipelago late Friday evening.

This same Friday evening at our home was when we were starting our opening prayers with John and Carol Leary. With the many words of knowledge we had all been receiving before then, we had arranged a conference for this weekend.

Mark and I let people know of the conference with John and Carol on Friday at our home, Saturday with Fr. David at the Knight of Columbus Hall, continuing informally at our home on Sunday – which, incidentally, continued into Tuesday!

People were drawn from the north, south, east and west! Could we please save them a seat?

Why sure!

...*That Ran Right into an Epic Weekend!*

(September 8-11th, 2017)

As Irma got closer and closer to landfall on the eastern seaboard, prayer warriors were all gathering at our home in Southern Indiana. People came from all over. Almost 100 of them arrived from seven states on that Friday evening.

And we were headed for a fight with destructive forces.

Don't worry, saints, we were used to winning....

"Do you think we've made enough food?" I asked my compatriots Katie Yocum, Deb Grimes and Mary Smith.

Between the three-day conference totals, we would be feeding over 100 people breakfast, lunch and dinner.

"I think we will be fine, Deb," Katie reasoned. She and Deb Grimes were always the calm warriors. I was, and am, the jumper.

Mark was on his way to the Louisville International Airport to pick up John and Carol Leary, and their friend, Linda who would be meeting Fr. David that afternoon at our home.

I set out our fall decorum as we waited for our company to arrive. And of course, when they walked into our home, I was the one with my hands in dish water.

They were introduced to everyone else first. It went something like this:

"Hi! I'm Katie!"

"Hi! I'm Debbie!"

"Ohhh! Debbie!"

"Uh, Debbie Grimes! I'm not the lady of the house."

Drying off my hands, I said, "Here I am. Welcome to our home."

Since I knew John and Carol, I said, "You must be Linda."

Again, "Ohhhh, Debbie! It's so nice to finally meet you!"

Of course, hugs and smiles were exchanged all around. Carol gave me a hug that felt like it was from a long-lost friend. We showed our New England friends to their bedrooms and allowed them time to settle in. I set out snacks for everyone until it was time to go out for lunch. Dinner was still cooking....

Conversations over fish and fries went quickly to the deep things of God, and concern for those in the wake of Irma. I let our company know we had children and grandchildren smack in the middle of the state, staying at a Walt Disney World resort for safety.

I had let Andy, our youngest, know we would be lifting them all up in prayer for the whole weekend. His response to me was, "Momma, do you think God has forgotten that we still live in Florida?"

Thomas Andrew's complete faith was on it.

The weekend events were set...or so I thought.

Friday evening, John Leary was scheduled to speak at our home. Saturday, Fr. David would be speaking at the Knights of Columbus Hall in Lanesville, Indiana, on the topic of the Immaculate Heart of Mary, all day until 4 that afternoon.

We assumed Sunday would be a day of rest and thanksgiving. Fr. David and Linda would be leaving that afternoon. John and Carol had scheduled to go back home on Monday evening.

Well, so much for the plans we could see. God's plans and ways are always much higher than ours. And longer....

We all agreed we would begin and end the evening with prayer for Florida. When Fr. David arrived Friday afternoon, he joined in with offering two masses for everyone in Irma's path. Divine Mercy Chaplets were said over and over for the same intention.

If you could force a weather system into submission through prayer, we were well on our way to doing just that.

Friday evening I prepared three roasts for dinner, supplied by Katie Yocum. It had all the trimmings and was several of our guests' favorite meal of the weekend.

The Gospel of John and Carol
(September 8-12th, 2017)

As dinner wound down, people started arriving for John and Carol's talk. We were able to seat 50 in our basement. There were a few ladies that could not navigate steps, so we compromised for their situation and came up with a great idea! I called Carol's phone and we put them both on speaker. Her phone was at the podium where John was speaking. I ran my phone upstairs to the waiting women in our sunroom. They were ecstatic! They weren't left out at all! I was sure it was a divine inspiration.

John opened the three-hour meeting with a prayer for the people in Texas and Florida, those suffering in the wake of one hurricane and the impending landing of the other!

He opened with a warning against powers that be who wanted to take our guns. He also gave an update on refuges across the United States.

John spoke on warnings of major events to pray against. After all, prayer can stop a lot of things except one thing — God's will. Even our prayers cannot stop that. But everything else is fair game.

John spoke of the life-review and mini-judgments he felt were coming. He warned not to take the chip in our hand or forehead no matter what they tell you. And if you think they will never pass that law, they already did. It was written into the Obama Care Bill.

John was also told by the power of the Holy Spirit, that a world famine was coming. And there would be a great schism in the Roman Catholic Church.

There could also be a crash of the dollar, calling for martial law to be set up as a possible dictatorship. Along with this, there could be major disruptions in services and supplies—just like in Venezuela.

John also felt there was an antichrist figure waiting in the wings (2017-2018) ready to take the world stage. Because of him, John felt we were close to the start of the Great Tribulation by merely observing world events. He felt that as these events unfold, he and Carol at 75 years old, would live to see the rise of this man.

John said, in that time-frame, look for a chastisement comet to hit the Atlantic Ocean. It will appear like two suns in the sky. It will be seen on the day of the warning. This is all based on the Book of Revelation and revelation of the Holy Spirit. There will be three days of darkness. The devil will lose the battle and be cast into the Lake of Fire. The Lord God will recreate the earth and Jesus will reign for a long time on the earth. Then we are all Heaven bound as we are purified.

Through August and September of 2017, there have been two category-5 hurricanes, a 50-inch flood, and an 8.1 earthquake in Mexico (prophecy is fulfilling before our eyes). God has told John He will protect His people at the refuges.

When we look to Scripture, we know that the Father in the Old Testament always protected His people before He destroyed the unfaithful. Noah was in the Ark before the flood. In Ezekiel 9, the angels were told not to destroy those with an "X" on their foreheads. In Sodom, again the Lord led Lot and his faithful out before it was destroyed. The Exodus also saw the Israelites led into the desert.

On September 3rd, John received another "download" from the Lord regarding North Korea. Their leader was trying to put war in motion. They detonated a hydrogen bomb underground causing a 6.4 earthquake under the mountain they were in. John felt North Korea could start a conventional war with South Korea and move to an EMP attack on America. It could devastate our land. America wouldn't be able to large-farm produce. Millions would die by starvation.

There is a study/document given to Homeland Security saying the threat of an EMP attack is very real. Up to 90% of Americans could die within one year from no food/mass starvation. No chips would work — cars, trucks, banks, appliances, communication devices, etc.

John asked people to pray very hard that none of this start nor escalate. If it became a nuclear war, millions would die suddenly. He went on to say, this past week, there were black skies over parts of our planet that were not evening-associated. John reiterated to pray for refuges to have enough food, water, heat and shelter throughout this winter.

John also saw in another vision, buildings falling from an earthquake. He saw the San Andreas and the New Madrid faults associated with it. He knew there would be a cluster of earthquakes over the summer in Yellowstone (which there were.)

John felt these would be a direct result of mortal sins being committed and not being repented of. This country needs more than one day of prayer. We need to repent. We are at the crossroads.

Items John encouraged everyone to buy were: kerosene, warm clothes, water, candles, food, wind-up flash lights, old ringer-type washers (they make those now with foot-pedal power) a camper-stove, a grinder, a propane tank, a one-year supply of all your needs, and a carbon monoxide meter. And make sure, wherever you are, you can get fresh air daily. These items were all for independent survival.

You will also need Spiritual items such as Bibles, rosaries, scapulars, holy water, blessed salt and a Benedict's cross. (Remember, John is speaking to the Catholics and the items they would specifically need.)

John has seen demons come out of people. Evil spirits are attached to addicts, killers, abortionists and their providers, homosexuality, transgender, personality disorders, pornography and the occult. Look at all the people that are suffering. There are demons for all our sins.

John asked, "How can we come against these things? Use blessed salt, the prayer of St. Michael—especially the Long Form, and holy water."

As John finished that portion of his talk, Carol got up to speak. She spoke on action and involvement. "Get organized! When you have a lot of people at your refuge, give out assignments. Everyone must have responsibilities and chores to do. This will keep order in your area. Make sure you have enough fuel to get through the winter. Have "balances" for stress and high-stress times. When you share distraught times or troubles, you can help each other. When people arrive, they will be distressed."

Carol went on, "Consecrate your property. Whether it be an interim refuge or a large refuge. Angels will bring a shield of invisibility and protection. These will all be helps to you and your group."

John took over from there once again. "In August, I recorded a message that vaccines are causing autism in babies. I am not saying don't get your children vaccinated. I am saying space them out so they don't hurt your children. If you can, avoid flu shots. The side effects are too many. And pray for your children's health."

John paused for a moment, then went on. "I have seen a vision of hell and of purgatory. In hell, I saw the top level were the lukewarm. In the middle, I saw those who sold their souls to satan for fame and fortune. And on the bottom, those who proselytized others to go to hell. The very bottom of purgatory is like hell, but you can get out of there. There are many levels as Jesus is just. The people there need your prayers. There are different levels in each area including heaven."

John also spoke of a priest he knew in Canada. He was in the process of building a monastery. This priest would be holding a couple of conferences in America later that fall. He is a gift for this time, this season.

John mentioned the US dollar —that he saw a change coming. Our passports are already "chipped." At first, they will ask for voluntary chipping of people—then there will be mandatory chipping required. This will be in our bodies.

John strongly advised people not to take the chip for any reason, because they will use it to control people's minds and free will. He expects soon after they start the voluntary chipping, it will become mandatory—especially for the military.

There is a one-world evil and antichrist-spirit out among the people.

Then John told a story.

"St. Maximum Kolbe was in a monastery near the destruction of Nagasaki. Yet his building was not hurt and no one got sick. His Monastery was protected. Fr. Maximum later died in a German Concentration camp giving his life for another man."

John mentioned the possibility of war with North Korea. He said, "Pray to end abortion, and just possibly peace will come with North Korea and they will not start a war. Abortion is the main cause of our judgement."

John asked us if we knew we could fight the devil with prayers and good deeds. He said to ask Jesus to multiply our prayers, too.

I responded, "You know, I never thought of that, but it sure makes good sense." I hoped in my heart, I had gotten it right all along.

John said, "Be watchful of churches and prayer groups being shut down. We are living in tribulation times. Satan and his demons are

116

setting in for a last stand. But God will only allow them to go so far. Satan knows his time is short."

John waited for the effect of his statement to settle in. He went on.

"President Trump is a temporary reprieve. He is God's man. He is trying to turn the tide around. He's fighting the NAFTA treaty, and finish good projects he is starting.

The hands of the clock [indicating the timeline of events] have slowed down. Minutes and hours are fast on our own timelines. But God lives outside of time. [There will be a warning in which] we will see our mini-judgements and then go back to our bodies. This warning is His greatest act of mercy since His death on the cross. Hopefully we will improve our lives and learn from our mistakes."

John paused to gather his next thoughts and took back off again.

"The war and tribulation with the antichrist will only be a short reign. Have no fear. When you see it coming, get to a refuge. Have a backpack ready to leave after the warning. There will be about six weeks for conversion after the warning given."

Comments were made about the Biblical flood of 50 inches of rain in four days with Hurricane Harvey in Texas. It was a destruction that would last a long time. Yet there were many acts of kindness that surfaced. The Cajun Navy from Louisiana showed up and kept hundreds of families from drowning. The goodness of the Lord outshone the destruction of the devil. People experienced God's love through other people's actions and gave it back out to everyone they met.

Toward the end of John and Carol's talks, we were reminded to keep pictures of our family around us. This is requested by our deceased relatives. John spoke about the vibrational energy of the Holy Spirit (just as we have vibrational energy) and said to love God and your neighbor as yourself. Reconcile to all and be saved for the coming battle.

God has helped President Trump to get him where he is today. But, there is a resistance out to get him. It is the "One-World" people who do not like patriots.

John said, "Look for them to first try to impeach him or call him unfit. And if that doesn't work, they may indeed try to kill our duly-elected president."

After that, John started on a completely different topic: purgatory. John has seen purgatory as a grey area. He has seen Heaven and levels of hell. The top level of hell is for those who ignore God. The mid-level of hell is for those who have made bargains with lucifer for fame and fortune. And the last level of hell is for the satanists and luciferians. The mere thought of those places made me shudder.

At John's closing remarks, he touched on each of these—chemtrails are black-ops, since 1998 HAARP has been used to *enhance* hurricanes and earthquakes. There are many refuges in South America and Europe. God is getting His message out about help. CERN [a French acronym – a European Organization for Nuclear Research] is real, and it has satanic rituals attached to it. There are such things as evil rosaries that have curses attached to them. Their crucifixes have serpents on them.

The last thing John said was, "When the time comes, we will all have to drop our phones and electrical devices and head to the refuges."

We closed that portion of the conference with prayers for the people in Cuba and Florida in the direct line of the hurricane. We asked God to take control of the weather and ease it down from a category 5 to one that was survivable for everyone.

I received a call from our women pastors who came all the way from Wisconsin to attend our meetings. Linda and Sherry had arrived at their hotel and wanted me to know they had made it in safely. They would try to make it to part of Saturday's events (which they did) but most definitely would be at our home for dinner that evening.

The thought of Linda and Sherry joining us and our conversations about the imminent return of Jesus brought excitement to my spirit. I could hardly wait to give hugs that next afternoon.

Much to our delight, overnight, the big Category 5 hurricane that destroyed islands and wreaked havoc in Cuba, eased down to 120 mph winds as it headed through the Florida Keys. At the start of Saturday morning, Irma began its turn toward South Florida as we were starting our day for the big conference with Fr. David.

The Gospel of Mark, Part II
(That evening)

By 4:30 mass was over and we started the arduous journey of packing it all up to take it back to our home. What we didn't know was, our journey together was just getting started.

And what God had planned, as usual, was much higher than our plans....

Katie greeted us as we arrived. "Come in! Come in! Dinner is ready!" She cried.

"Oh, you jewel! What a help you are!" I responded.

Beef stew and chicken & dumplings awaited us. Along with the left-overs from the conference, a feast loomed before us.

Everyone gathered around for the evening prayer of thanksgiving. We bowed our heads anticipating "amen!" and a meal together. As soon as the quick prayer was over, chatter rang among our guests as they helped themselves to dinner. Our visitors represented almost 1,000 miles worth of a gathering. From New York to St. Louis, to Wisconsin, people came and sat, once again, in our home. And we were mighty glad to get to know them, each and every one. The count was twenty-something by then, not the 12 we'd planned for. But the meal held out—with left overs. A remnant was seated in our home: they came from Catholic, Christian and denominational churches—all coming together to hear the good news of the Gospel of Jesus Christ.

I remember one family in particular. They were from West St. Louis. They wanted so badly to understand the times we were living in. They had asked their local priest over and over for help. He refused to answer their questions. But there in our home, their questions were answered and they were not turned away.

As dinner wound down, our kitchen crew went to work. Linda, Carol, Deb, Katie, Mary and Mark started the clean-up. As we worked together in our kitchen, conversation of a higher sort was going on in the sunroom.

When we joined the folks in our sunroom to settle in and consider the deep things of God and how they related to the times we were living in, questions were being passed around. A couple of our people had met our neighbor.

They whispered, "Do you think he will come and talk to us?"

They asked Mark, "Would you mind to please go over and ask your neighbor if he would come over for just a bit?"

Now, our neighbor had just had as big of a day as we. He is a one-man army when it comes to yard sales. And it was almost 9 p.m.

While we were busy discussing whether our Mark (Peyron) should even go over there to bother him, he had already slipped out of our house and across the street. He stood on our friend's porch and knocked. Mark came to the door wearing shorts.

"Hi, Mark." He said.

Mark Peyron just smiled and replied, "They're waiting. Won't you come and speak for a little while?"

Mark nodded his head and asked my husband to wait for a few minutes while he changed. Then they walked back across the street and into our home. He promised he would speak to our group for a few minutes.

Mark told our neighbor he would be speaking in front of Christians of all denominations, including a Roman Catholic priest and two female pastors. They were all of great faith.

As the men walked into our home, whispers began. "He's here! He's here!"

When they walked into our sunroom, Katie jumped up and ran out of the room. While they positioned themselves for the talk to begin, Katie was back in an instant dropping paper and pen in my lap.

Katie whispered to me, "You'll need these."

"Thank you" was in my eyes. And once again*, this is where the Gospel of Jesus Christ met the Gospel of Mark...

Mark started the conversation with, "I'm sure you've heard about and seen the "Great American Eclipse" that just happened. It will cross America again in seven years — April 18, 2024."

Heads nodded including his. Then Mark's conversation went in a different direction.

"The Jews in Israel are very secular— especially in Tel Aviv. They are non-practicing in faith and modern in their thinking. The Jewish faith has 613 commandments. We also have dietary laws. There are things that are permissible and things to eat that are beneficial. So there are differences in traditions of people with the same heritage.

*See MI-V, "The Gospel of Mark" for the 1st story.

The Zionist Jews who are democrats are not for Donald Trump —even though Trump is for Israel and Jerusalem as their Capitol city. They are more pro-democratic party than they are pro-Israel."

Mark asked for a glass of water and went on with his ten-minute talk that turned into an hour and ten minutes.

"I would like to teach about some of our Jewish celebrations and our words associated with them. *Awe* - means to stand in awe of God. *Rosh* means "heard." And *ha' shamah* means year. *Rosh Hashannah* - the Feast of Trumpets.

A *shofar* is a horn blown to call people to synagogue, or at a time of warfare. A horn taken from a ram, gazelle, or antelope was used as musical instrument. The term was taken from Abraham: When Abraham took Isaac up the mountain to sacrifice him as the Lord commanded, the angel stopped him from taking the boy's life. The horns of the ram tangled in the thicket was sacrificed instead. Its horns became the first shofars. Jews believe one was for the earth, and the other is in Heaven. It will be blown when Jesus comes back a second time."

As understanding hit our crowd, "Ohhh's" and "ahhhhs" went up in the room. Mark went on.

"Many major events have occurred on Jewish Feast days. As of the 21st century, we are in the 6,000th day of creation."

Just like watching a well-told movie, our group was translated from Corydon, Indiana to Israel, and back and forth as in a time continuum. You bet no one moved from their seats. We buckled in and scarcely breathed.

"In Jerusalem there is a small building with ancient writings in it. It is practicing this mystic writing where men learn how to make creative power without God. They are using creative power wrongly.

"Since the 1960's, science has been trying to figure the age of the universe. Socrates taught there was no beginning to the universe. Years later, scientists found there was a signature 'echo' of a bang. This beginning is where the Bible and science come together to prove the words, 'In the beginning...'"

Polite clapping went up with approval of Mark's message. He went on.

"There was a Jewish professor of cosmology of nuclear science at MIT who proved a theory that took 13 billion years down to 6,000 years. In the vastness of creation, the Talmud —our oral tradition — looked at created man and the planets in the sky. With all this knowledge and the Hubble telescope, they can see the edge of the universe— where time started, the edge."

I was taking so many notes so fast I thought my hand might cramp up!

More ohhhs and ahhhhs swept through the room with each bit of information Mark shared with our group.

"Were you aware the angels look at man in awe about our faith in God? Angels don't understand choice. (For the rebellion had been preplanned upon.) There really are sons of satan."

Mark paused and people gasped as the realization of the fight between good and evil settled into their minds.

I had personally felt that way too. *(As explained in the beginning of book VI, "Warn Those Who Will Listen," in story, "The Death of the Soul.")* Long ago, I spoke to one of these on the phone. The angel that guards me cried out, *"Hang up the phone! You are speaking to the damned! Hang up the phone! You are still speaking to one of the damned!"*

Mark continued, "Over in Europe, Muslim refugees rape and murder. They worship a god of war. Which can be traced all the way back to King Og, who was 19 feet tall.

"Our world is prophetic without even knowing it. There will be a millennia reign. The 'Days of Awe' are near the Feast of Trumpets, in 2017 the 21st-23rd of September. 3,650 years ago there was an exodus out of Egypt. Moses had an almond staff — it looked like a golden wood."

As we "travelled" back and forth in time, hearing how it all related together, Mark spoke on many more topics. Including Planet X and how it is associated with "Wormwood." The state of Arizona and Project Lucifer — how scientists since 1984 have been watching a brown dwarf star with the appearance of 'inbound wings' with its trajectory toward Earth.

"There will be a lot of magnetic upheaval to the core of the earth. A few years ago, radiation had gone up 12% and coming from within, not without. It has risen 24% in the last two years. This has been a great rise of concern with people on our planet."

Mark also believes Planet X is between the sun and the earth. It is at least 9 million miles away. It will not be a direct hit, but he thinks the earth will run through its tail, causing plagues from toxic elements. "If the poles change—it could cause a flash freeze on parts of our planet."

Mark has come to the conclusion that the Illuminati is a real entity. It does have to do with satan. And they are trying to pick presidents and world leaders—as they have been for centuries.

"Donald Trump is a phenomenon. The enemies of America are fighting him all the way."

Mark cautioned each household to have enough food and water to last at least one month in our homes. He reminded us that the Year of Jubilee would end at the end of September, 2017.

Then we went on a history lesson. "The Ottoman Empire ruled what they called "Palestine" for 400 years from 1517 to 1917 until the end of World War I. The English took, what would later become the land of Israel, without a shot. They created the Balfour Declaration giving the land back to its rightful owners. All the way to 1917, it was desolate land – barren. But once the Jewish people began coming back to their homeland, the land itself began to flourish. Now the whole world is focused on Israel. The Dead Sea has so many healthful minerals. They make soaps, bath salts, facial and body creams from the salt and Dead Sea soil.

In Israel, every day they are finding in that region, gold, oil and natural gas. As the middle-east runs out of its resources (water, oil, money) watch, in 20 years, all those rich countries and families will be Bedouins again. Tent dwellers."

The whole room took on a collective sigh as Mark took a drink, only to start up another amazing discourse once again.

"September 23, 2017, Revelation 12:1-3 lines up – Jupiter [the star of the Messiah, the star of the King and called the "King Planet"] has been for the last nine months in the womb of constellation Virgo—the virgin. It is another sign in the heavens."✶

John and Mark commented on how they felt President Trump could be the last president to come against an antichrist. We all wondered if we would be here to see the end of days or rapture out — when the Holy Spirit is removed from the earth. John had previously seen in a vision the "taking up" at the end when the comet hits earth.

Mark once again took us to historical and biblical perspective. "In India, everything's a god. And that is why they are starving to death. Food all around them that they can't eat.

"Goliath was a Nephilim giant. He had poor vision and couldn't move quickly. His blood line was cursed. How do we know this? The Hebrews were still working with bronze weapons—swords. Goliath's sword was made of refined steel. It was a real weapon of war. It was the technology of the fallen angels brought down to earth."

> ✶ *The planets Jupiter, Mercury, Mars, Venus and stars aligned to make 12 stars around the head of the Virgin constellation, with our Sun on her shoulder and the Moon was indeed under her feet – just as described in Revelation.*

Mark chuckled for a moment and shared an observation. "Americans treat crazy as bad. Other nations in Europe and Africa call them, 'touched by God.'"

He moved on to other subjects.

"King David was a prophet, King, Priest. Jesus was a prophet, King, and Priest, too." (Yes, Mark believes Jesus, Yeshua, is the Son of God.)

"I know, all you hear about on American television is how much Muslims hate Americans. And they do. But Muslims hate Hindu's the worst. If they could, they would fight each other first."

Mark and John carried on a discussion as to who they thought the antichrist was and if he was on the earth now. As they put their information together, each asking the other more questions, we all began to wonder if indeed there was validity to their assumptions.

I tell you here and now, I believed them. We all believed that all those in that sunroom would live to see the antichrist make an appearance on the world stage. And I am grateful to say, we believe he is not an American nor associated with America. (Thank God!) John believes the antichrist is a man named [L.M.] who lives in London, England. He is of both Muslim *and* Jewish heritage.

Time flew by and before we knew it, we had kept our patient young neighbor way past his agreed time limit. People clapped and thanked him for his time and Mark walked him back to his home. Meanwhile, we were all so excited over our new-found information, sleep was far from us for hours to come.

John, Carol, Linda, Mark and I ended the evening saying prayers for Florida, as Irma had sustained winds of 130 mph over Key West. We prayed for the "giant of giants" to turn from the major portion of the state. We knew, millions of people were praying with us for lives to be spared.

A Much Needed Vacation
(September 26- October 7th)

My Lord! How can I tell you how weary I was? We were? Mark and I needed a break. He was cast head-long into this "prophecy" which had been trailing after me for months.

We had prayed day and night against a nuclear attack on American soil. I had seen open visions of a bright light early in the morning with an exact time of 8:15 a.m. I had cried.

I heard from several different sources that the same vision had been seen by other people too. One a priest and the other an ordinary lady such as myself.

If only I had indeed told all the right people. And dear God, let that letter I had sent to our president through a visiting pastor, have made it to its goal. The warning had stood in my heart, all through September and October. I felt, if we made it past fall without an incident, then I would have indeed told the right person.

For months, we had taken every waking daylight hour to work landscape jobs and painting jobs in order to afford the two weeks off. Because of the visions, we wanted to go and see our children in Florida – especially then. It was that important to us.

In our eyes, it all fell together for the second two week vacation we'd ever taken. Surely, we thought, it would go much better than the last one.

Don't count your "betters" before they arrive...

"Frick frack! Frick frack!" I yelled. (And that is the closest interpretation you will get from me, thanks for asking.)

"What's wrong with you!?" Mark asked. Frustration had settled in before we had even got out of our driveway!

I had everything packed — which was monumental for a two-week stay away from home. Plus we had books packed for the conference during the second week of our trip. And that money was to be used to go to a conference at the end of October down in Louisiana. Not quite like "robbing Peter to pay Paul."

"I can't get the rental car started!" I cried. Literally cried.

"Calm down!" Mark shouted. "You are too wound up! Give me the keys!"

Shaking, I handed over the keys. For Mark, the car purred to life. Sigh. I was in mid-repentance to the Lord when Mark spoke again.

"Let's go honey. You are sure you have everything? For the whole journey?"

I meekly said, "Yes." but I was feeling pretty humbled.

Off we went. Our first day, we travelled to Tennessee to spend the night. Then the next day, a long 12-hour trip to arrive at Andy and Sam's. We were to spend one night with them, and for the next five nights we would be staying on property at Disney. We had even arranged for Andy and his family to have the room next to us for 3 days too. The last of our savings well spent.

The weather was calm all the way down. Yet, we saw remnants of Irma's damage the farther south we traveled. High stacks of palm tree leaves and debris were on every corner. We knew that by prayer alone, Florida had "dodged a bullet."

We were greeted outside our car as we arrived at their new apartment home. Lily had Sophia on her hip and Matthew was bouncing all around. Papaw and Grammy had come to visit!!! All three children were shouting, "Grammy, Papaw! Grammy, Papaw!!"

As soon as Mark had stopped the car we fairly jumped out and ran to them with open arms. Those sweet dolls have trained us well. More subdued than the children, but still happy to see us, Andy and Samantha met us with smiles and hugs. Sweet kisses were exchanged. At last, we were all theirs as they showed us around their new apartment. Baby Sophia had to show us "right now, Grammy!" — her new big-girl bed.

Dinnertime came and Andy asked us if we had seen the newest Disney movie — which we hadn't had the chance. In just a few minutes he had it up on their television screen. In my mind, I flew back in time as I remembered running home from the grocery store on Friday evenings, shouting for all to hear, "I've got it! I've got the newest Disney flick, you guys! Movie night! Family night!"

We spent most of the next day with them, then headed into our resort reservation late that afternoon. Mark and I had decided, months before we left home for this trip, we wanted to be good to our son and his family. They had been so good to us through the years, we thought giving back to them in the form of a mini-vacation with us would be a nice way to repay their kindness. We paid for them to join us for the weekend – Friday through Sunday – our hotel rooms next to each other. And our grandkids could stay with us.

For the first time, in 20 visits over 40 years, standing at the check-in reservation desk, I asked a question I had never once asked before.

"What you got going around here?" I didn't realize the words had come out of my mouth until I heard them.

The woman eyed me for a full minute before answering me.

"We have the flu – Influenza – from people coming in from other countries. Hospitals and clinics are full of it. Be careful."

I replied, "Thanks for the warning...."

Mark and I checked in and took the entirety of our week-long luggage to our rooms. Then we went to the boat dock to take a ride in to Disney Springs to meet our children for dinner. Pizza was on the menu. We'd promised we would buy all their meals during our time together. Their money was no good.

Dreaming in Disney
(September 28, 2017)
(5:30 a.m.)

After a nice meal and walk around together, the kids went home to pack for their weekend with us. And we went back to our resort to rest for the busy weekend ahead. Even as urgent as the message had been that had brought us there, I went to sleep at ease, to finally rest...

My "Telling" Time

I went to sleep and opened my eyes. I saw hell. It was all around me. I was in hell but not a part of it. It was as if I was falling down a long, black hole, into the earth. I saw what I thought was coal glistening and flash firing in the walls of the cavern as I fell endlessly downward. I soon found I was being directed where to go.

In this vision/dream, I reached a large cavern, bigger than I could take all in. I did not stop there. There was a second cave, farther down into the depths of hell, off to the side. As if it had been dug deeper into the very pit of hell. I was aware of a stench, horrors, sorrow and despair; but they were not a part of me nor of my experience.

I realized I was with an angel and it brought me great comfort. We slowed our progress and came to a room lit by a single candle. There was a table with no chairs—for there is no comfort in hell.

On the table were plans of a sort. Much like you would see in a situation war room. Out of the darkness to gather around the table, came hideous demons dressed in general's uniforms. The most ugly of all—ha' satan—lucifer himself—walked up to the table and spoke.

"Get ready. I am starting the war soon." His raspy voice seethed with venom giving me chills up and down my spine.

As soon as he spoke, I was back in our bedroom wide awake, heart pounding.

Immediately I was given revelation. I felt in my Spirit, "Imminent! Days! Weeks!" And I felt I knew why. The devil was trying to start a war before the second coming of Jesus Christ. Satan thought the body of Christ couldn't stop his plans without the Man-Jesus physically on the earth. Satan was once again trying to usurp God.

I gasped. "What do you want me to do?!"

In my Spirit, the reply came quick. **"Pray the Lord's Prayer! God's will. For the devil can't win against God's will!"**

I shook my husband awake.

"Mark! Get up! I've seen hell! Been to hell! I've heard the devil's plans! We have to pray! Get your Bible please!"

The urgency in my voice got Mark's attention. He quickly grabbed his Bible and we went to Ephesians 6:10-16 - the armor of God, as a sword and a shield.

Sundown of that very day, was Yom Kippur - the Day of Atonement.

I believed it.

I found out later, Katie Yocum was also up at 5:30 that morning praying. Sleep finally came back to her at 6:30.

Birds of a feather prayed together 900 miles apart!

103.1° What?!

(Tuesday, October 3, 2017)

Mark and I hadn't been to breakfast yet. We were too busy packing. I would pack a stack of luggage and Mark would take it to our car. I packed another stack of luggage and he took it to our car. The third stack of luggage was all small bags and blankets that would go in our backseat.

Mark came back into our resort room just as I was finishing up.

"All's ready honey." I said, "We can go down to breakfast now."

As I was talking, and turned from him, Mark got back in our bed, shoes and all, grabbed the covers, pulled them up to his neck and preceded to shake the bed.

I cried out, "What is wrong with you?!"

Mark stammered, "I don't know. I hurt all over and I'm so cold!"

Our bag with medical supplies, including a thermometer, was still in our room. I touched Mark's forehead. He was hot!!

"Oh my!"

I dug out the thermometer and put it in his mouth.

Mark was saying, "I hurt all over...," as I put it under his tongue.

"It sounds like you have caught the flu." I went straight into nursing mode. I took his blood pressure and his oxygen stats – all normal. His temperature was 101.2°.

"I don't understand it. You don't shake like this unless you are over 102. You are nowhere close to it. This doesn't make sense. Maybe my thermometer isn't working. I'll call Sam."

Mark laid in the bed, miserable while I got our daughter-in-law, the ex-emergency room nurse, on the phone.

"Samantha? This is Momma. Something's wrong with Mark. He is showing a fever of 101.2, but he is shaking the bed like crazy! I think my thermometer is on the fritz. Do you have a thermometer?"

Samantha put on her nursing hat right away. "Yes I do, Mom. Come on over. I'll be waiting at the door."

"I'll be driving sweetheart. It may take a little extra time. I don't know the way like Mark does. Even with directions on our google maps."

"I'll pray for you, Momma."

"Thank you, sweet doll. See you in a bit. We are checking out and getting Mark a bit of breakfast down as fast as I can."

I practically carried Mark to our car and bundled him up in our extra blankets. I drove us over to the main building at Port Orleans, where were to check out and grab breakfast. I knew Mark would need medicine as soon as we got to Sam's. He would also need something on his stomach, whether he liked it or not. I walked Mark in and sat him down next to the fireplace.

I checked us out and ran and got us each small plates of breakfast. Mark could barely walk. He legs were cramping up in pain.

"You need to eat a little something honey. You are going to have to take medicine to bring your temperature down."

Try as he could, Mark could only get a few bites down.

We walked slowly back to our car, and I bundled him up once again. I put in the kids' address on my phone and off we went to their home. I could feel an emergency room visit coming on...so much for Tennessee that day.

When we arrived at Sam and Andy's, Samantha was already at the door — waiting with a thermometer in her hand ready to go. She was all nurse.

"Open your mouth, Dad. I already called Andy. He is aware of the situation." Boy, she was on it!

Sam hustled us over to the couch. The she read Mark's temperature.

"103.1°. Dad, you've got to be seen right away."

Samantha dug around through their cabinets for acetaminophen, handing him 1,000 milligrams.

"Take these right away. I am calling and making you an appointment right now. Mom, I'm sending the link to the directions to your phone."

Boy that girl was on it! Within minutes, the "situation" was handled.

"Go now, Mom. I'll keep Andy informed."

"Thank you sweetheart!"

Weakly, from on the couch, Mark said, "Do you think this is necessary?"

Sam and I just looked at him with our jaws dropped. He nodded his head and gave us no more fight. I walked him to the car.

Sam called out from her doorway, "Call me when you know anything!"

"I will!" I promised.

Four miles never seemed so far away.

As we walked in, I said to Mark, "I'll fill out the paperwork for you, honey. Sit down. I'll be right over there."

I approached the reception desk.

"Thank you for seeing us right away. We are here on vacation to see our children when Mark woke up sick this morning."

"You are out of town visitors?" The young man inquired. Two nurses looked at each other. "Do you have any health insurance?"

"No, sir. No, ma'am," I said looking at them across the desk.

They looked at each other again.

Did I ever tell you I can read nurse language? "What's wrong?" I asked.

"There's a $500 charge for out of town."

"Oh no..."

I quickly gave my own credentials in the nursing field and asked if there was anything they could do about the cost. We put our heads together.

"Well," they started. "You say you are here visiting your son? So, it's a Florida address we could use, especially if you pay your whole bill today?"

Smiles were on their faces.

"How much would it save us?" I asked.

"Almost $200." They said with a grin.

I called Sam to make sure it was okay with them, and it was. Instant part-time Florida residents we became. Thank God!

Shortly after that, another nurse called Mark back to his room. They took his temperature. Still high at 102.9. They left with a report for the doctor on-call. He came in shortly with an update. While the kindly, elderly gentleman examined Mark, he gave out orders.

"600 milligrams ibuprofen now. Culture for the flu. And get him a blanket."

All was done in an orderly manner. Mark and I remarked about the serenity that seemed over the urgent care center. How peaceful it seemed.

Mark had felt compelled to pray for a young man with a broken collar bone in the waiting room and for the attending physician that saw him. The doctor was so touched by Mark's prayer, he held his hand and smiled. He told Mark he did not know how close he had come to the actual prayer on the man's heart.

"You don't leave until your temperature starts to come down. Then go to the pharmacy nearby and get your prescriptions filled. Get rest and lots of liquids." Doctor's orders.

His diagnosis: the Influenza of 1917. Oh boy.

I started myself on Silver Shield right away.

It was late in the afternoon when I called Sam with an update. She had good suggestions for us.

"Mom, you can't drive all the way to Tennessee or anywhere with Dad that sick. I'm calling Andy. I think we know where to send you. It's only four hours away."

Of course Sam was right. The couple gave us information to their favorite hotel to stay at on the road just on the other side of the Georgia border. I made our reservation. And I called our reservation in Tennessee for the suite we had reserved and let them know what was going on. They were very understanding. The desk clerk said they would hold our room for us. Please take it easy on the road. I sure did.

Before we left Altamonte Springs, I picked up Mark's medications, some lunch and made sure he had his first dose down before 50 miles out. I drove three more hours and made it out of Florida and started looking for our exit. We arrived shortly after dark.

I checked us in to a beautiful hotel and room. To our blessing, there was a restaurant right across the street. We walked over to eat, with Mark in his jacket and hoodie pulled up around him. He ordered hot tea. I shoveled food and his medication down him for a second time that day.

The next morning we slept in until Mark felt he could travel another five hours to get to the Tennessee border—our next stop. It did not look like a good start to our week-long conference and Fall Festival scheduled for Saturday a.m. Katie and Nick Yocum were supposed to join us on Thursday for the conference and fall festival on Saturday. How was I going to tell them our plans were rapidly changing?

We arrived at church that evening with a very rough-looking Mark Peyron. One of our favorite people greeted us at the door. She knew immediately how sick he was. That's when she started shouting, "Oh no! We have already had that flu in these halls. We like to never got rid of it! Go and buy your DVD's of the conference, and go back to your hotel and rest. Maybe you can come by Saturday for the Festival. Go home!"

And we did just that. On the way back to our hotel, we stopped at the grocers. Our suite had come complete with a full kitchen, living room, separate bedroom and bathroom. Home away from home.

Over the next two days, Douglass Inn fixed breakfast, I fixed lunch and dinner. We stayed in our room, only moving from bedroom to living room to watch a little television and eat meals in the kitchen.

While there, we would go into our praying time together. It was during that time that Mark saw a tsunami wave coming from the ground itself, not water. He also saw a big cloud over a city that was near water. Part of the cloud dropped down engulfing the city. But it wasn't violent. It was a very interesting vision.

I called Katie Wednesday evening and gave her an update on our situation. We were still registered for a booth at the church Fall Festival. I was sure I could sell all my books, and Katie her soap, to make money for our next planned trip to either Ohio or Louisiana at the end of October. And we were hoping to meet up with the man we had sent the letter with back in July, to find out the rest of our story.

Mark and I made the best of the situation with his temperature going down day by day. By Thursday afternoon, we heard from Katie again. We thought for sure they were well on their way to Tennessee.

I heard a heavy sigh on the phone. "I have bad news."

I cried, "What's wrong?"

"Our van won't start. I've got Chris coming over later tonight to check it. But it doesn't sound good Deb."

I could hear tears in her voice—and mine.

If the Yocum's couldn't arrive, I had very little to put out on a table. No decorations either. She was bringing everything. And I most certainly couldn't leave Mark for a full day to fend for himself. I have to admit, I cried like a baby.

By that evening, Chris confirmed the bad news about her van. It was going to cost $600 to fix. And the Yocums couldn't fix their van and come to Tennessee. They had to do one or the other. Sadly, I told them we would head home Friday morning. At the time, I didn't realize how early that day we were going to have to leave...

5 a.m. Friday

"What's wrong with me?! What's wrong with me?! My throat is so sore, I can't swallow or talk! And I have a fever!! How will I ever get us home?!" I shook Mark awake. Panic was in my eyes.

Mark cried out, "What's wrong?!"

I put his hand to my forehead and clutched my throat. I whispered.

"We have to leave now before I get worse, or I won't be able to get us home."

As we quickly packed up the car and checked out, I thought to myself, "Gosh, will I ever confirm my letter getting to the President?" At the time, it was the least of my worries.

I started out driving. But after a couple of hours in, I was feeling so poorly, I couldn't drive anymore. As sick as he was, Mark took over. I kept taking my Silver Shield to ward off what was taking over in my body.

By 9 a.m., we hit the Kentucky border, and I put in a call to our doctor's office.

I croaked out, "You guys! This is Debbie and Mark Peyron. Mark got real sick with Influenza while in Florida. It has taken us days to get this far. I woke up at 5 this morning with a horrible sore throat and temperature. Too weak to drive. Mark is driving. I need to see the doctor as soon as possible!"

"When can you be here? Can you make it by 11:30? We will hold your time for you! Get here but be safe!" What jewels they were! And we made it with ten minutes to spare. Thank God I did not have the flu. Our doctor figured I picked up a virus while at the hospital with Mark. He gave me medicine and sent us both home to rest.

Well, needless to say, Mark and I spent that whole weekend at home taking care of each other. Due to the extremely untimeliness of these events, we had no money to go to either Louisiana or Ohio for conference. But we still had a date for the last week of October to Michigan with Deb Grimes. Nothing was stopping that.

During our resting time the first weekend in October, Mark dreamed of money. He dreamed of three checks coming to us. Two have come true just as he saw. One was at Christmas time and one was during the summer. Both blessings that came down the pipe.

But that third check, the blank check, has yet to make its appearance. And where that money comes from, only God knows....

Confirmation of a Sort
(December 16 and 17th, 2017)

Let's recap the last two books of the *Miraculous Interventions* series:

Miraculous Interventions V The Small, Still Voice and *Miraculous Interventions VI Warn Those Who Will Listen.*

The warning in the fall of 2017 was about a possible nuclear strike from North Korea, although the first warning came three years before with Pastor David Becker, culminating at the end of book V for me. The verification came at the end of writing that book. All of book VI was about the fight to tell someone who would listen and do something about it. After all remember the conversation that started it all...

[Me: "What?! What do you want me to do with this information?!"

Holy Spirit: "For this, you have to do something. You have to tell someone. Tell all who will listen to you."

Me: "Pray?! What can I pray?" (Because I was panicking, quickly.)

HS: "Yes, you can pray against it. Pray for duds. That they are to be duds."

Me: "Yes, Sir! Duds, duds, duds, duds, duds -- duds in Jesus name!"]

My hope against hope came in, as higher and higher sources came around at just the right time for me to send the information up the ladder.

God sent the first confirmation that my message had reached the intended audience from a pastor in a small church in New Albany,

Indiana. His visiting pastor had a word of knowledge that was so specific, there was no escaping it.

"You sent a message with a man of importance to a man of great importance. God wants you to know it got there."

I was sure when I went to Tennessee for a conference, I would get a second confirmation from their people there. Yet unfortunate occurrences struck. Mark was so ill (103.1 temperature) I was unable to leave his side and go to conference by myself. I thought I would have to be content with the word of knowledge from the evangelist.

And by the way, he prayed for blessings and protection over me and my family. We were going to need it.

Questions remained in my mind until the beginning of the third week of December (17th). I happened across an obscure eight minute you tube video. I have transcribed it here:

Title: North Korean defector says even a limited attack by US would trigger all-out war.
PBS News hour
Title of Article: Out of North Korea
This was viewed and transcribed from the airways and a public site on YouTube.
Transcribed here:

"As we reported earlier, President Trump departed today for a lengthy trip to Asia. At the top of the agenda will be coordinating pressure against North Korea. The regime of Kim Jong Un has made significant advances in its nuclear missile programs. The core message of the President's trip, 'We will not allow North Korea to have the capability to launch a nuclear-tipped missile that can hit the United States.'

So how does North Korea view its weapons programs and the Trump administration's approach?

We turned to former North Korean Diplomat Thae Yung Ho. He was once North Korea's Deputy Chief of Mission in London. He defected last year (2016) and now lives in South Korea."

"Mr. Thae, thank you very much for joining us. You were telling us that you led a pretty privileged life as a diplomat working for the North Korean government. Why did you defect?"

"It's a complexity of reasons for my defection. First of all, I did not agree with Kim Jung Un's desperate race of nuclear and ICBM programs which can finally make North Korea totally destroyed, and secondly because of my future of my sons. I thought as a father the best legacy I should leave for my sons is to let them free."

"We know this is a regime that takes defectors very seriously. Are you and your family safe?"

"At this moment I am not quite sure where they are. My family members and relatives are safe."

"The ones who are still in North Korea?"

"Yes. I have one sister and a brother in North Korea. And for propaganda work, last

April, North Korea invited CNN team to have interview with my brother and my sister. In that interview, they cursed me a lot but at that moment I was really happy to see their faces again because I didn't imagine that I could see them again in my life after my defection."

"So as someone who worked in the diplomatic field for the North Korean government through many years, what can you tell us about the mindset of Kim Jung Un?"

"Kim Jung Un is not a madman. He is intelligent guy. But with a (muslis, *unclear word*) mind. So the past five years of his stay in North Korea proved that he want to destroy anything in his way no matter whether it is a country or human being. He has persecuted hundreds of city leaders in North Korea in his five years including his family members like his uncle and his half-brother."

"His own half-brother. What do you understand to be his view of the United States? We have seen his nuclear build up. The missile build up. What is your sense of what he thinks he can accomplish when it comes to the United States?"

"He has kind of an illusion that if he acquires these nuclear weapons and ICBM he could be able to compel Washington to pull US troops out of South Korea. And once US troops leave South Korea then foreign investments would follow troops out of South Korea. And if that is the case, then the South Korean business also would leave. Then he can stabilize the whole South Korean system with his nuclear weapons."

"But we haven't seen that happen of course. And we are seeing is this administration, the Trump administration pursuing a very aggressive policy toward the North. What do you see as the effects of that on the North?"

"I think the Kim Jung Un has been very desperate to develop its ICBM and nuclear. And he even sent a lot of rhetorics, warnings and provocations of nuclear tests and ICBM tests. I think we should admit that some rhetorics by President Trump and the unpredictable character of President Trump actually worked to some extent to stop his desperate escalation of the conflict. For instance when Kim Jung Un want the possible test around Guam, the American territory, then President Trump respond with fire and fury."

"That comment."

"Yes. And that kind of very strong response by President Trump actually stopped Kim Jung Un to have a test around Guam. That's why he changed the direction of ICBM from Guam to Pacific Ocean over the Japanese territory."

"So you are saying to some extent, that it's had a positive effect on the North?"

"Yes, I believe its so."

"And we know now from reporting that there are those in the Trump Administration who have put forward the notion of the possibility of a limited strike—an

151

attack against the North in order to punish the North to keep it from developing its nuclear missile program, in the belief that that could be effective. How do you think the North would respond?

"I think even a limited strike like kind of strike by US can bring a full-scale conflict or war on Korean peninsula because all North Korean military have been trained to fire back anyway, if one of their army very small part of North Korea is attacked by the US. And given the fact more than ten million of South Korea population are living within one hundred range of tens of thousands of North Korea artilleries, missiles, I think it not, if that kind of immediate and automatic response from North Korea military can create huge human loss on South Korea side. And if that's the case, then I think America and South Korean forces may retaliate in full scale. Then that's why it will easily escalate into a full-scale war on Korean peninsula which would mean huge human sacrifice."

"Huge? Almost unthinkable?"

He nodded.

"You've also talked to us Mr. Theo about what you think would be effective. You are saying some of the tough talk from President Trump has been effective? But you've also said that there should be a better effort to communicate with the North? To reach out to the North? What do you mean by that?"

"I think we should engage in and even try a dialogue with Kim Jung Un and also we should engage to break the isolation of North

Korean people. I think we can disseminate the more outside information to educate North Korean people so that we can help North Korean people to make a change."

"Fascinating to see where this is going to lead. Thae Yung Ho thank you so much for talking with us."

"Thank you very much for this opportunity."

Between January and August of this year (2017) 780 people escaped from North Korea. 57% were farmers and manual laborers.

Site: PBS News Hour
PBS New Hour You Tube video
PBS is a publically-funded American broadcaster.

This was taken from the common airwaves making it public knowledge.
Used with general permission.
(Verbiage transcribed as exactly as possible.)

To me, in my heart, this was the verification I—we—had done all the right things. From the Indiana pastor who put it out over the airwaves to get everyone praying, to my doctor who believed me, to our local law enforcement official who took a copy of my letter and two books! To the pastor who we believed took my letter to the President of the United States. Every one of us had a piece to help with in this. Not to mention all those I'd had praying, family members included.

From over four years ago with Pastor Becker, to this past summer with my friends from up north, and all in between, I believe we all had and have an integral part in the ongoing Saving of America.

And it's not over yet...

A Final Confirmation
(Long after I thought
I had finished this book!)

While Mary and I were editing this book, and I was waiting for page reviews to come back from New York, a package arrived.

In it, was a copy of a report to Homeland National Security. It was regarding the likelihood of an EMP threat from the North during the fall of 2017. And it was dated during the period of time which we were all getting alerts from heaven to pray like crazy against an attack! Even the date of September 30th was mentioned, just like in my dream!

This was the same month that North Korea detonated an H-Bomb under their mountain. (It caused a 6.0 earthquake, bringing down internal parts of the mountain, trapping and killing a hundred people.) And it released radioactive fallout over their area.

There was much more in the report that was way beyond my ability to explain here. Suffice it to say - we got it right. The threats had been real and the warning came just in time.

Epilogue
(December 31, 2017)

(Laughing)

Well, it appears, I have tried to say "the end" to the *Miraculous Interventions Series* with the last couple of books. I figured, "What else is there to say?" I wasn't going to share a warning, God said to share it. So I did. And I have told you what I know to date about it all. So when these last four books came to a close, I thought I was once again, "off the hook." But the Good Lord kept naming more.

If this tells me nothing else, it tells me that these books don't belong to me anymore – as if they ever had. They belong to all of us – you, me, everyone involved. To John and Carol Leary who have joined our team – or we joined theirs! We are all on God's team together! Amen.

By the afternoon of the last day of the year, 2017, I was deliriously happy we (the world) had made it through the fall mostly unscathed. No planet had knocked the earth out of its orbit (I believe because of prayer), and because of all our efforts and faithful prayers, nuclear war was averted the fall of 2017.

It seemed to me, the Good Lord in *The Saving of America,* was as concerned about the saving of souls as He was the saving of countries. After all, He has a vested interest in all of it. From the smallest of detail to the largest, He is in charge.

I have recently met a gentleman who thinks America is "toast." "Be prepared," he said. And I reminded him that "toast" is for another season, not yet here no matter how close it may be. He nodded in agreement.

We will live on to fight the good fight for another day, another season—no matter how short or long. But in my opinion, the last days or years are upon us.

And the surprise of surprises, Mark would be going into business during this new season. No rest for the weary. Because of it, I was sure my writing days were coming to a close. After all, how can you top saving the world? If even just for a season?

That's when the Whisper came, as always, out of nowhere. ***"Miraculous Interventions VIII, Extraordinary Miracles,' Look not only in your life, but all around the world...***

"My Spirt is moving..."

Oh my, it looks like I will be doing a lot of researching in the coming months.

And the dream I had on Easter morning 2018, of land splitting wide open on the east side of Tennessee, like an earthquake, with bright light rising out of the earth and into the heavens. Then huge cracks all over the earth had started. A light shone simultaneously from everywhere, reaching to the third heaven. It seemed as close as ever to coming true. Revelation?

The Holy Spirit was moving like lightening!

See you in the next book!

Love, Deb

Miraculous Interventions™ *VIII*

Extraordinary Miracles

Deborah Aubrey-Peyron

*"What I tell you in the dark,
speak in the daylight"*
Matthew 10:27

**"Look not only for you, but all around
the world. My Spirit is moving..."**

PRAYER FOR AMERICA

That she not fall in one hour.

That the Democratic Socialists do not steal any more elections.

Patriotic citizens stand up for our country.

That our president have two full seasons. That Donald Trump complete his mission by God and not be stopped.

That President Trump not be impeded by any communist manifesto (in my opinion it is not and has not been Russia.) But the Deep State that is involved in both parties.

That the patriots of this great Republic HOLD OUR TERRITORY!

That the American citizens wake up and stop listening to the agenda of fake news with their lies and deceptions.

That the Lord God remember those that are good to the nation of His people, Israel. That she and we prevail as in scripture.

And last for the safety and security of our President Donald John Trump, our First Lady, Melania Trump, their family, our Vice-President Michael Pence and his wife, Karen, their family, and for the conservatives of not only our nation, but all nations on this earth.

For the battle we wage is not of this world. It is against the princes and powers of the air, principalities and darkness that reigns on this earth for a season.

And that the people of the world understand time is short. This season is winding down, Jesus is coming back soon for His bride. As John the Baptizer said, "Prepare ye the way of the Lord. For His time is at hand."

Revelation 20: 1-4

And I saw thrones and they sat upon them, and judgment was given unto them and I saw the souls of them who were beheaded for the witness of Jesus, and for the Word of God, and which had not worshipped the Beast, neither his image, neither had received his mark upon their foreheads, or in their hands and they lived and reigned with Christ a thousand years.

DEBORAH'S SONG
by Mark Allen Peyron
(November, 1997)

After knowing Mark Peyron for a mere two weeks, he decided to write me a poem. The first poem he had ever written in his life-and since. After 20 years of carting it around in books, my wallet, and other assorted areas, I thought it would finally have a wonderful resting place right here.

Your faith in Father, Son and Holy Ghost
Is of true trust and love.
Faith in men is hurt and lost.
For it is not gone deep inside
Deborah's Song.

Take your time,
Take your time,
Friend of mine.
Trust in your heart
Then in your mind.
This is a good thing, inside
Deborah's Song.

Walls of fear and pain
That hold tight your heart,
Did melt for a time
To let me feel just inside
Deborah's Song.

Take your time,
Take your time,
Friend of mine.
Trust in your heart
Then in your mind.
This is a good thing inside,
Deborah's Song.

For only a moment, you let me in.
Feel did I
The offer of the touch of your hand,
The love in your soul.
The feel of one with me a man, just inside
Deborah's Song.

Take your time,
Take your time
Friend of mine.
Trust in heart
Then in mind.
This is a good thing inside
Deborah's Song.

We will see
We will see.
Time not short.
Time not long.

For I hope to see,
I hope to feel

Deep inside
Deborah's Song.

Take your time,
Take your time,
Friend of mine.

Trust in heart
Then in mind.
This is a good thing inside
Deborah's Song.

A WORLD'S BACK DROP
2018

Politically
By 2018, patriots world-wide were fighting back against a gathering Democratic Socialist party agenda. Some called it Deep State, some called it New World Order, but I called it what it was. A pack of lies and destruction from the underworld itself.

In America, Democratic Socialists raised their ugly heads seducing college students with their indoctrination. I couldn't believe the amount of naiveté in our youth that would allow them to swallow the garbage they were spewing. I wondered, had our high schools stopped teaching the lessons of a hundred years ago in Europe and Russia, China, Korea and Cuba? America had lost a half-million lives (*DOD and NRA stats*) fighting wars in other countries against the very agenda that was rising here.

I heard young people on alternative media saying, "That's not the same kind of Socialism we will have. They didn't do it right."

In their vernacular, "OMG."

I wanted to scream back at them, "Oh yes it is!! Do you not understand, Communism eats Socialism for lunch?! What they give you in Socialism, they take away in Communism!"

Oh for gosh sakes.

And these same people who rejected America as a Republic in their understanding, used the same tactics against us as they were used against people in 1920. Lines were being drawn between Patriots in our great republic and the radical left actively politicking for Socialism to take over in our federal and local governments.

In two addresses to the Nation, (2018 and 2019) President Trump stood firm and told the House, Senate and our nation, that "America is a Republic, and it will never be a Socialist country, ever."

Praise the Lord.

Around the world, we watched as the "yellow vests" in France took on the rise of Socialism and Islam in their country. They were ready to throw their "baby" president out with the bath water.

In Venezuela, where after two elections in which they had voted in Socialism, their country had all but gone to the dogs. From what I'd heard, starving people were eating them as fast as they could catch them.

Spain was also having political unrest as Catalonia pushed for independence.

Weather

Mexico suffered an earthquake of an 8.0 magnitude.

Volcanic eruptions in Hawaii were almost non-stop for months.

With all the crazy weather around the world, America was on tap to have the wettest year ever in our recorded history. I really did wonder if there was a planet invading our solar system that was causing everything to go topsy-turvy. Was it really vapor-locked behind the sun, waiting for its appointed time to come and bring an end to mankind? And I wasn't the only one wondering.

Everyone from political pundits to religious psychics a like were asking the same questions. Was there really a meaning for mankind in all that the heavens were displaying? Were any of those events portentous for the planet earth and its inhabitants? With all the mass die-offs of animals in the sea, air and land since 2005, it was another way for folks looking for Jesus to say He must surely be coming back soon. Only time itself, would tell.

South Africa suffered a severe drought in their most recent history. Kenya was politically unstable. There was a constant Muslim-Buddhist tension in Myanmar.

In Yemen, eight million people were on the brink of famine. They had one million declared cases of cholera. And to make matters worse, they have three million displaced persons due to the Yemen War.

Wars and rumors of wars

The Houthis were continuing their violence across the Saudi home front firing missiles toward Riyadh and other Gulf States. The Taliban still enjoyed their ties to Iran and Russia.

In Syria, they have reached the seven year mark of war under President Bashar-al-Assad's regime. All due to the propping of Iran and Russian-backed forces and air power.

In Eastern Syria, the fight was with the Kurdish-led Syrian Democratic Forces (SDF) backed by the United States-led anti-Islamic State Coalition. With the Islamic State gone there, the Kurds are pressing for maximum autonomy.

Israel viewed Iran-backed militias near the Golan Heights as a direct threat and may take military action to push them back off of their border.

Terror attacks are increasing all over the world from Barcelona to London to Sweden.

CIVIL UNREST AROUND THE WORLD

France was all but burning down under Macron and the people have had enough. It has evolved to a "yellow vest protest." It started with a fuel tax protest and morphed into patriots wanting their home life back as the Muslim invasion had taken their toll on their city streets.

Since the rise of the middle-eastern population in Paris, 46 Christian churches have been burned to the ground.

Hyperinflation in Venezuela has starving people eating animals off the street as fast as they can catch them. The world looked on as they are unsure of who really is president, Juan Guaido — opposition leader or Nicolas Maduro. The opposition-led national congress declared the election illegitimate calling Juan Guaido's fight for democracy over dictatorship elected and 50 nations recognized Guaido as President over Maduro.

While all this went on, children were actively dying from hunger. Rumors of zoo's being emptied were rampart over the air waves. My husband, Mark, wondered if the good people of Venezuela were a 'test run' for bigger fish from the globalist agenda. I told everyone who would listen, 'Communism eats Socialism for lunch.'

All this anarchy stemmed from the election in 1998 when the Venezuelan people elected Socialist Hugo Chavez. He died in 2013 at 58 years old from cancer. His Vice-President Maduro assumed office.

Venezuela's economy collapsed partially due to the decline of international oil prices in 2015. Oil was

95% of their revenue from exports. They had reached an all-time low of 35 out of 100 on the Regional Political Risk Index Chart. No one else in the world came close to their low.

Germany's Angela Merkel's approval ratings declined as Chancellor significantly since her fourth election. It is possibly due to the rise of non-European refugee's and the rise of Islam attacks on German women not being dealt with by the police or politics. Angela Merkel is head of the Christian Democratic Union and Christian Social Union. They took in one million refugees at the height of the crisis in Europe. It has taken its toll in the political arena.

In the European Union, Britain in 2016, voted to get out. Teresa May, the Prime Minister agreed to it. More than a year after the people of England voted for Brexit, in 2018, Parliament failed to deliver it on time going against the will and the vote of the people. As I write, this may well cost Teresa May her position. And it did.

Poland has turned their backs on globalism with the rise of the patriot movement in their country with the refugee in crisis. They closed their borders to being overrun like many of their neighboring countries such as France and Germany. They want to pay the United States two billion dollars to bring in a permanent military bases in their country.

In parts of Africa, native Africans are going on rampages against white families. Farmers were beaten and killed – their families were thrown off their land. As of 2018, white farmers have appealed to President Donald Trump of America for help. An appeal to the civil authority has wrung out.

The rise and the real threat of war loomed all over the Middle-East. Syria has all but been "blown off the map" with world powers jockeying for influence over that region. President Assad's regime was backed by Russia and Iran. The rebels were backed and supported by America. Why? We were helping our ally, Israel, to keep their borders safe.

There is the constant risk of conflict between Israel, Hezbollah, in Lebanon, Hamas in Gaza, and a Palestinian uprising at all times.

(Source: *Brenden Weber Truth in Media 5/30/2018*)
(Source: *PRS Group August 9th, 2018*)

END TIME HARBINGERS
(Last week of January, 2018)

One evening, Mark and I listened to Pastor Paul Begley (look him up on YouTube, he is a Pastor on alternative media. He's great.) These were some of his points he made that night in his sermon that I felt compelled to share with everyone.

"In the end times there will be false Christs and false prophets. Those who don't know, will be tricked. How you will know them is they will have no Biblical scripture in them.

"The next way you will know that we are in Biblical times, there will be wars and rumors of wars. Look at the Middle East, North Korea, Israel and the Muslims, a war could blow up over caliphate, there are two areas claiming it. This is a time bomb.

"There are famines and fights over water. 26% of world can't get clean water. Most of it is caused by war. Venezuela and North Korea.

"There are pestilences and plagues. They are in Africa and Madagascar. The bubonic plague has mutated to a pneumonia and within 24 hours they are dead.

"There are earthquakes in diverse places. For 2018, 2019 and 2020, scientists are expecting record high earthquake levels especially over a 7 on the Rictor scale. The gravitational pull on the earth is changing. Could it be Planet X and the binary system? Something is literally moving the earth.

"And I wonder, From August 21, 2017, the date of the first United States Solar Eclipse to the second United States Solar Eclipse on April 8th, 2024, where it creates an X right in the middle of America, could it be the harbinger of the Age of the anti-christ? Is everything getting into position for apocalyptic events during then?

"What about sin and iniquity and persecution? While sin abounds everywhere all over the earth, there is great persecution of Christians and Israel that hasn't been seen for 2,000 years.

"And what about the Revelation 12 alignment in the constellations?

"We haven't even talked about the abominations yet. Will it be set up by the anti-christ?"

In my head as he spoke, and I wrote as fast as I could, I thought of the confusion of trans-genders, the illegal, immoral and egregious actions of pedophiles, priests that were and are raping children, Islamic terrorists murdering Coptic Christians by the villagefull, and the satanists that were coming out of the wood work, as if this was the season for them to be "loud and proud" of their evil deeds. These and much more are the fruit of idolatry. Paul went on.

"We are under the Great Commission headed right up against apocalyptic events. The third temple is ready to be built and then the anti-christ will show up.

There are four major harbingers that will happen once all this is in place. They are listed in Isiah 24.

"A pole shift will occur. It is already shifting now. All the seasons are off by a month. There have been sounds heard round the earth for the last five years, especially since 2012-2013. Strange noises coming from the sky. Major booms are felt. Scientists say it is the earth itself changing.

"Lastly, in The Book of Revelation, it states the earth will dissolve, it will rock to and fro. These are mega-cataclysmic events. They have been seen by many visionaries down through the years. Especially the last two generations."

Pastor Paul took an altar call with an emphatic, "Jesus is coming back soon! Whaaattt?! You better be ready! Are you serious!?"

Side note:

May of 2018 the Sanhedrin and the Pharisees put up an altar where the third temple will be. 70 nations were represented and invited to be witnesses.

Folks, we are living out the book of Revelation as I write.

AN 'OVERNIGHT' SUCCESS

The Word of Knowledge that came down quickly, interpretation
In five seconds.

I was picking up something off the floor. A conversation started.

"Do you remember when you were young how no one liked you?"

"Yes, Sir."

"Then as if overnight, they all wanted to know your name?"

"Yes, Sir. It did seem that way."

"This will happen for you again."

"Oh."

I felt impressed, (and hoped) it would be from my books. I would be an "overnight" success.

CELEBRATE HARDSHIP
(Jan. 31, 2018)

I've always told the Lord, "If You will name them, I will write them." This is one of those titles He named, and I will try my best to make it understood.

"Rejoice in the Lord for He is good."

Celebrate hardships, oh boy, here we go. I'm called to write about something I didn't expect to put in any miracle book. Here goes nothing, 'cause that was all we had at the time. This story walks through time until 2018. I realize it takes you readers a little out of the book time-line but bear with me, it's worth the read.

The fall of 2017 was my 59th birthday and I wanted to spend it with our children in Florida. We had done pretty well that year financially and could swing it. Andy even helped us with tickets to Disney saving us hundreds of dollars. How could we repay him? By getting him and his family a room next to ours!

It was Mark and my first two week vacation in ten years. And the first week with our children was wonderful. The last week was terrible! Mark had picked up the Influenza our last day there. He was so ill it took us four days to get home and missed our planned trip to Tennessee (in the fall, sigh.)

But that same fall we had several nice things happen out of the blue. I was offered a nice job at our local hospital, we were given an opportunity to enhance our faith walk by helping a young couple by giving them our car and cash. In response, God gave us an opportunity to buy a truck with the last of our savings and me a car with no money down. Both were great deals. We got $34,000 worth of vehicles for $17,000. Half of their worth. We praised God.

Within a month of all this goodness going back and forth, and us taking a $4,000 vacation, hardship hit our lives that we still haven't recovered from (as of May of 2019.)

I lost both my part-time jobs. The end of December 2017, Mark came home with the news that Albin Jewelers was closing in April. Mark was two years from early retirement and we had just spent the last of our savings on vacations and vehicles, and helping another lost soul out. At the time, it looked like we were headed for the 'poor soul' territory on a one-way ticket.

Instead of Mark looking for another job to supplement our income, he and his co-worker decided to go into business for themselves. Build it from the ground up literally.

And we were sure somehow things would work out to our benefit through the winter. We saved as much money as we could while paying down or off small bills that we owed.

As April of 2018 loomed over us, we were sure Mark would be eligible for unemployment until they got their new store opened and able to start weekly paychecks again.

We also thought, for all the years they had worked for their employer, 50 years between them, they would receive a monetary gift of some kind.

Severance pay, vacation pay, sick pay, something. None was offered. But their old boss did offer them an interest-free loan for business start-up expenses and 20 years to pay it back. At least it was a leg up.

And unemployment turned both of them down flat. It seemed opening up your own business is frowned upon when unemployed. They were no help at all.

April of 2018 found us in great hardship. But the end of April I knew I had to do something to help out our situation. I signed us up for food stamps and Medicaid. One heck of a way to head into our 60's. Again, I was sure it would be temporary. Surely I could get a job somewhere. I updated my resume and made 50 copies.

The same office worker that had told Mark a resounding "No, you are out of luck here," turned to me and said, "What's wrong with you? Can't you work?"

Mark looked at me as if to say, "Well, can you?"

Within five minutes I was filling out paperwork up to my ears.

"We are having our biggest employer hiring fair ever in two weeks. Be here early!"

"Yes, ma'am!"

I showed up early with my best business attire on and 24 resumes. I was sure someone there would hire me and get us out of our situation. None came that day.

And there were jobs to be looked at in the newspaper. I was on a mission to save us if I could. There was one that was just perfect for me and my background in patient advocacy work. My hopes were high with anticipation. I was interviewed twice, filled out all background checks, and offered to go for a tox screen. I waited. I called. Nothing. It seemed being 60 years of age was getting in my way.

Over the next three months I gave out the remaining 24 resumes. I took tests, interviewed on line and on Skype. I went in person, received second interviews, etc. As the months went by, I heard over and over, "I'm sorry, you were our second choice." Five times out of six, I was a 'second choice.' Somehow it was not a comfort to hear. Both times they had chosen 40 year olds. On that, I couldn't compete.

And it seemed businesses in Corydon that I applied to all expected me to go to work for my husband. When I told them my husband wouldn't hire me, I might as well have hung out a sign that said, 'worthless, no hire.'

By that summer, all my suffering internally caused my gallbladder to give out. August and September found me recovering with no job at all and no prospects. We were living on below poverty wages as Mark's new business was growing roots and making it through its first year. Fall held no promise for us as I recovered.

Our sweet friend Deb Grimes tried over and over to tell us as bad as our financial situation was, we were the richest people she knew. We hung onto her words like they were gold-lined.

At the same time, one of my longest friendships, Mary Smith, and my publisher, had her 24 year job come to an end. She was to receive six months' worth of severance for all her years. Boy did we have severance envy. Mary and I decided to put all of our energy into the books and the business. Over the fall, we lined up four fairs. We were used to doing well at those too. In all my ten years of booking, I had never failed at four in a row. Never. But that is exactly what happened. It felt like something was sitting on my worth. Mary fell despondent and I had to work my way up to despondent!

Physical challenges hit on all sides. In Mary's family, cancer hit the young! Divorces hit and all-around mayhem followed. As hard as we tried, we couldn't get more than a couple of her books to e-format.

On Mark and my side, counseling was in order for us. We were desperately trying to hold onto our car, our home and each other. The strain was showing.

And to top it all off, if Mark and I made any more money, we would lose our health insurance and food stamps. We were trapped like rats in a maze. If we could just hang on for a year, or until Mark turned 62 the next year, he could draw social security. Then we would make it just fine as far as we could see. But how in the world could we make it another year like this?

Only God knew.

To be continued…

DREAMS FOR AMERICA
(Feb. 17, 2018)

I saw buffalo, as a storm cloud on the earth, running hard and fast through the mid-west of America. They moved with power and fury across the land.

Interpretation
Strength
Abundance
Gratitude
Sacred

It is also the symbol of survival. Pay attention to the path you are following in your life. What if this is the larger picture. The dream was meant for America, not just me. God said look at not only in my life….

Mark and I were throwing a party. Lots of people were there. We were there to solve a mystery. Mark and I had been given all the answers and were there that night to give all the answers.

To get people's attention, I hollered for them to be quiet. They laughed and hollered for me to "shut up!" They eventually got quiet and listened. I noticed two men in the room. They were undercover, spying for the enemy. Mark started after them and they took off running. We had brought them out of cover. Just like the prayers Mark had been praying for America. That all be exposed and set out.

6 A.M.
(Easter morning 2018)

Dreaming in my telling time.

I saw the earth from high above. It was quiet in the darkness of the outer space. I could feel a presence standing next to me. I was sure it was the angel that usually accompanies me on this walk through the veil of time. I saw the continents. I saw particularly the North American and South American continents. The vast oceans spread out to their shores. In an instant, the scene changed.

The earth broke open like a tremendous earthquake had happened. Out of it, came a brilliant light that shot up to the third heavens. I bent down peering into the darkness to see where it emitted from.

"Wow, uh, that looks like Tennessee. It looks like that light is coming from the south-eastern border of Tennessee."

I thought for only a few seconds.

"I, I believe that is Cleveland, Tennessee! Why that's Cleveland!"

As I spoke those words, great lights split the earth over and over again until it looked like a pin cushion. Lights emanated from all over our planet. It was bathed in a glow that was other-worldly. Simply breathtaking. Revelation hit at once.

"This is the light of Revelation as it goes across the earth one last time."

I could hardly wait to type it up and send it to the good church that we frequent there. I am sure, the best revival yet, will start there.

As if to confirm all of this, I watched a meeting of the church I felt this represented a few days later. The pastor was hot on fire about Cleveland being a hub of the last time revival being there. I knew I had seen their verification in my vision.

The next afternoon I called their office and told the receptionist what I had seen. She asked me to please email everything I could remember about it to them. It sure sounded like verification to her!

Absolutely it was. Get ready church, Jesus is coming back soon!

REVISITATION
(August 10, 2018)

One week before my gallbladder surgery.

It had been four months since Albin closed and seven weeks since Mark and Lana had opened Capitol Jewelers. Mark barely had a couple of paychecks under his belt with 1/5 of his old pay.

Katie and I were sitting at my breakfast table. She had come over for an early morning visit. But there were not just two people in the conversation.

Katie spoke.

"You are reliving 2008 when you and Mark went down. You were devastated. Please don't do it again. Praise God while you are in the fire."

It was the same message the angel had told me 10 years before that I couldn't do at that time. Evidently, the circumstance came back around for me to remedy.

"I think you are right, Katie. It sure feels that way again. I'll tell Mark. Maybe I can get it right this time around."

While at dinner that evening, before I could bring the subject up to Mark, he brought it up to me. It seemed, great minds were thinking alike.

Soberly, Mark opened the conversation.

"You know, this situation feels just like 2008 when everything was taken away from us."

I told Mark quickly about Katie's Word of Knowledge that morning.

I added, "God said praise Him during this time — and don't despair!"

We reasoned we had been totally dependent on Him the last five months. What was another five months of 2018?

We hadn't gone under or been late on one payment. Just maybe, miracles really were happening and going slightly unnoticed all around us. After all, we were still afloat.

WAKING FROM OUR SLEEP
(August 11, 2018)

As Mark and I were having morning breakfast, we were listening to a YouTube pastor from Ireland. I heard from the Lord God again, out loud:

"THOSE WHO ARE SLUMBERING, I AM WAKING."

"Oh, oh, yes Sir!" I cried out.

I felt the power of the Holy Spirit from my head to my feet.

I then heard the Lord call me "Little One" and Mark "Pastor."

Of course I told Mark.

GALLBLADDER AWAY! Or "TABLE FOR ONE PLEASE"
(August 17, 2018)

I had a peace concerning my surgery. I'd known my surgeon as a great doc and dad to our youngest son's good friend. We had all grown up together.

(3 weeks earlier. Sitting in his office.)

Doc walked into my waiting room. He started talking as he looked at my chart. He looked up once and I smiled at him. He was in mid-sentence when he stopped. Perplexed he said, "Don't I know you?"

I smiled again, "It's me, John. Andy Merk's mom."

"Deb!"

"Hi, buddy!"

We talked small talk and caught up with each other's children. He scheduled my surgery and said, "We'll take good care of you, Deb."

I knew he would.

The Rest of the Story

8:17 a.m. The day of my surgery.

I had called my family and friends and asked them to pray for me. For some, that was good enough, living in separate states. But for others, they had to be there.

"Have we got everything?" I asked.

"I think so, honey." Mark replied.

Oldest son, Ben called out too, "I think so Mama."

Grandson Edward walked between friends and family as his momma, Amanda was watching close behind.

Pictures were snapped, hugs were given as more friends arrived before time to leave. Let's see, who all came to my surgical event?

My beautiful daughter-in-law, Amanda!

Mark, of course, Ben, Amanda, Edward, Mary Dow, Katie, Nick, and met us at the hospital, Deb Grimes. Larry and Marilynn Crosier. And Mark's sister Susan came in from New Albany. Twelve including me. We sure looked like a party as we walked up to the registration desk.

I had opted to show up in my pajamas. I smiled as I walked up.

"Peyron, party of one, please." The lady at the front desk laughed. I stood in my pajama gown surrounded by family and friends alike.

After the paperwork and tagging me, we all went and sat in the waiting room.

Within a few minutes, I was called back. Hugs and kisses abounded. The nurse assured everyone they could come back in a bit to be with me before surgery.

My nurses were wonderful! I sure wish I could remember all their names. It took them just a minute to "grab a vein." Blood pressure and respirations were normal—check. Every nurse that attended me I told them about my son, Ben the PTA, physical therapy assistant.

Shortly in walked the anesthetist assistant. He took down all my information and then stopped. He asked me an interesting question.

"What do you want to remember?"

"I'm sorry, what?"

"What do you want to remember? Do you want to remember going into the surgical room? Or the recovery room? What are you comfortable with?"

I laughed and answered him, "I don't want to remember leaving this room and I want to be in here when I wake up."

He nodded his head and left with the instructions he came in for.

That was when my lovely set of nurses brought in my family. Everyone gathered around. We held hands and prayed for all the staff and me. The mood in the room was fabulous! Dr. John stopped by to say hello and that all was go.

He asked me, "Deb, do you know what you are here for?"

I searched in my mind for the correct medical term and replied, "A cholecystectomy?"

The good doctor nodded his head and laughed replying, "Gallbladder surgery is good enough."

He asked us, "Does anyone have any questions or anything to say?"

"Yes, sir. I do," I replied. "I'm asking you as a member of the medical community and as my friend, do your best. Don't get in a hurry. I have heard stories from other people (not his patients) that have had this surgery, about fluid, other things, and I don't want any complications, no tubes later, none. You take care of business no matter how long I have to be under."

With a sober look, Dr. John replied, "I am a very conservative doctor. You won't have any problems."

"I believe you."

Last call was given to the family for goodbyes and to head out to the waiting room. I gave one last instruction to Ben Merk.

"I want to hear my favorite Christian songs playing when I come out from surgery."

"Yes, ma'am."

As family was leaving, two nurses and an assistant came over to my right side.

"We're ready to unhook you and take you back now."

"Okay."

While I was busy with them, out of the corner of my eye, I saw a man slip behind the staff to my left, moving toward my IV. Before I could say, "Who are you," I saw him inject liquid into my IV. Before they moved me out of the doorway, I was out like a light.

My eyes were still closed, but I could hear voices in the room.

From far away, I heard, "Honey, open your mouth, I have ice-chips, you're thirsty."

What trust I have in my husband! With eyes closed, not even coherent, I opened my mouth like a little bird waiting for my ice-chips. After the third or fourth chip, I opened my eyes.

There were Mark and Ben smiling at me. I was filled with love for them. Ben piped up, "Mama, we played your funeral song for you."

"What?!" I cried. "Was something wrong? Was I breathing?"

Mark and Ben looked at each other in surprise at my outburst.

"No, Mama," he replied. "Your song, "Spirit in the Sky."

By then a nurse had come in and was checking on me. She smiled at the conversation. I finally recognized what Ben meant and broke out into a big grin. With the first line, the nurse joined me in song.

"That's where I wanna go when I die. When lay me to rest, I want to go to the place that's the best."

The house was rocking!

More nurses came in and out of the room checking my vitals as I woke up for longer periods of time. Mark and Ben stayed at my side. Finally, it was time to try to stand up.

The nurse spoke, "We are going to turn you to the side of the bed and sit you up. We just want you to sit there before you try to stand, okay?"

"Yes ma'am. Will do."

I was able to sit up by myself with little discomfort. I took a deep breath and nausea permeated my being.

191

"I may need an emesis basin."

My nurse immediately handed me an emesis bag. I took deep breaths as she gave me IV promethazine. I stayed in a sitting position.

"Are you ready to stand up?" she asked.

"Yes, ma'am."

Before I could move, Ben stood up first. I watched as he walked over to the glove station and put on a pair of gloves. They all knew Ben was a physical therapy assistant. (I made sure!)

As Ben walked over toward me, both RN's took a step back to let him through to assist his mother. I was so proud I wanted to cry.

"Ready, Mama?"

"Yes, pal."

I took a step onto the floor. Ben's feet were right there to steady my stand.

Immediately, I said, "You're blocking."

Ben chuckled. "Very good, Mama. Your nursing training has kicked in. Now, why do we block our patients upon standing?"

Foggy headed, I searched for my understanding.

"We block to keep our patient steady so we can help control their movements."

"Very good Mama."

With help, I took a few steps forward and a few steps back. I sat back in the bed.

"I'm just so tired. Could I sleep a little more, please?"

"Sure," replied my nurse. "How is your pain level?"

"A four maybe," I responded, "out of ten."

"Would you like something for pain?"

"No, I'm good. Thanks. If this is all it will be, Tylenol will handle it."

By then, my antiemetic kicked in and I slept.

When I woke a few hours later, Mark and Ben and my nurses were packing me up to leave. The nurses that tended to me were very caring.

One of them said, "Now remember, if you get sick, nauseated or hurting, we can wheel you right back in here and get you a room for the night."

"Oh, thank you for taking such good care of me. But I believe at home, there are a whole bunch of people waiting to take care of me. I'd hate to disappoint them. I think I'll be fine."

They wheeled me out to our car, instructions in my hand. I was ready for healing to begin.

A houseful of people were indeed waiting for us when we arrived. Mark pulled up in the drive. He and Ben walked me to the house and onto the couch.

After a few minutes of reassurance that all went well, I was led back to our bedroom and I slept the rest of the evening. Every once in a while, I could hear them playing cards….

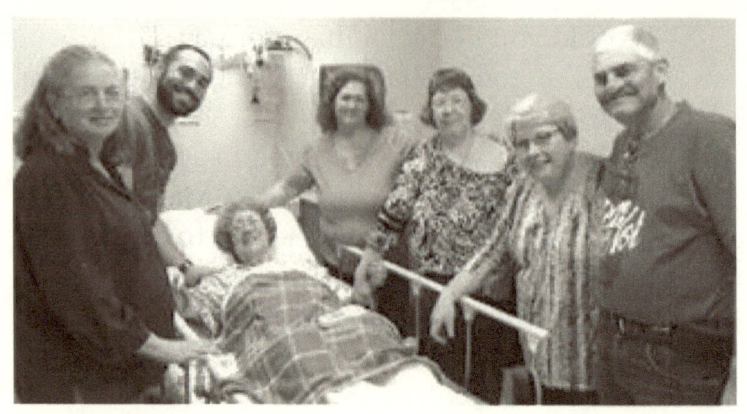

From left to right: Mary Smith (Publisher and best friend of 27 years and counting) Ben Merk-our oldest son, (me) and our dear friends Katie Yocum, Deb Grimes, and Larry and Marilynn Crosier.

SURPRISE, SURPRISE
An Accidental Call
(December 13, 2018)

I was innocently working on my computer, catching up on fb, emails, twitter and instant messenger all at the same time. It can sure be a full-time job. Sometimes, I get "confused" and think I am on one site and can be fully on another site. That is what happened when I clicked on a "face." I thought it was to reply, but instead, quickly, it started ringing. I panicked so much I forgot how to stop it from going through.

"Make it stop," I cried!

Then I heard, "Hello?"

Oh boy, here we go…

(Laughing) "I'm so sorry! This is Debbie Peyron. I thought I was replying to your concern by text and it called you instead…"

"Oh Deb, this is Deborah! We're in a situation and need help."

She told me all the circumstances and waited for any help I could give. I told her a story of a similar situation and how we resolved it. Then I gave her a bit of wisdom and knowledge to stand on.

"What fear should a Christian have of a witch or warlock?"

The Word of Knowledge for the whole world had been delivered. This is the recognition of the Word of God.

Thanks be to God.

THE PARALLEL OF OUR LIVES

Debbie, Mark and Vicki

You know how "they" say, the longer you are married to your spouse, the more you look and act like each other? Well, could it be that way for others around you too? Do you think our lives could mimic ones we've loved that went before, with, or after us? Say like my son's godmother who had been my dearest friend for over 45 years.

"Oh you never know...but this story might say otherwise."

The parallel of Vicki Sampson's life and my life got more uncanny every year.

November, 1974
Freshman Fall Dance, Angela Merici High School

"Well, bring her in Gary! Let's see her!"

I heard a cheery voice greet me at the top of the stairs of my new boyfriend's home. I was meeting his parents for the first time.

There stood Miss Vicki and Mr. Ralph—all smiles. I smiled with a big, bright "hello!" standing next to Gary. I had on a floor-length dark blue dress. I was five feet two inches, 110 pounds, with long auburn curls just the way my momma had fixed my hair. At first glance, Vicki and Ralph were enamored with me and I was with them.

Ralph Sampson owned three different companies, the largest being Hart Furnace. He was tall, six feet and lanky to Miss Vicki's five- feet-three-inch frame. She was immaculately dressed-beautiful with big, brown, expressive eyes that danced as she spoke. The Sampson's had three fine sons. The two oldest worked for their dad. And I was dating their youngest.

As our high school years turned to Gary's college years, the attraction he had for me waned.

After over four years of dating, one fall afternoon, he said to me, "There's a big world out there, Deb! I can't marry the first person I dated. Boy do I feel better getting that off my chest. See ya!"

I was floored. I never saw it coming. I spent the whole fall of 1979 in sorrow and heartache. And so did Gary's family. One afternoon, Vicki called our home.

"Hello?"

"Hi, sweetie. Ralph and I want you to know we miss you. We're sorry Gary broke up with you."

Tears welled up in my eyes right away.

"Oh, Vicki, I miss you and Ralph and the boys so much! Do you think it would be alright if we saw

197

each other sometimes? I have a car now and could come and see you."

"Like for an ice-cream?" I could hear Vicki smiling over the phone.

"Ice-cream?!"

Now both women were smiling. My own momma breathed a sigh of relief. I'm sure she thought we might all live through the break-up after all.

Gary went on to college and moved to the big city of Chicago for many years. He and I managed to stay friends and remembered each other on our birthdays. I married a man from Indiana two short years later. I invited them to my wedding.

Gary and one of his aunts attended. Vicki and Ralph were out of town on a business trip. Their generosity came in an envelope with a $100 bill. At the time, it looked like a thousand dollars to us. My new husband knew I came with the Sampsons part and parcel.

With the death of my father a year later, Ralph became even more important in my life. It was like he instinctively knew it. If I needed anything, he and Miss Vicki were there.

When I was in labor with my first son Paul Benjamin, they were right there with me. By the time our second son was born (in Florida) they were godparents to David. They stayed four days to help me with our growing family.

By the time Thomas Andrew came along, we were back in Louisville, Kentucky. By then, they were known as godmother Vicki and godfather Ralph to all our sons. Just like my best friend, I had ended up with three fine sons too.

Even though life could be a little trying sometimes with "Ralphie boy" he liked a good card game, he liked a good drink and a good horse race, Vicki knew she was loved. At that same time, my marriage was falling apart (due to chronic abuse and drugs on the part of my soon-to-be ex-husband) Vicki was saying goodbye to the love of her life. Ralph was losing his battle with emphysema.

Within a year of Ralph's death, and after my 14 year marriage failed, I filed for divorce. Of course Vicki was right there with me. I went back to school when Andy started kindergarten. Vicki and I visited each other frequently. I found solace in her calming words and prayers. She really was my role model to hold me and my little boys steady. Of course, we all had our Catholic faith.

Another year went by and I was invited to a party of people that were going through annulment classes as I was. I happened to meet a six-foot tall, lanky man my age. He had a really nice smile and seemed, as the evening wore on, was everywhere I was. By the end of the party, Mark gave me his phone number.

Within the month, he had to meet Vicki, "my other momma" over the Christmas holidays. We all went bowling together. They were fast friends and she had to have a picture of us. Mark, unknown to me at the time, was already falling in love with me. He was all for a picture of us. Why? That was evidence! We were a couple.

"What?!"

He finally had something to show his family. I was real and so were we. As our dating turned to marriage expectations, I asked Vicki to be my Matron of Honor.

"Oh no, sweetie," Vicki cried. "I'm too old to be in your wedding."

I bawled like a baby. I hadn't expected her to turn me down. She rescinded quickly.

"Oh, oh! I don't want you to cry! Of course I'll be your Matron of Honor!"

How could I do anything of importance without her? Our friendship held strong for 22 more years and counting.

Why even the unpleasant things of life seemed to occur at our same ages. At 60 years old, both of us had gallbladder surgery. We both came through it with flying colors.

As I headed for my 61st year, there were a couple of tiny calcifications on my right breast on my mammogram. My husband sat with me as I spoke to the doctor in the lab.

"Well, do they have any earmarks of cancer?"

"Well, no…"

"And there are no clusters?"

"No, just a few more single ones. No jagged edges either. I just want you to see a surgeon and get an MRI. That way everyone knows you are okay."

"Sure."

It was practically nothing. I came home and looked up "calcifications." Common in women. 85% are benign with no tumor markers whatsoever. Still the wind was out of my sails. There would be no dance instructions from Vicki and her friend that day. They would have to wait a week for us to have more dance lessons with them. All I wanted to do was take a nap with Mark. It was noon when I rang her up.

"Hi Vicki."

"Hi honey. Uh oh, what's wrong?"

"I had my mammogram today, then an ultrasound. Now they want to do an MRI."

"You don't feel like dancing today, do you?"

"No, ma'am."

"Okay honey. Call us next week and we will reschedule."

That flew for almost 30 seconds.

Vicki was back on the phone with me. Before we knew it, we were all going out to eat together. Cracker Barrel here we go!

Vicki listened over lunch and told this story.

"I almost had a biopsy too, one time. I prayed and prayed. When I went for the biopsy, they x-rayed, nothing. They did another mammogram, couldn't find anything. The doctor looked at me and said, "Well, okay. You can leave." No biopsy. God took care of my breasts. He will take care of yours too."

I knew it was a promise. And thank God, especially then, I wanted to be just like my godmother. She was with me through all this too.

To be continued….

A WORLD'S BACKDROP
2019

2018 went down as the wettest year on record, in Kentuckiana, ever. 2019 started in its wake to beat it. The start of January and February saw eleven inches of precipitation fall as rain, with barely a trace as snow. Yet in Las Vegas, Nevada, they saw more snow than we did in Southern Indiana. It was a significant snowfall on the ground in mid-February. It rained so much that arsenic showed in ground water because of saturation. That was most certainly a lousy place to be.

By spring, there were blizzard warnings in six states. Cattle froze where they stood. In the Sierra Nevada mountain range, winter still held them with snow clean into the summer months. What seasons were we in? And in Russia, they saw black snow. How does that happen? (*Reported WDRB blog 2/27/19*)

Political

February 26, India and Pakistan traded airstrikes. An emergency meeting was called -they are both nuclear nations. The world asked, was this a final hour? (*News channels*)

Israel warned the world that 150,000 ISIS members were being deployed around the world.

The Daily Wire reported on February 25th, Iran claimed they broke through America's military computer system and took command of our drones.

And in Venezuela, over three million citizens had fled from poverty and starvation. Their money was now worth zero. People were taking down their homes for the copper and steel to sell in Columbia. They were desperate. Chavez' Socialism disarmed the population in 2012. They were desperate and unarmed. America has sent tens of thousands of pounds of food-aid to them and the government burned it in front of their eyes. (*CBN-March 6, 2019*)

Religious
From the years 2008-2014, abortions dropped by 25% (*reported by the Prolife Movement.*) Abortion clinics were down by 79% with only six states having one abortion clinic in them. Twenty states only have three clinics and 25 states have only five. They were on the decline. Seventy percent of our nation is either trying to ban abortions or target restrictions on the clinics that perform them. Planned Parenthoods are being refused leases. *(Too controversial)*

As most of the country was fighting that battle, less than a half dozen states were endorsing the right to kill live babies on the table when the abortion doesn't work. And New York's governor Cuomo signed into law (2018) the most gruesome of abortion laws. A baby could now be killed on the way out of its mother. Dead on arrival. Not to be outdone by him, the states of Vermont, Virginia and Rhode Island were all vying for legal end-stage abortions.

Quote Dr. Ben Carson, "As a surgeon, I have operated on infants pre-birth. I can assure you that they are very much alive."

(Articles from *Pro-Life Vision* and their website, quoted by Dr. Steve Turley, who has a YouTube Alternative Media with 123k subscribers.)

Planned Parenthood, in my humble opinion, has gone completely off their rocker. It is my personal opinion that these states that support them, see that Roe v. Wade may well be overturned, sending it back to each state to rule on. They are trying to supersede this landmark-to-come ruling and set themselves up as abortion on demand states. So now just as America has "sanctuary cities and states" we will now have "abortion on demand states." And I wouldn't live in any of those places for all the tea in China.

Medical and political

It now appeared Measles and Smallpox were being transported across the Mexican border into America by the illegal immigrants. And Typhus has run rampart in major California cities such as San Francisco, San Diego and Los Angeles. California is now labeled as a sanctuary state.

Religious

(Article by *Cherie Vandermillen, Feb. 8, 2019, for Pulpitandpen.org reported by Charisma News*)

"Pope Francis has signed an interfaith covenant at Abu Dhabi with Inman in Sunni Islam, Sheikh Ahmed as-Tayeb, head of Sunni's most prestigious seat of learning, and considered the Grand Iman of al-Achar. It is not just for Catholics and Muslims. It was signed in front of a global audience of religious leaders as reported by the British News source article titled "Christians, Islam & Judaism." It is calling for peace between the nations, religions and races. They are encouraging all believers from all religions to shake hands, embrace, kiss and pray for one another. The only problem with this great effort, there is no dissemination of the term god and allah."

To round this section out, 100,000 child porn videos and photos were found on Archbishop Jozef Wesolowski's computer. He is being accused of raping numerous children in the Dominican Republic and in Poland. He is a Progressive Secular Humanist. And he is an archbishop for the Roman Catholic Church. (Source: *Patheos.com/Minutemen of America*)

CHURCH AT THE DOUGLAS INN
IHUB Church
(January 1, 2019)

From 7 a.m. until 8 a.m. I was talking with God. I was reviewing my life in my head. Had all my experiences, all my books I had written in obedience been for naught? Why had I been stopped at every turn? Would things ever pan out? I cried silent tears as Mark slept through it all.

Mark and I woke to daylight. *After* we moaned, we got out of bed, dressed quickly, packed and ran downstairs for a fast breakfast. We were sure we were getting back on the road early, after all we were in a hurry to get home –so much for hurry. We hit the kitchen at 8:40.

While we were eating our meal, a group of young men came into the breakfast area.

Mark immediately said, "I like your shirt!"

I turned around and looked at the young sojourners. Well, he could have been speaking to any one of them!

"Lion Tribe of Judah."

"BBS" with a picture of Jesus on it.

At that I had to ask, "BBS?"

The young man replied with a smile, "Be back soon."

I squealed for effect.

I gave them the five minute version of our story. Two minutes of my birth and three minutes of writing books for Jesus. In a collective, they said, "Wow."

The young man named Corey, who we found out was a seer and a hearer since a child, spoke quietly to Mark. Mark looked at me.

I asked, "What is it? What did he say, Mark?"

Again to Mark, "Your season isn't just yet."

Then he turned to me and said, "God has seen you. He told me to tell you, you are on the right path. It is just not yet. Soon, it is just not yet. Oh, and don't give up."

I dropped my jaw.

He sat there as if listening to an unseen visitor. Cory dropped his head, then nodded, and continued, "Yes, don't stop."

I stammered out, "I didn't get it wrong."

He replied with sincerity, "No! Keep going!"

I simply cried. I knew what his words of encouragement were. I knew why now, it did not matter what time we left that morning.

"Thank you, thank you, thank you!"

Then God spoke to my heart, **"This is why you were here specifically. Why you can't just jump up and leave to go home."**

Cory reached out his hand, "I'm Corey Grippin."

Mark and I smiled. I said, "Nice to meet you young man."

I gave out all the cards I had with me. Just like young people do, they all went looking for me on Facebook. Soon, my phone was pinging away. I responded and friended them. I wrote Corey first.

"Hey Corey! God bless ya, buddy! So very nice to meet you and our other brothers and sisters in Christ Jesus. Have a great year. Mark and I hope God allows our paths to meet again soon! Many blessings, call anytime. Ya'll have friends in Southern Indiana."

Five minutes later, Corey replied.

"It was definitely a divinely orchestrated connection! I get the feeling this was only the start of something bigger. I pray this year is a mind blowing one for you both!"

Two minutes later I replied.

"Corey Grippin, I agree. And I hope it involves you all too!"

ROBERT & DONNA JACKSON
(Jan. 15, 2019)

Robert Jackson is a good friend and brother in Christ. I met him on a wonderful group site called "Prophecy Watchers" because we are all prophecy watchers as the days get shorter until the return of our Lord and Savior, Jesus Christ. We have so much in common we kid about being siblings from other mothers. So be it. He always asks about Mark and I always ask about his wife, Donna. Lovely folks, one and all.

Well, I have made no bones about being a seer and clairaudient with our group. Many of them on the site have gifts of the Holy Spirit. But until that day, I was unaware of the gifts Robert possessed until he made confession. One of the most powerful stories in this book, comes from his mouth.

Aren't I glad?

A strong earthquake was reported on Prophecy Watchers.

Deb: That's getting up there guys! Eeks!

RJ: Deborah Aubrey-Peyron, Sis, I believe the gravity of the moon will have a series effect on our fault lines. I hope my vision does not come true, pray for no major tsunamis.

Deb: Robert Jackson, brother, I know I have visions, I knew Perry Stone has visions. I was not aware you are a visionary. You see visions too?

RJ: Deborah Aubrey-Peyron, about two years ago, I saw a vision of a Tsunami hitting Florida, a huge high wall of water. It really stunned me. On Perry Stone's next broadcast, he talked about it too. I think I may have told you this before, but about 3.5 years ago, Donna and I was visited by an angel in the guise of a loan officer. We sat at the table for hours. She revealed to us Trump would be our next president. Almost a year before he even considered running and revealed a few other things. But she did say there will be a major tsunami hitting the east coast but she did not give a time frame. She did elegantly say Trump is chosen by God and he is the great key to prophecy being fulfilled.

Deb: Wwwwwwwooooowww!!!! Yes you all were visited! I have had two occasions like that myself. Wow! Brother, may I put your story in my next book? These are the kind of stories that the Lord God said He was bringing to fill *Miraculous Interventions VIII*. Call me this evening or at your convenience. Thx so much!

RJ: I just want to add Donna and myself felt the Holy Spirit and without a shadow of a doubt we knew she was an angel. She explained other things that only with supernatural knowledge would know. Our bodies was tingling when she left.

Deb: Robert Jackson, I bet! Boy have I got two stories for you! This is not a coincidence!

Two nights later, 7 p.m.

Robert Jackson is a 60-year-old artist and sculptor of wood, just as his Scott-Irish great-great-grandfather was. Robert works with a chain saw. He makes animals, faces, bird houses, etc. He does a lot of his woodwork for an Indian Village and museum. Robert's work is sold all over the United States. He worked for Kroger Company for 31 years until he had to go on disability 11 years ago.

He and Donna had married shortly out of high school. Donna has a business with home decorations. It is her passion. She also went to School of Cosmetology. She was a stay-at-home mom for many years to their son and daughter. Two granddaughters are also counted among their fold. All are among the saved in Jesus name.

The first time I called Robert's number it didn't go through. Mark sat beside me at the kitchen table. I had pen and paper in front of me.

Mark said, "Try again."

That time the call went through.

Within seconds, I heard Robert and Donna's voices loud and clear. He had "warned me" that they were just country folks, and I would hear it in their voices. But to me, they sounded a little bit like the South Side of Heaven.

"Deb? Is it you?"

"Robert! Yes it's me! My husband Mark is here with me."

"Hey Mark! How ya doing? This is my wife, Donna."

"Hi Donna!" Mark and I said together.

"Hi ya'll! It's nice to meet you over the phone!" Donna's cheery voice warmed our hearts immediately.

Over the next several minutes, Mark and Robert led conversation. They spoke about West Virginia and the vacations to his grandparents Mark used to take not far from where the Jacksons live. The world seemed smaller and homier the longer the guys talked.

Then the real conversation that I had waited to hear, started.

"Now Robert, I am ready to hear about your angel."

"Well, Deb, this was about three-and-a-half years ago. And there was a tingly presence, an angelic presence around her."

It was the year before Donald Trump had announced he was going to run. No one on earth knew, but the angels in heaven did.

"What was the lady's name?"

"Her name was Mary. She looked to be in her 40's. She had a spray of silver in her long, black hair. She had dark eyes, petite and very soft spoken. And she was a loan officer."

"What time of the year was it?" I asked.

"It was May, early spring of 2015. She came to our house early in the morning. She just started talking about what was happening in the world and the biblical implications of it all. She said in this world people needed an intervention. Someone who would stand up for good people. That was when she said that Donald Trump would run for president and win. At the time we didn't know he was a professed Christian. But now we know. Trump is armored and clothed. They can't get to him. God prepared him for this the last 10 to 20 years."

"Wow," I breathed. "Is that the way your meeting started?"

Robert went on.

"No. Mary showed up with the papers for our loan application. But Donna and I both knew as she stepped into our home, she had a presence about her. She had a calming, knowledgeable presence about her. She wrapped up the material part of our conversation for the bank very quickly. Then she very quickly changed the conversation to the Bible. She talked about the same things we believed that would come to pass. She informed us on Biblical events."

Mark and I were taken aback by all that the two of them had to say. We couldn't believe our ears.

"Deb, we knew we were sitting with an angel! The meeting was between an hour-and-a-half to two-and-a-half hours long. The loan was just a small part of it. Mary went through the events that were happening now in scripture. She came in, introduced herself, helped with the papers for the loan, and closed her book. Then started talking about prophecy and Donald Trump. She said the Bible says the Last Trump will sound. Mary kept saying it isn't a coincidence that Donald Trump will be the next president. She said it several times. Then she said things in the future."

"Oh my!"

"There is going to be a great calamity. A wall of water, a tsunami will devastate, flood all the way to Roanoke, Virginia. The only thing that will stop them is the Great Smokies."

My heart felt sick with anticipation of the events spoken of. We have children and grandchildren in harm's way. A long with about 80 million other people.

Robert began again, "Even scientists are talking about Super Blood Moons, the pull of gravity on the earth's plates--how they will move. When she spoke about the great earthquake and tsunami she did not put a time frame on it."

"She also mentioned the verse with the trumpet, the '67 war in Israel. God sent to the Rabbis a device to make and they made it by instructions by Yeshua. When they were overwhelmed, the priests called for the device to activate, and a special sound went out. As it went forth, their enemy dropped their rifles and ran screaming. When they were captured, they asked them to make it stop. They told the soldiers when they heard the sound, they saw flaming angels next to the Israeli army and took off running."

"Holy cow." I whistled. "Donald Trump was chosen by Yeshua Himself for this time." I whispered, "I believe you."

Robert went on, "Then Mary asked me a question."

"Wow, what?"

"She asked me why I feel like, after 1,000 year reign, why the Lord lets the devil come back. Robert paused as we considered the question.

He replied, "God gives everyone a chance to choose either way. The people that are born during the 1,000 years will have to choose God or satan. These choices are for the people that do not have their glorified bodies and choose to be born again or die with satan. It must be their final choice. Mary told me that was a very good answer."

Robert got quiet for a few minutes as if thinking something over to tell me.

"Two years ago, in 2016, I saw the East Coast in a vision. I pictured Florida as plain as day. I saw a tsunami totally take Florida out. It is coming. Then I heard the sound of shofars and horns. I heard trumpets in the Eastern sky. I was in my workshop at my desk. I put my foot on the step and felt instantly close to the Lord. When I walked in my house, I felt the presence of the Holy Spirit. I bowed and knelt. I was not scared. It was peaceful, unexplainable."

"Glorious."

"Mary also said Trump would surround himself with good Christians and knowledge. And she said Trump may be the last president. During his presidency the Last Trumpet will sound. It will be the end. Donna and I are praying for another four year term. I think he will win and toward his last four years, all will come to a head. In our last lingering years revival will come."

"The last thing Mary said was time is short."

As Robert spoke those words my mind wandered to the time the angel had told me time was short. And the time that Andy was told by his friend that had gone to heaven, that time was short. It was my third verification.

As I pondered these thoughts, Robert spoke about his father, a Pentecostal. Robert spoke about his gifts to be able to see and hear and listen. Once he asked his mom why him.

She replied, "It was meant to be. Dreams and visions."

Robert and Donna are humble people. I am proud to know them and call them family. Robert is gifted with understanding when he hears.

Finally Donna spoke up.

"Deb?"

"Yes, ma'am?"

"We are so glad to have met you. We can relate to you. You won't think we're crazy. It is so good to know and hear knowledge. To know the truth is out there."

"You are most welcome."

Robert piped in. "Can I ask you somethin'?"

"Sure!"

"Do you think that America is Mystery Babylon?"

Before I could answer, Mark spoke up as if on cue.

Mark said, "No. That's Mecca."

Robert replied, "There are great arguments on both sides. But I'm leaning in Mark's favor."

Donna said, "I think America is close to it."

Robert went on, "The antichrist will be from Rome, the city of the seven hills."

I spoke of the dream I had on Easter of 2018 at 5:30 a.m. About the earthquake and the great light that reached to the third heaven. Robert said he was told in the spirit I am a warrior.

Robert spoke of his father who was a Pentecostal Evangelist for 30 years. He asked Robert many questions. When he is asked, answers come to him. Robert felt like he and I are gifted.

Mark told about the spirit of corruption that was on America. We need to repent and pray against it. And to pray for discernment. Robert said he already prays hard for it.

By the end of the meeting with Mary, Robert and Donna had to pick their chins up off the floor. They had been overwhelmed by the presence of an angel. They had been visited. As Mary left for the door, she turned around and gave them one final word. She told Donna to remember these things. "Everything will be alright. Don't worry." Then she hugged her and Robert, then she was gone. Peace fell over their household and they shouted and praised Jesus!

Now, the warning had sounded. After telling me their story, Robert's burden had been lifted.

Mine had begun.

UPDATE ON THE WORLD
2019
(February, 2019)

This is just a smattering of updates on the winter around the world.

In Japan, the ocean water was freezing and dolphins were freezing in it. *(Japanese television station – Heidi Begley reported on her channel)*

Siberian polar bears have moved into towns and are killing people. They have never done that before. I wonder, if the pole shifting is influencing their behavior?

And could this be part of the reason for more violence among men?

(Mr.mBB333 YouTube channel aired 2-12-2019 5 p.m. EST)

Maui –

Storm of record proportions. 191 mph winds and it wasn't a hurricane! They had snow in lower level areas.

This same storm sent flash floods all the way to the middle-California coast line.

It ended up as Snowmageddon in the Sierra Nevada's. They had six to ten feet of snow.

85% of the Euphrates River has dried up. It started eight years ago. In Revelations, the Kings of the North's army will be able to cross it into a Jerusalem war. (*As reported by Paul Begley, Indiana preacher between two corn fields/a YouTube Salvation Station.*)

There has been a Typhus outbreak in San Francisco and the homeless in Los Angeles are reported to be greater than 150,000. They carry dysentery and other communicable diseases in that area. The number of Muslims there is still on the rise.

Patriots are standing up in countries now. Examples are Poland, Hungary and the United States.

There is a "Cali-exit" going on in California. The middle class can't take it anymore. They are leaving for Texas.

Mindless violence is rising around the world. In New York, a man murdered a pregnant woman. He kicked and stabbed her to death. Sheer madness.

On the up side of things, the "Covington Boys" who were alleged to have caused a fight and it spread like wildfire over the internet and all the news about the horrible white boy Catholics, were finally found to have done nothing wrong. They had been set up and did not fall for the trap that had been set against them. Now they are fighting back with a very good lawyer. Pray that truth pays off real big for them in the end. To me, they were the heroes of the situation.

And as a side note, Christian stores are back on the rise from when they were being threatened.

It has been confirmed by the CDC, Black Plague is rising in New Mexico, Mexico, Texas and Los Angeles.

(Prophecy Update with End Times News headlines. 2/14/19 per Warren Cleaver Prophecy Update videos. 127,000 subscribers, titled, "Our Time is Short.")

Synopsis:
The Middle East Peace Conference was held in Warsaw, Poland. Prime Minister Netanyahu met with Arab leaders on how to combat Iran — the destabilizer of the region. Our VP Mike Pence also attended, lashing out at Europeans over Iran. *(www.reuters)*

Pence states Iran's Mullahs were at that very time plotting a new holocaust to erase Israel off the map. *(dailymail.co.UK)*

"Iran vowed to raise Tel Aviv off the map if US attacks them." *(www.express.co.UK)*

"PM Netanyahu warned Iran, 'Attack Israel, and it will be the last anniversary you celebrate.'" *(www.timesofIsrael.com)*

Moscow and Tehran are arming Hezbollah with Iranian defense missiles. Jared Kushner stated a Mideast peace plan is expected after the Israel election. *(www.foxnews.com)*

The Palestinians are still stating without 1967 borders, they will sign no treaty. *(Israel National News)*

Russia backed them and warned the United States, their peace plan will set everything back. But Prime Minister Netanyahu is looking forward to seeing it. *(The Times of Israel)*

Russia, Iran and Turkey are combining to talk a peace deal in Syria—which is a heap of ruins as stated in the Book of Revelation.

Luke 21: 11, 25-26 "And there will be earthquakes in diverse places, plagues, famine and pestilences; and fearful sights and great signs from heaven."

There were eighteen 5.0 and larger earthquakes in a day's span. Five volcanoes went off at once in mid-February. And eight more the next day.

Yellowstone was, and still is, being closely monitored as fire and brimstone light the sky all over the earth.

Weird winter weather was felt all over America. In the Ohio Valley, it felt like spring one day and winter the next. Actual temperatures ranged from 60 degrees one day to all the down way to -10 the next day.

From the end of December through the middle of February, weather through Indiana and Kentucky was all over the place. Highs and lows went from one extreme to another. People suffered from headaches with the barometric pressure acting like a yo-yo. Cockeyed at best.

In Queensland, Australia, 50,000 cattle drowned in a massive 'water-bomb' of a storm. *(theguardian.com)*

The second largest outbreak of Ebola cropped up in January 2019.

Rapidly dying insects are happening all over the earth with catastrophic results for mankind.

As of late, (late winter, 2019) Iran is claiming that death is coming to America. That is right up there with what I've been told in the Spirit. *"In the fall of 20--, an attack will befall America. And it will be fed by the money given them from President #44."*

Churches are going wild as they open breweries in common areas to influence people to come through their doors.

Pope Francis has signed a covenant with the leading Iman pushing toward a 'fellowship religion.' *(www.Charismanews.com)*

Abortion has become the leading cause of death worldwide in 2018 — 42 million infants. *(www.theisraelwire.com)*

On the other side of the world-coin, 1,000 scientists signed a statement dissenting from Darwinism. *(www.christianhealines.com)*

And DC comics had to cancel their blasphemous *'Jesus'* series after 220,000 patrons signed petitions for them to stop production. *(www.christianheadlines.com)*

There is a new Bible translation technology helping to spread the Gospel of Jesus Christ faster than ever before. *(CBN)*

Matthew 24:27 "...for just as the lightening comes from the east and flashes as far as the west, so will be the coming of the Son of Man."

The best news, we who are in the body of Christ, have been pre-approved for Heaven, but you still have to "put the application in!"

Radiation in California has increased 13%. It was up three years ago by 18% and 13% four years before that. It is becoming a big problem and affecting biological life. There are radiation-driven plagues. The particles have arsenic with them. The symptoms are being felt all over as people become physically weaker.

Arizona and New Mexico have been saturated with floods. From Texas to Quebec, to Ontario, Canada, thunderstorms spanned the United States. People are beginning to fear water. *(Paul Begley with Mike around the world YouTube)*

(Forbes Magazine, 2/21/2019) NASA reported a collision of two neutron stars, which they named a Kilataon, has sent massive waves of energy over the earth. The first wave was in 2017. The second wave was in early 2018. The third wave hit in November of 2018 all the way through the winter of 2019. Radiation levels were high all over the earth.

The third week of February four huge hail storms hit in San Diego-with no thunderstorm attached to them.

And in July, of all things, a Hailstorm of Biblical proportions hit parts of Mexico. Three feet of stones buried cars, some buildings and trapped people for miles and miles.

BOWING TO THE WILL OF GOD
Even the toilet…
(Feb. 10th, continued 7 a.m.)

I still had the tummy ache and the stuffy nose. Not only was my head as stuffy as our yard, our toilet was "stuffy" too. No matter how many times I flushed, it was to no avail. I figured I'd tell Mark when he woke up.

I took a natural stress relief pastille, spray for my nose so I could breathe, and went back to bed. I read until my medicine kicked in and I could go back to sleep. It was a wonderful little book by Dr. Sizer. It was on his life in the healing ministry. Francis had started out as a priest with a heart on fire for God. Eventually the Good Lord called him out of the Roman Catholic church so he could pray for all of God's children — the exact same calling as I had.

Francis Sizer's call started in 1975 and I have no idea if I ever had a start. It has been with me all my life.

I sat in bed, reading while waiting for everything to feel better. The more I read, the more Dr. Sizer's sweet little book spoke to me. I saw many similarities between miracles, faith walks and prayers answered. As I read further, many questions I'd had asked over the years, were answered. Then I read about attacks on him, especially after anointing services. I paused and put the book down and pondered all the arguments and fights Mark and I have gotten into after the same glorious meeting with the Lord at Holy Services. I woke my husband.

"Honey, I think I know why we get into fights after prayer groups. They really are attacks stemmed from familiar spirits of oppression and wounds and willfully mad. I know you don't want these anymore and I don't either. Please let's pray together to stop this."

Mark got out of bed to go to the bathroom for a moment to gather his thoughts, and relieve his bladder. When he came back, he was ready to pray.

Mark led, "Lord God, we pray as a married couple, with the authority Jesus gave us, to bend the spirit of indignation and cast it off of us for evermore. Any smaller spirits of hurt feeling and oppression have to leave as well. In Jesus name."

I added, "And where these empty places are, be replaced with the increase of the Spirit of Compassion and Love in us. Especially with each other. In Jesus most holy name, amen."

We smiled and kissed. Mark turned over to go back to sleep.

I asked, "Honey, when you get up, please help me with the toilet. I think the lines are backing up because of all the rain."

I heard a muffled reply. "But I thought we were going back to sleep?"

"Oh, yes, when you get up. You don't have to get up now."

As Mark fell back asleep, I felt called to the bathroom once again. I hadn't walked a few short steps from our bedroom to my bathroom when a conversation started. God had joined me in the hallway.

"I can fix your toilet for you. Why don't you (pray/ask) me?"

I giggled and replied, "Okay, Sir, if you say so. I'm glad the thought doesn't offend you."

I opened the toilet lid and saw it still stopped up. I spoke to it as a child.

"Now toilet, I know you're having a hard time right now with all the rain and flooding, but in the name of Jesus I want you to work and work correctly, the way you were made to work. Flush and flush well."

I flushed the toilet with all the high, murky water and extra toilet paper. I watched as it all went down the pipes as if it had never had a problem to begin with.

I thanked God and chuckled that even toilets had to bow to the will of God.

PRAYING THROUGH A STORM
(Feb. 15, 2019)

Preface:

It had been a hard day. Something had happened that had not happened since I was healed of a heart arrhythmia almost 16 years before. I had gotten up early that morning and weight-trained with Mark. Then I went to the pool with Deb Grimes. I knew something was up. My coffee didn't sit well. Being at the pool didn't sit well, eating didn't sit well, etc.

Finally, at home, I checked my heart rate. I had gone into tachycardia. (My heart rate was into the 130's. Normal is 70-90 bpm.) For more than seven hours I battled it.

I started with Deb and myself in prayer. Then when Mark got home, he joined in the prayer battle. Finally, Sylvia from northern Indiana got in on the act.

I became weak from diarrhea as my own body battled back against the physical fatigue. I knew eating would exacerbate the problem so no eating. The best I could do was to keep electrolytes moving through my body. Finally at seven that evening, victory was won.

Boy was I exhausted. But in that exhaustion, I sat still. It was then a 'word of knowledge' came down from above. Here I share that word.

"The first Christian/Catholic Church was filled with Jewish men who stepped out of what they knew and stepped into what God knew."

Boy, did they!

And that night, I dreamed…

228

As If to Dream

The scene opened and we were in my office.

I could see me writing. Working on my newest book. Mary was with me helping research. My house phone rang. I picked up the receiver.

"Hello?"

As I said hello, I went into a vision. I could see the person at the other end of the line.

He looked to be an elderly, Jewish man. I could see the room he was in. It was dimly lit. An office. He was seated at a desk with books and papers all around him.

Once again, I said, "Hello?"

Mary piped up, "Who is it?" She could see concern on my face.

I shook my head 'no' for "I don't know." I was still in a vision. The old man on the other end of the line said not one word. I knew he wanted me to know he was there. My heart was pounding in my chest.

I could see him sitting at his desk, staring intently, listening to the sound of my voice.

I tried one last time to make full contact.

"Hello!"

With no reply from him, I slowly put the receiver down and hung up.

As I took the receiver away from my ear, I could see him turn from his phone and write furiously in a large book that was opened before him.

I looked at Mary in bewilderment.

Mary asked with concern, "What just happened?!"

I replied simply, "I don't know."

As the dream-vision faded (within my dream) as if from a long distance-or time, away, I heard, *'The early church was filled with elderly, Jewish men who stepped out of what they knew and into what God knew.'*

Yes sir.
I now had a better understanding.
Get busy.
Get into what God knows.
Yes Sir.

WHEN NO ONE WANTS YOU
BUT GOD
(Third week of February, 2019)

The title was given early that morning. I already knew what to expect for me.

On paper, it sure sounded good. And it is. God wants you above all else. But many times, it is a lonely walk.

Spring of 2018
When Mark's old boss (literally old, 80 years) decided to retire the jewelry store April 2018, he did so with no severance or vacation or sick pay for his employees. He had been good to them over the years, but his money, at the time, was caught up in expenses of closing the store. It's not cheap to go out of business.

Mark and Lana decided that very day they would open their own store, but it would be months down the road. We were staring zero income in the face.

In the meantime, I went out for job interviews, took tests, signed papers for background checks and still came up, time after time, in second place.

"We'll keep your resume' in case anything comes up."

Sure.

To this day, over a year later, I have never heard from any of them.

Fall of 2018
My publisher, Mary Smith watched all of this with dismay. We struggled for months until it took a

toll on my health. Then, while I was in recovery from gallbladder surgery, 'lack' struck Mary's household. Her position of 24 years was downsized to nothing. She, at least, received six months of severance pay. That was a big help to their family of seven living under one roof.

Mary and I decided for six months to make a go of her business and my books. But at every turn, something stopped us. People were sick and needed Mary. Children came out of the woodwork for her to babysit.

In the meantime, Mark and Lana opened their new business to a great success. After the first month, they were able to pay themselves a small salary. Mark's share was almost two-thirds less than his previous salary. We were consigned to live below poverty wages.

Before we knew it, Mary and family were in the same boat as we were. Financially, we were all taking on water.

A conversation occurred one morning as Mary and I were working together putting published books in e-book format.

Mary said, "I'm going to a job fair next week. Could you help me with my resume'?"

I piped in, "I'd love to!"

I made some suggestions on how to organize her talents on paper—which are many. Then in a soft voice, I whispered, "Maybe I'll go with you."

Mary Dow squealed with joy and hugged me. That was a yes in my book.

Over the weekend I updated my own resume and had 10 copies made. I just had a feeling that this fair was not for me to help our family, but to get Mary back out there. It was all about Mary.

Thursday arrived and I picked Mary up early that morning. She looked as nice and crisp as her resume'. We went to the unemployment office job fair and filled out more paperwork. We walked around to the different companies represented. I have to admit, I talked more about Mary than myself. Truth to tell, she didn't need me at all. Two of the companies thought she'd be a good fit after looking at her resume' and gave her the suggestions of what to apply for. And one of them was a recruiter. We left with our spirits high for Mary's success.

It was not a surprise to me that I was not qualified for even one position that day. I sorta knew. That morning before I left our home, I felt in my spirit, today was to be all about Mary. And I was for it.

In my heart of hearts, I felt the only one who wanted me for service to others, helping my family out, prayer for people on short notice, and writing, always writing, was God.

Ever-patient while I veered from my path, He waited for me to come back and pick up pen and paper once again.

Unfortunately for my husband, none of my good qualities helped him pay our mounting bills.

SIGNIFICANT
(First day on the road back home)

We started out late afternoon. I couldn't leave the state without all the gifts I wanted to find for Trinity, our oldest granddaughter. I couldn't leave her out. Once all was accomplished, we were on our way home.

"I don't understand it." I sighed.

Mark commented, "You know, I think you knew this was a possibility. Remember, Andy did this the last time a baby was born. When he got home, Andy took over the chores and sent you home."

I whispered, "I know, I know." I was still crying when we hit our first traffic pile up. The traffic we had run into on our way down was nothing compared to the traffic coming home. We barely made it out of the state by dinner time.

At the Georgia Welcome Center, we pulled in for a break from the drive and to relieve ourselves from all the coffee and pop on the road. On the way back to our car, we gently kissed as Mark opened my door. That was when I heard singing coming from a few feet away from us. We looked over in question.

There stood a smiling, 80-something year old man, singing his heart out about, "*young loves, being in love…having their whole lives in front of them….*"

The elderly gentleman serenaded us for a full two minutes. When he finished, I clapped my hands joyfully and thanked him. I couldn't place his accent. But I knew immediately, he was a brother.

He thanked us for showing him love was still alive on the planet. At that, he began to tell his story….

GOD'S HAND
(March 29th, 6:30 p.m.
at the Georgia Welcome Center)

Now, the Lord said this book, these stories would be from all around the world. Knowing my dislike of travelling outside of America, how could our Father in Heaven get stories of His goodness from world-wide to me? Evidentially, on the way home early from vacation.

"This song is from a play in London, England. I was born in Berlin in 1935. In my first grade, two-thirds of us did not make it to the next grade. My family and I went on vacation and came back to our home. Nothing was left of our home or street. Nothing but bombs were around us."

"Oh my…"

I assumed from the song he sang, he and his family had spent some time in England, eventually coming to America. His story continued.

"I finished school at a Christian College in middle America. I worked as a plumber."

Then his eyes sparkled.

"I sang on radio in the late 1940's and early 1950's."

"Wow," we replied.

His last story was even more significant than that.

"On 9-9-01 I stood in the Trade Towers on vacation. Two days later, they came down."

He let out a deep sigh and said, "When God's hand is upon you, the devil can't stop you."

By then I was crying.

"Yes sir, yes sir."

This example of a life well-lived is not just for the 84-year-old gentleman standing in front of me. It's for me, Mark, ours, yours, our country, and every free Christian on the planet. Please remember *When God's Hand is upon you, the devil can't stop you.* Keep going.

And this was why we had to leave Andy and Sam's early. They prayed and God knew.

WINNING
(Spring of 2019)

Finally. After 45 years. We're winning against abortion clinics. There used to be 2,176 clinics all over America. Now as of 2019, there are 697. That's a 79% decrease. We are now life-supporting.
(Mommy Activist)

There is an unclassified report of a deep impact coming. And I believe it. I will tell why later in another chapter. Pastor Paul Begley from West Lafayette, Indiana has been reporting on this for almost five years. This past April (2019) a meteorite exploded over D.C. And several have exploded over Russia in the past. And for the last nine years, Paul has been reporting on the hundreds of thousands to millions of deaths of animals. And don't forget about the Apocalyptic Dust Storm (April 2019) that killed 103 people. All too coincidental. Paul also reported on the Five Waves of Energy, earthquakes, sink holes, droughts, monsoons, typhoons, volcanoes, locusts at the Red Sea and Mecca, Hawaii, Japan, and the End Times. He is one busy pastor. Mark and I are honored to call Paul and Heidi Begley, friends.

Paul Begley also reported on this topic: National Near Earth Object Preparedness Strategy Action Plan—the hazard of near-earth objects in the next ten years. It specifically talks about the federal departments and what they would cover, our government's resources and existing assets, our nation as a whole, the internet, the public and private sector. Under this 'Agency,' sits NASA, and the Department of Homeland Security. Their possible agenda? Is there any chance we can prevent a disaster of that size catastrophe, and if we can't, then what?

Were you aware before President Obama left office, he started an office called The Armageddon Office? And President Trump just signed for another office titled 'Space Agency' for trouble in space, or any enemies from space — or earth.

Asteroids are increasing as debris from our galaxy collides with our planet. *"And great signs in the heavens will melt men's hearts for fear of what is coming upon the planet…"*

The Inuit Elders issued a warning to NASA and the world: The Earth has shifted. The changes in our climate is not due to Global Warming, but to the Earth shifting. It has tilted and wobbled. The sky has changed. The Inuits live near an artic region of Canada, the United States and Greenland. They are known for their superb weather forecasting skills.

And the rise of earthquakes is not from 'global warming' either. The Sun is rising in a different position. There are longer hours of the days. The Sun is off by a full half-hour. The sun set is also in a different place. Our axis is tilting. Last but not least, the stellar constellations are changing positions in the sky. The Earth has moved from its place in the galaxy. --- *(YouTube channel, The Real MLordandGod — Athens, Greece)*

I remember the dreams I had for so many years in my young teens, running out of the house, looking up to the night sky, shouting, "The stars are falling from the heavens! The stars are falling from the heavens!" It seems closer now than ever before.

A CALLING OUT
A Queer People in a Perverse Generation

Scripture states that we should be a queer people. In the Old Testament that means to stand out, shine, have love, show compassion, show all you meet who you belong to. Do not go with the flow.

Many times, God's people were in the middle of difficult circumstances — and were still called on to be different than those around them. It seems to be always in the middle of a perverse generation that God's people are called to stand tall no matter the consequence or circumstances around them.

Just like now, you will know the perverse generation that surrounds us. As they push to murder babies born and pre-born, many states are signing "heartbeat" laws saving the lives of the least of us. They have drawn the battle lines.

"Not here. Not here."

Churches are dividing over these same issues — homosexuality, sexuality of all kinds (LGBTQ etc.) abortion and murder of the after-born babies, the loss of nuclear families, the list goes on and on as good and evil separate like a chasm formed between them. That is where God will divide the sheep from the goats — even those in the church pews.

Remember, I beg you, love what God loves, and hate what God hates.

OUR OWN 5/11
An Attack of a Different Order
(May 12, 2019)

Katie Yocum and I were excited to be on a road trip together. The weather was fair as we took off for Cincinnati, Ohio. It was to be a day-long seminar on the heavens, celestial bodies' courses, and how and if it will impact the Earth in our near future. Doesn't that sound spectacular? It sure does to a watchman.

I will not give much of the information we learned here. But I highly recommend you go to Pastor Paul Begley's site on the internet: **Paul Begley Prophecy** –YouTube and internet.

Look for the four-part video *The Heavens are Shaking.*

Paul felt the Lord press on his heart to put this conference together. He knew all these speakers personally. He knew they all had the different parts to the puzzle. And it was time to put it all together. People came from all over America to capture one of the 300 seats available that day. Over 350 showed up. Paul had his people go to the local store and buy more chairs for folks to sit in. No one was left lacking a seat. Not even the man in the audience from the CIA.

They recorded all the speakers and you can get it all for $40. (I got permission to promo them!) It is absolutely worth your time and money. In my opinion, the whole world needs to hear what these four brave gentlemen had to say.

The first to speak was Clyde Lewis of Ground Zero Media. He can be found on the West coast on IHeart Radio and Soundcloud. He also has a YouTube channel. Look him up.

Clyde spoke passionately about earth science, the changes in our poles, the celestial bodies in our solar system, and what it all means to be alive on this earth at this day and age. He spoke of a planet named Hierapolis. He spoke on love and faith. Be prepared, not afraid. You can hear his talk in its entirety on Paul's four-part video.

The next gentleman to speak is a decorated Green Beret who also won the 2017 Prague Peace Prize. His name is John Moore. And we thank him for his service to our country. You can find John's information at **The John Moore Show** on YouTube. And on Internet-Radio.com, Republic Broadcasting Radio Stations. Please look up **John Moore's TheLibertyMan.com.** You will never regret listening to his teachings from his life, and how it all became a warning to the population of the whole earth. He is also an author of several books and videos. This was not something he sought out for his own fame and fortune, all the information came to him. I believe he was predestine for this very time and season. He spoke on the Gulf Stream, the warnings that have come through movies, and a revision of the world map. He was the second speaker at Paul's conference.

The third speaker was a gentleman named Steven Ben Nun (DeNoon). He is the founder of DeNoon Institute of Biblical Research, author of books including *Israel, Are they still God's People?* and *Yam Suph, Israel's Final Exodus.* He is the reporter for Israeli News Live, a YouTube news program. He has over 300,000 subscribers.

Steven also worked for the United States Federal government for a while. But the information he shared that day had little to do with his work history. His information was from a happenstance meeting, if there is such a thing. He spoke of a Chilean astronomer that lived at the turn of the last century, Carlos Munoz Ferrada. (Born 1901, died 2001.) Please research his work. He must've been one of the most brilliant men to ever have walked the earth. And Steven found out about him on a little green disk, given to him this past spring; and in front of everyone, he gave it to Pastor Paul Begley.

Steven spoke on the 100% accuracy of Carlos' predictions. And in 1923, Carlos made a prediction 100 years into the future. For the year 2023. A comet-planet that would have tremendous consequences to the Earth and everyone living on our planet today. If you buy this DVD set for nothing else, buy it for this.

I hope everyone who reads my books, will support all of these fine gentlemen and their programs. Their research has changed our lives and how we live and prepare for the future here as we wait the coming of our Lord and Savior, Jesus Christ, whom I call Yeshua Ben Elohim, Son of the Living God.

There were vendors there that Katie and I bought supplies from. She bought food and I bought a surgical kit. (Imagine that.) I was able to meet two out of three presenters that day. I have to tell you, out of all the conferences that we have been to, *Heavens Are Shaking* was the best one I have ever been to; no matter who put on the others. Like they say, "the information is priceless! Get your copy now!"

After the conference, Katie and I left around dinnertime. We stopped at a lovely restaurant in Cincinnati. As we were leaving the area, I watched rain clouds form on the horizon. An hour-and-a-half into our journey home, rain started falling. The thought that kept running through my mind, that I told Katie over and over was, "If we can get to the bridge, we'll be okay."

Three miles before we would have crossed the Sherman-Minton Bridge into Indiana — and safety — havoc happened.

As night descended over Louisville, Kentucky, and rain was lightly falling, Katie was on her phone to our friend Eva as I was watching the road carefully driving in the middle lane — out of everyone's way. Or so I had hoped. We were going through downtown Louisville on I-64 West at what's known as Spaghetti Junction. We were in a bright red car on a straight road in the middle lane. In an instant, our life changed. As God as my witness, I saw none of it coming.

"BANG!!" It sounded and felt like a bomb had just gone off.

Katie and I screamed as we felt the impact to our car. My car almost lurched sideways as we were hit hard in the passenger side door. Some idiot had tried to pass us on wet roads on our right side.

Katie screamed, "We're hit! We're hit!"

I cried out, "I know! I know!"

The air bags all down the passenger side deployed. Time crawled to a standstill.

I held tight to the steering wheel to keep us from hitting another vehicle. And kept driving looking for an immediate exit off the highway.

I could not see out of the passenger side window. I turned and looked out the back window and saw everyone coming behind us scrambling to get out of the way of a white car doing circles all over the road. He had lost control entirely.

The Third Street Ramp was right in front of us. To me, it looked like it was blinking *"here I am! Get off here!!"*

I felt in my heart if we had stayed on the expressway, we might not make it out alive. I got onto the ramp immediately.

Our phones had flown from beside us. I couldn't find mine. They had both disappeared on impact. We were two hysterical women crying out to each other. When I stopped at the light, the car died. It took me a second to recognize the car was speaking.

"Airbags deployed. Calling Ford Sync now."

I was still shouting orders to Katie when Ford Sync was coming up.

I shouted, "Katie! Call Mark and Nick! Then call an ambulance! I can't find my phone! Call the police!"

Katie cried out in exasperation, "I can't do three things at once!"

I stopped and said, "Oh! I'm sorry. I'm on overload."

That was when I heard another voice shouting above the fray.

"Shut up! Shut up! We are the police! This is Ford Sync! Calm down! Do you need an ambulance?!"

I looked at Katie and with tears, she nodded yes.

I replied, "Yes, please. Hurry."

The Ford Sync representative spoke again.

"The police say they can't find you on 64. Where are you?"

"We are at the bottom of the Third Street ramp heading west."

"We will stay with you on the line until they arrive."

I was never so grateful to hear another human voice.

While I was on with Ford Sync, Katie called her son Nick, who was with Mark at our home. He was downstairs watching television while Mark was balancing our checkbook.

Katie said, "Nick! We're hit! We're hit! We're in Louisville. At the end of the Third Street ramp. Come quick!"

Nick shouted from downstairs, "Mark!!"

By the time Nick shouted "Mark!" again, he met Mark at the top of the stairs.

"They've been in an accident! We gotta get there now!"

Mark grabbed his wallet and they ran out of the house. I won't tell you they got from Corydon to Third Street in 22 minutes. I'm sure, they were flying low….

It wasn't a few minutes before the police and fire department were by our side.

As they were jarring the passenger car door open, they spoke to Katie, "Are you alright?"

The police on my side said, "What happened?"

We both spoke at once.

Katie told the paramedics "I'm hurting. I have a heart condition and am a diabetic."

I told the police the best I knew.

"This car came out of nowhere! He was passing us on our right side. He must've spun out on the wet road. It sounded like an explosion when he hit us."

Katie heard them speaking outside. They wondered if it was the same white car they'd had reports on going down I-71 south headed for 64 west. He was all over the road. It was reported that he was slumped over the wheel of the car. Driving slumped over. And he hadn't stopped after the accident. It was a hit and run.

The ambulance arrived shortly after and started administering to Katie to get her out of the car.

That was when Mark and Nick arrived. Mark literally parked his truck right in the middle of the triangle divider at the stop light across from us.

I tell you now, they looked just like Batman and Robin walking across the street. Nicki ran to his mother. But not my Mark. I saw him walking toward me, hitched up his pants and surveying the situation.

The police backed up and let Mark near me. In his calm, cool manor, he said, "Hi hon." He kissed me gently on the lips.

Nick leaned over to Katie and said, "Are you alright Mom?"

Katie replied, "No. Something's not right."

I started, "Oh, honey. Someone hit us, hard! And I think Katie is going to the hospital. I'm alright."

Mark walked over to the other side of the car to survey the damage. He shook his head slowly.

The ambulance packed Katie up to take to the University Hospital.

The police looked at me and asked, "Is it drivable?"

"I have no idea! I'm not driving it! I'm scared."

Mark agreed to take it to the nearest parking spot until we could get help bringing it home and to a body shop.

In the meantime, Katie had Nick call Debbie and Dave Grimes.

"Hello?" Debbie answered.

"It's me, Nick. Mom and Debbie have been in a bad accident. Come quick! We are headed to University of Louisville Hospital."

Deb and Dave just happened to be in New Albany, right over the river from Louisville.

"We will be right there, Nick!"

In the meantime, Mark walked me over to the truck and helped me in. Then he went and started our badly damaged car to take it to the nearest parking spot. I sat in the truck and waited for him to walk back. After ten minutes, I called him.

"Where are you?" I asked. "I'm getting kinda scared out here." My nerves were finally taking hold of me.

"I had to park a long ways a way. There was nowhere close by. I'll run back."

"Thank you sweetheart!"

Ten long minutes later, Mark came running up to his truck. I unlocked the door and he jumped in. He was panting really hard.

I asked, "Are you alright? You're panting really heavy."

In between gasps, he replied, "You said, (pant) you were scared. (pant, pant) I ran all the way (pant, pant) back. (pant) I haven't ran in (pant) ten years."

My hero.

Mark went from Batman to Superman in two sentences. He started up the truck and off we went to find the biggest hospital in downtown Louisville. We arrived ten minutes later. Dave and Deb weren't five minutes behind us. Once again, we were all together.

Deb asked, "What happened?"

I told her the story beginning to end.

"And now Katie is in the ER being checked out."

That was when I happened to look down and noticed Nick's feet. It was Deb who asked the question.

"Where are your shoes, Nick?!"

"Uh," Nick started. "I ran out of the house so fast, I forgot to put shoes on." We all had a good chuckle as we waited for word on Katie.

In the meanwhile, Mark and Dave thought of a way to get our car home. Dave would drive Mark's truck back and Mark would drive the car back.

"Is it drivable?" I asked.

Mark replied, "It started up just fine for me. I think I can get it home."

"Please be careful."

After Mark and Dave left, I walked up to the aid station. I was tired of waiting.

"Katie Kost Yocum?" I smiled.

"They are still assessing her." She smiled back.

"I'm her patient-care advocate."

"Oh please! Go right back!"

I sure did.

They gave me Katie's bed number and I walked back to her room. I found her by herself forlorn, laying in the bed with a neck brace on.

"Have they done the x-rays yet?" I asked as I approached her room.

"No," Katie replied. "They are really busy back here. People and patients. I've seen so many wreck injuries!"

I hugged her gently and we talked a bit. I went back to get Nick. Then I went to bring Debbie Grimes back. I figured we should all be together.

By 11:30, and nothing else had been done for her, we were all getting tired and edgy.

Deb, the one who always perks us up in situations, said, "We might as well sing 'Kumbaya!"

I thought she was kidding until Katie took off singing. I joined her in the middle of the first verse. We were in perfect harmony. We were sure, it was the angels singing alongside us. It broke the weary atmosphere around us. Smiles were finding their way back to our faces and hearts.

By 12:30 that morning, they took Katie to X-ray. I called Mark.

"Are you home?"

"Yes, I haven't been home five minutes."

"Please bring Nicki his shoes and come and get me. I'm exhausted and can't stay any longer." I was ready to sob. Mark was back on the road five minutes later.

Mark brought Nicki his shoes and picked his weary wife up. Deb, the wonderful friend she is, agreed to bring Katie and Nick back to our house when they released her.

We arrived back home by 3 a.m. Katie and Nick were right behind at the top of the next hour.

"Results?" I asked.

"No broken bones, no concussion, no muscle tears, just gonna be achy for a couple of days."

"Thank God. Me too, sister. Me too."

We found out two days later our car was totaled. The man that hit us, hit us so hard that he cracked the frame of the car in two places.

I said it again like I said it that night when the car came to a stop at the light at Third Street.

"I hate the devil."

On the way home from the body shop, I asked Mark to stop at Heritage Ford, where we had bought our car. I told the young lady at the counter what happened. I was in tears as I wrote the general manager a note explaining that their car had saved our lives over the weekend. I left my phone number.

Remember, what the devil intends for evil, God will use for good....

Bert Hodge called me at 6:30 that evening.

"Deb! Are you okay!"

"Yes, Burt. A little banged up, but okay. Do you remember who you are talking to?"

"Yes! Yes! We had Bible study together after you bought your car from us."

"That's right." Then I started to cry. "Bert! I'm so sorry! Your car gave its life for us this past weekend. It's been totaled." (Sobbing) "I don't know how in the world we will ever get a car that nice again." I was devastated.

"Well, I am glad you are going to be okay. Now you know what we really do. We are in the people business, we just happen to use cars as a way of reaching out."

"Yes, sir."

"Do you mind if I change the subject?"

I paused for a full minute.

"Well, no Bert." I giggled. "What would you like to talk about?"

Mark was smiling too.

"The timing may not be perfect, but we have five positions coming open in the next couple of weeks, would you like to put in an application for one of them?"

I dropped my jaw. "Sure, pal. I'd love to work for the company that built the car that saved my life. Can you give me a week to heal up?"

"That would be perfect. In the meantime, go online and fill out your application. Download your resume."

"I'll do it."

"And by the way, I get to pick out your next car!"

Laughing, I said, "It's a deal!" I could see a tank in my future.

Mark was jumping and down for joy.

We had just come off our poorest year ever. Living off food stamps and Medicaid.

The day I started there, Mark and Lana got their first year raise. We went from a meager below poverty wages one week to well into upper middle-class the next. And we knew it was all God's timing.

And the insurance ended up not only paying off our car loan, but paid us almost $4,000 above it. Instant saving account.

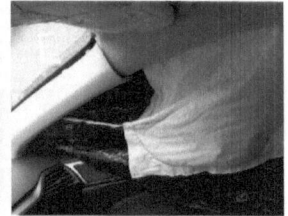

The totaled car, outside (left) and inside (below)

Over the next six months, Heritage Ford taught me, with great patience, all about the vehicles they make — and why they make them that way. Everything from the newest safety features to what was hot on the market each year. At 60 years old, I was keeping up with youngsters [30 years olds] all around me. They set the pace and I ran to keep up with them. One and all, a fine lot that I have grown to love and admire.

But it sure did speed up the passing of time.

ONWARD CHRISTIAN SOLDIER
(Last week of November to December 15th, 2019)

Every Catholic friend I asked to go with me to see an anointed priest from Canada, Fr. Michel', for one reason or another, could not go. It was a ninety minute drive one way for those in our community. To my knowledge, there was some "slight" weather to come home in—less than three inches of snow. And if that had been all it was, it would be no trouble. But that was not what came down the pipe that evening for myself and two of my sweet Christian friends that agreed to go up with me to the middle of my home state, above Indianapolis. But we are in the middle of the story here. Let's start back at the beginning….

I had been in contact with my dear friends from New York, John and Carol Leary. I'd sent Carol the notes from my newest book draft and was waiting to get her revision with added notes from their stories. As of the end of November, I had not heard from her. So I called.

"Hi Carol! It's Deb. Thanks for taking my call."

"Oh, hi Debbie! Yes it's good to hear your voice too. Boy we've been so busy! On the road all the time. We feel like this is our last year to do this. We've been with Fr. Michel'."

"Oh I wish we could meet with him too."

My memory went back to the trip Deb Grimes, Mark and I had taken all the way to Michigan to hear him speak two years before. At that time, I had been asked to leave a letter and a book for him — which I did. He knew me as "the Indiana author."

As Carol and I chit-chatted about where and when my wayward notes would make their way back to me, Carol mentioned Fr. Michel' again.

"You know, Deb, I can check his calendar. I think he's coming to Indiana very soon. Maybe next month."

"Wwhheee!!!" I squealed across the line. "Let him know I will start politicking to see who all wants to come with me to see him. I have plenty of friends that would line up for that, I'm sure."

"I'll call you soon and let you know what I find out."

"Okay. Our love to John!"

It ended up being just a couple of weeks before Fr. Michel' was to arrive. And I needed another minor miracle - as of the end of November, Mark and I had no car to go up and back in. I was going to have to hitch a ride myself — or so I thought. But God was already in the mix in all of it.

The beginning of December, two weeks before the meeting.

"Yes, Larry, he's the anointed priest from Canada. The one we brought you the video to see."

Our precious Christian friends from Salem, Indiana were very interested in a road trip together.

"I know Marilynn will want to go see him, Debbie. I'll have her call you."

"We'll set up a time we can meet at our home and take the expressway all the way up."

Ten days before the meeting.

Mark and I still had no car to make the trip in. And it looked like Mark himself couldn't go either. No car, no husband. It wasn't looking good for the home team. It looked like Larry would be driving.

Until Bert Hodge, General Manager of Heritage Ford—where I had worked the past seven months, stepped onto the scene. He and I had been looking for a car for Mark and me. I thought it would be one that we would 'settle for,' – as in I wanted to settle, and Bert wanted us to have the best we could for a price we couldn't refuse. The conversations between Bert, Jerry (our pre-owned General Manager) and myself got more interesting by the day.

Bert requested, "Deb, remind us once again how much is our ceiling for everything?"

I spoke with Mark. I gave them an amount.

"And do you have anything to put down?" The men inquired.

"Yes, sirs. Two thousand dollars."

Bert and Jerry grinned. They had a plan up their sleeve. Glee was in the air.

Bert asked a final question, "We need to know one more thing. Does Mark want a family car, or a sports car?" I could see hope in both men's eyes.

I laughed as I replied—being so sure of the answer. "I'll call and ask him. But I'm sure at 60 years old, he's going to want an economical family car."

So much for my sense of what I knew about my husband.

Mark Peyron immediately responded to my inquiry. "Are you kidding me?! They can get us a real sports car for that price? I've never had a real sports car! Yes, yes, yes!!"

Bert and Jerry were the new super-heroes of the day in Mark's eyes. They had captured his heart in one fell swoop.

Two nights later, the dream of a 'sports car' came straight into view. And Bert and Jerry were on it.

That day, my fellow KBB employees were off and I was manning that part of our BDC department alone. Not a problem. I'm not afraid of hard work. That left free computers all around me. During the afternoon, Bert joined me in the office at Scott's desk. As I worked through the afternoon and into evening, so did Bert. He was searching diligently for our next vehicle. For your information, vehicles are rated from 1-5 at dealer auctions. Five being showroom ready — in perfect condition. And Bert had a criteria to meet for us. It would have to have AWD (all-wheel drive) able to withstand any ice or snowstorm that would come around. Or be able to outrun any maniac taking straight-aim at us (as what happened to our last car).

At five minutes until close, Bert Hodge found a 'big catch.' He practically ran to see Jerry.

I calmly packed my lunch bag and purse for the end of the day, turned off my computer and put on my coat. I walked out of our office and onto the showroom to say goodbye to the guys.

There they were, Bert, Jerry and Chris, one of our product salesmen, looking at a computer screen with almost a green envy. Then, as if on cue, they looked at me.

I sighed. "I'm not going home right now, am I?" I asked.

In unison, the men said, "No."

I walked over to them. "What is it? Have you found our car?" I asked.

"I think so." Bert started the conversation. He spoke on where the car was being auctioned, from one of the best auto auction dealers in the country. And the hardest grading. If you find a '5' on their site, its showcase perfect. Bert Hodge was just sharing the pictures and information with Jerry and Chris. A '5' was being auctioned at that very moment.

"Hurry Deb! Call Mark! Tell him we've found "our" car! And it's in your price range!"

The men were salivating over a black, 2017 (birth month of May of that year) Ford Fusion Sport. It had every option Ford had to offer on a car. It was fully-loaded with the engine of an F-150 in it. An honest-to-goodness sports car.

I called Mark as fast as I could. As Mark picked up to say hello, Bert Hodge said, "Uh oh." I hung up on my husband.

"What's wrong Bert?! And it better be good. I just hung up on my husband!"

Jerry replied, "I think we just lost it." The computer had a glitch.

All the men in the room were crest-fallen.

I took it well. "It's okay guys. We can look again tomorrow."

I walked out to our borrowed 20 year-old mother-in-law's car. I lovingly called it Fred Flintstone's car. With roll-up windows and push-in-place seats, it had no options except the option of starting every morning.

As I was ready to open the car door, Chris came bolting out of the dealership hollering my name! I didn't know he even knew my name!

"Debbie! Debbie! Bert says come back! Run! Run!"

Both of us went running back into the showroom. Before I could get to Bert, he shouted, "It's still here!"

"Hit it!" I cried. "I'll get Mark on the phone!"

Bert hit the button and waited as I got Mark on the phone. He answered on the first ring.

"Hello?"

Bert and Jerry shouted into my phone. "Mark!!"

I chimed in, "Mark, Jerry's to your left and Bert's to your right."

"Hi guys! Do you have us a car?" Mark sounded hopeful.

Jerry replied, "We've put in the bid. Ask us what it doesn't have that Ford offers. Go ahead, ask us." Jerry's eyes were twinkling.

"Okay," Mark laughed. "What doesn't this car have that Ford offers?"

In unison Jerry and Bert replied, "Nothing!"

We all laughed. And within two minutes Jerry's computer screen popped up with a great big **"Congratulations!"**

All three men shook hands and clapped each other on the back as if we'd just had a baby. With a smile, I shook my head at the wonder of 'moving metal' our way at the speed of a computer's glitch.

And it would arrive in detail three days before our trip. It had all-wheel-drive, just in time.

Just like God.

Sunday, December 15th, 2019 Noon

Mark took off for work as Larry, Marilynn and myself took off for areas known only to our GPS. At least we were riding in style.

The ride up—which I drove—was very pleasant. We arrived early and ate a late lunch at a close-by restaurant. I was hopeful, since it was not snowing, it might go around us. We walked into the venue as they were setting up for the meeting. We went straight for the front row seats.

Fr. Michel' had a message specific for those there that night at that meeting. He knew it would be a special group of people coming. All would be called by God. No coincidences in the bunch.

After an introduction and a song, Fr. Michel' spoke about being from a family and family community. He spoke on the first time he heard Eternal Father speak to him—and the first time the devil did.

Fr. Michel' told us that the Lord God told him that sickness was a consequence of original sin.

Father warned us to be wary of the flu shot. He feels they put some things in it that causes other diseases in man including autism.

Fr. Michel' is also an exorcist. He gave us tidbits of how to fight the devil throughout his talk. "Sing 'Gloria Excelcius Deos', the devil will flee from you."

"Everything the Father wants, exists already. And *you* are here to serve."

[*Wow!*]

The good priest has now become an Abbot of his own order — as per instructions given to him by St. Labre' in a vision late one evening in 2009: **The Apostolic Fraternity of St. Benedict Joseph Labre'**. It is an emerging religious community for the New Evangelization. They are preparing priests for the future church.

And this Canadian had some very spot-on things to say about President Donald Trump: "Did God choose Trump? Yes! Why? Because the bad guys don't know which leg he can dance on. They can't control him. The Eternal Father has chosen this man to block the world government and block all plans of the enemy!"

Fr. Michel' sees troubled times after the election in 2020 for America — and even the world. He said America will come under attack. There are sleeper cells here now.

At the middle of our time together, before we took a break, Fr. Michel' spoke on the Second Coming of Jesus Christ and how close it really is.

It was during the break, I was finally able to approach him. Unlike many of the others there who asked for a blessing or prayer, I didn't want anything from him. I had two stories I thought he needed to hear, and quickly. It was a three minute conversation.

"Hi, Fr. Michel', my name is Debbie and I'm from Corydon, Indiana. I'm the *Southern Indiana author* they've told you about. I gave you a book and a letter while in Michigan."

Fr. Michel' nodded his recognition.

I smiled a bit, "I've been trying to catch up with you for two years. I won't take up much time. I have two stories I'm supposed to convey to endorse what you have just spoken, about the return of Jesus."

He nodded again. On I went.

"A couple years back my and husband and I were shopping at a department store for his birthday present. While he was looking around, I went over to a bin of kitchen towels. I was approached by a very ordinary-looking lady. Very nondescript."

"Without looking at me, she said, '"What is the exact day and time of Jesus' return?"'

"Immediately I knew I was in the presence of a demon. But just like in scripture where Peter is told by the Holy Spirit he will be given the right words in the face of his enemies, so was I. I drew my breath in and replied, 'I would be a liar if I told you I knew the exact day and time Jesus is coming back.'

"She tilted her head upward, her eyes rolled up in their sockets, moving from side to side, like a snake. With a curt nod of her head, she acknowledged my answer and she left stage right. I took stage left running after my husband yelling for him.

"The second thing I have to tell you is we have much in common sir."

With my stories done, Father nodded his head in recognition of the information I'd given him. I started to walk away from him. That is when the good priest touched my arm and stopped me. He said, "God bless you."

I was overwhelmed. I knew it was not a simple blessing he was conveying. I knew there was 'power' behind it. I smiled my full gratitude. "Awe, gee. Thanks so much."

Five minutes later the rest of the meeting started. And so had the snow, in earnest. And it was piling up in inches by the hour. We were 120 miles from home.

Father Michel' started the second section of the meeting. He spoke of some specific prophecies he had received. Father also spoke of Garbandal, Spain, St. Michael the Archangel, a warning, a miracle and a great chastisement that is to come. [*He was speaking so quickly, I could not get it all down on paper.*]

"Be careful of 'new christs', false messiahs, UFO's, vessels of satan, communism, sorcery and masonic temples. All these want to destroy America. They want to destroy humanity! They are against the Holy Trinity.

Everyone in the room gasped, mortified at the very thought.

"Do you know the devil has no set gender? That is why he is perverse and loves homosexuality."

(*Because I believe all this absolutely, that the Church has been attacked by the devil. The resignation of Benedict was a big blow. The fire at Notre Dame was criminal. It should never have burned.*)

One of Fr. Michel's final messages was this: "Eternal Father will invite humanity to return to Jesus. Confess your sins, say your rosaries and go to communion. The blasphemy against God cannot stand. Sins are multiplying and purification is coming. In your hearts, wonder at all God does for you. And has done all your lives."

[I most certainly have. With every book I write, I wonder and praise God for all he has done and continues to do. For as He is not finished, nor am I.]

"Remember even the simple words He gives you; breathing, waking up daily. We are never satisfied. We are always looking for the best. It is a ploy from the devil — be careful! It is an illusion."

Fr. Michel' took a breath, a drink of water, and went on.

Fr. Michel' exhorted us to increase our prayer life and dedication to God. He reminded us that, in order to give a good confession, to remember to confess our sins of omission.

From there, Fr. Michel' went on to some very practical suggestions. "Have three months' worth of food reserves for your family."

He reminded us to be careful, watchful and respond to the Lord's call *when* He calls you.

It was at that time, Fr. Michel' became very specific to everyone there that night. He pleaded. "Eternal Father will inspire you. He has chosen you to prepare His mission. How to help people endure and be saved."

He added, "Remember to mark your foreheads with the sign of the cross always."

I thought about how many years Mark and I had been doing that to and for each other. At least eight years. We knew it was important when we started and even more important now.

Fr. Michel' went on with his personal message to all there that evening. "We have been chosen to be here now. You are messengers of the Lord. You are chosen to be here! Don't shun your destiny. You have even braved the weather to be here."

At that, we all looked at the dark sky, which had let loose a barrage of snow. All of our cars were covered with inches deep of it. You couldn't see ten feet outside the front door.

Fr. Michel' readied himself to pray a Rite from Exorcisms to bless items, Crèches', Rosaries, water, pictures of people's families, etc. Some of those gathered, came up to speak to us.

One lady said, "Aren't you the ones that have come the farthest of all of us here? We've been talking, you can stay at my home. Or at (someone else's) home. Please we want you safe. You were called here for a reason."

Marilynn and I were for it. But Larry was not. He said he would drive us home...in my brand new car, in all that snow....

To quote my marvelous editor and publisher, "Crummy buttons."

Information on how to contact or contribute to the Fraternity of St. Benedict Joseph Labre:
      163, Route 109
      Saint Dominique-du-Rosaire (Qc)
      JOY 2K0
      819-444-6710 or 819-443-2891
        fabl.adm@hotmail.com

READIED FOR HEAVEN

(Third week of December, 2019)

DREAM

I was out with my friend Katie, shopping. All of a sudden we heard a noise coming from above us. We looked up. As we looked up, we were being lifted off the ground. I reached for Katie to hold hands and could not quite get to her.

The higher we went the faster we flew. As darkness surrounded me, I saw all of my sinful times in my life. I had great sorrow and cried as they flashed before me.* By the time we arrived at our destination, a place brilliant white, I was standing in a gown with no spot or blemish.

A little later that morning, I called Katie to let her know I dreamed about her. When I got to the point where I was seeing my sins before me and crying, Katie began to shout.

"Oh, Deb!" Katie cried. "Do you understand what that means? As you were heading towards Heaven, your sins fell off of you. You were being readied for Heaven.*"

Oh thank God.

*This would be Purgatory -- editor

COMMERCIAL BREAK

The Misadventures of Igor and Ichus
By Sophia Jo Rose Merk (Age 3 years)
--My Granddaughter

Well, what do you expect, telling full-blown stories at three years old? After all, she is <u>my</u> granddaughter. (Laughter)

Over breakfast with Andy, Sam and their three children with number four on the way, while we were talking about Bible Study, Sophia started a conversation about her 'special friends'. It seemed the last couple of months, she had 'found' two new friends. As I inquired further, she told me their names and ages. The conversation went as follows:

"Grammy, Igor is a boy. He is three years old. Ichus is a girl and she is four years old."

I smiled.

Satisfied that she had answered all my questions, Sophia finished her breakfast and off we took to run errands for a day out. In the van, conversation resumed.

"Sophia," I cooed. "Tell Grammy an Igor and Ichus story."

Sophia Jo Rose jumped right into the middle of a story.

"Oh Grammy! Igor ran from a big bear!"

"Eeekkk!!" I squealed.

Immediately, everyone in the van was transported to the middle of a story. We looked all around to see a big hill with a big bear standing on top of it. And of all things, he was holding a camera. Sophia, being the bravest of us all, stepped forward toward the bear. He aimed the camera and 'snap' went a picture!

Sophia went on with the story, "He took a picture from top a big hill and tumbled down running away." We could all see him roly-poly flopping down the hill with Igor and the rest of us in high pursuit. But we were no match for a full-grown bear.

"Oh! Did he get away?!"

"Yes!" Sophia cried out.

"Did the picture come out okay?"

Sophia started to giggle.

"Yes." Full blown laughter erupted from her. "It was a picture of me!"

Everyone in the van laughed.

By the end of her story, we were 'all back in the van', back on the road headed to the biggest story-telling place in America, Walt Disney World.

"What a good storyteller you are, Sophia." I said. "I wonder where you get it from? I'm pretty sure you get it from your daddy."

(Now, where does he get it from?)

I'm sure we all knew that answer…

What does this have to do with a book of the supernatural and world events?

Consider it a commercial break.

Brought to you by Igor, Ichus, and Sophia Jo Rose.

My drawing of Sophia

CORDUROY, SILK & BLUEJEAN FOREVER
60 long years

As a child, I had two very good friends. They were Kae Smith, who I called Blue Jean, and Karen Clark, who I called Silk. I myself was Corduroy — nothing fancy, just comfortable, thanks.

None of us were big girls. Although I was the biggest of the three coming in at a size medium. Kae Kae and Karen were always smalls. And I was the oldest. Allow me to explain.

Kae was the youngest of the three. Both her siblings were boys. She grew up able to handle her own. You didn't want to get on the wrong side of her right fist. At 100 pounds dripping wet, she could throw a 12-pound bowling ball and knock every pin down! Stay out of her way! She had long, sandy blond hair and dark eyes. At five feet-two-inches, she was the smallest and youngest of us.

Karen, on the other hand, was very lady-like. She loved to wear dresses. That is where the nickname "Silk" came from. She also was the only girl in her family. She was adopted with three younger brothers. Karen had big blue eyes and cascades of long, blond curls.

If I wasn't with one, bowling, I was with the other talking, or Bible studying. We all played with Barbies, horses, games and went places together. We were good company for each other.

As I grew up, we went to different schools and led different lives. We all three got married and were several times, pregnant at the same time. Karen had one son, I had three boys and Kae had four girls.

Through circumstance and lives, we all ended up divorced from our first husbands, living in different states. Kae in Kentucky, myself in Indiana, and Karen in Florida.

As we grew older, in our 40's, I lost touch for the most part with them. I love them still and pray nothing but the best for them. If I ever find them again, I'll send them our story.

I believe God loves our memories and sweet beginnings. It has been my experience that at times, God allowed part of my life to repeat itself.

After a contentious divorce from my boy's father, and back in Indiana, away from my birth family, I was alone. The Lord God knew I would be in need of friends, and HE slowly sent me my "youth" replacements.

The first one to show up was Mary Smith. Yes, another Smith. But unlike the first, she was more corduroy. A comfortable fit as my first friend in a long time. At the time, I sure hoped she'd keep me. Mary was taller than I and just by months, older. She was very self-assured with three little girls. Laughing, yes this Smith had only girls too. She was divorced.

One evening, Mary came to prayer group wearing sorrow.

I asked, "What's wrong?"

She replied, "My best friend just died."

Moved with compassion, I said, "I'll be your best friend."

And so it was and has been ever since. Why Mary even started a publishing company because she believed in me and my books so much. Doesn't the Bible mention the laying down of your life for a friend? She has surely laid down her own ambitions, made them new, and picked up to help with mine. I am forever grateful.

The next "Corduroy" to come into my life was Deborah Grimes. A marvelous priest named Fr. Bernie Weber introduced us. Deb's perky in nature and very smart. Seems to be a trend in my life of smart people that come my way and decide to stay. Deb had a degree in psychology, had worked for doctors, and we spoke the same spirit-filled language. I was very glad when she showed up in my life too. And talking about laying down one's life for a friend. Listen to this:

For several years she and I discussed the need for a group of friends to come together. We both knew we were living in the time just before the return of Jesus. The only thing we differed on was is I am pre-trib (because the Bible tells us to pray to be kept away from the Great and Terrible day of the Lord; and I am a remarkable chicken, despite all outward appearances.) Deb is post-trib. That is what her church has taught her and she believes it.

Debbie Grimes strongly believes in community. Mark and I had lined up a couple of friends to look for a place together when it all hits the fan. I had never asked Deb if she wanted to join us because she had a big, gorgeous home that I didn't think she wanted to part from. I learned different.

In the meantime, my second in my life, Kae Kae showed up. A true Blue Jean. She came from a different manor.

I had a friend who was moving to Texas. She called the day she was moving and asked a favor of me.

"Deb, could you do me a favor?"

"Sure."

"Could you befriend Katie Yocum? She's the blind widow I've told you about. She has a young son named Nick."

"Sure thing. Give me her number. I'll invite them to our Christmas party."

I was pretty sure it was Biblical, being kind to the widow and the orphan.

Katie and Nick and friends ended up coming to dinner on a night all to their selves. Well, it was a good thing! None of us ever shut up! We all had so much in common. None of us at that table were 'regular' Christians. We all walked in the supernatural and through the veil.

By the beginning of 2015, we invited Katie and Nick to a Gathering. That was where Katie got the full indwelling of the gifts of the Holy Spirit as she was prayed over by Jim Carter, retired pastor.

Two weeks later, she came to my home and 'read my mail' without me saying a word other than, "Oh my!" and "uh huh," on and on.

Since then, we found plenty to get into. We've been to conferences together. We've helped each other when we were sick or injured. We haven't let each other down.

And when she found out my birth family 'divorced me' after the death of my mother, Katie, as well as Mary Dow, and Deb came to my rescue. I may have lost one birth sister, but I gained three eternal sisters.

Sold American.

Katie as well as Deb believed in community for the last days. When another family that we had included parted ways, Katie and I knew we needed a third family. Now comes the part I was telling you about Deb earlier — what she was willing to give up for friendship.

One evening three or so years ago, Katie, Deb and I were making dinner together. I explained to Deb that the other family had decided to 'opt out' of our lives. Debbie listened as I told the dilemma of looking for another family who might be interested. Finally, she spoke.

"Aren't you going to ask me?" She asked.

Katie and I stopped what we were doing and looked at her.

I replied, "Well we didn't think you'd be interested. You have that beautiful $400,000 home. We didn't think you'd want to give it up."

Deb quietly replied, "I've been waiting for you to ask me for two years."

I wept.

"You are willing to leave your home for us?!"

"Yes."

Three families became one that day.

My life had now become complete once again. I had two Corduroy's with Deb and Mary, and one blue

Jean with Katie. My second Blue Jean Katie. But where oh where was Silk?

Had I not told you until now? I myself had finally grown up and become the 'new Silk'. *(Laughing)* and I was now the smallest and the youngest.

Now how in the world had that ever happened?!

I reckon only God knows.

"Framily"

EPILOGUE

Prepare your body, but save your soul.
The timeline as I see it.

As I wound up this book, I found this; it has ranged from miracles, to prophecy to attacks not only in our lives but the world round. I will try to sum it all up to where we are currently in my view.

One last article to share that came across my desk as I was finishing up this last book. This is from Prophecy Alerts with Robert Rite Author. Warren Cleaver is a group member that keeps us current. He posted this to our group from Breitbart May 21, 2019. The title of the article is *Ramadan Rage, Jihadis Massacre 364. Injure 404 in two weeks.*

I have not mentioned the nation of Islam and Islamic terrorists much in this book. But if we can't get the word out on television about these horrific events—and we can't—it has to go through an alternative media and print. Consider me alternative. Here's a recap of the article:

"During the second two weeks of *May* 2019, or Ramadan for the Islamic world, Islamic terrorists carried out 76 attacks in 15 countries. They have killed at least 364 people and injured 404 so far. They still have two weeks of their 'holy month' to go. It is expected to last through sundown June 4th.

The countries the attacks occurred in are as follows:

Afghanistan, Benin, Burkina Faso, Chad, Egypt, Iraq, Pakistan, Kenya, Somalia, Libya, Mali, Nigeria, and Syria.

The Taliban is responsible for 40% of all fatalities. Isis is behind 30%. The vast majority of Ramadan attack victims are Muslims in Africa and the Middle East."

Can anyone explain to me, why they are butchering their own people during their holiest month? This is not religion, it is a monstrosity. And I am sure, there are monsters involved.

Politically, America is as polarized as I have ever seen in my 60 years. Just like the word of warning I received this past year, *Socialism is coming to America.* I watch as conservatives and Donald Trump Patriots line up against the Left-wing Socialists as they rose up in the ranks of the Democratic Party. 50 years ago, the democrats themselves would have thrown them out of America. Now, they have the audacity to boldly burn our flag and our Constitution and call it 'their right'.

For the first time in 19 books I will swear an answer.

Bull....!

Politically around the world, nation after nation are holding elections and conservatives are winning. Could the tide be turning in our favor? Can we forestall the inevitable that Revelation speaks of, or is the end/tribulation times on our doorstep in the next 2-5 years?

Australia, Bavaria and India as well as America are putting conservative candidates in their highest offices. The standing up for each one's nation, national pride and preservation of freedom are once again travailing up to the top as the thought of a One-World Order declines in popularity.

Religion. According to the Italian reporter, Leo Zagami, several of the Roman Catholic Church Cardinals are having a split over several issues with the current Pope. And according to Michael Voris, *The Church Militant* and *The Vortex*, half of all priests and Bishops in the United States maybe homosexual. And priests are dying of Aids. (Kansas City *Star*)

In another report, *"Clergy and Religious and the Aids Pandemic,"* the National Federation of Priests Counsels, 34 pages document discussing the Aids epidemic among priests today. They now screen seminarians for HIV across America. (In the last 20 years) From 1995 to now, the numbers are as high as 1,000 in 15 years. It is ten times the national average at the low end of this scale. 45% of 500 priests surveyed voluntarily told they are indeed gay and one in four has Aids. The percentage maybe as high as 58%. At 58% these numbers are 50 times the national average.

It is a homosexual cover up now being exposed.

It truly is a sordid mess.

Nature. (VOX)
The amount of Earthquakes and Volcanoes erupting has sky rocketed over the last several years.

In January 2018 alone, Mount Mayan in the Philippines, blew for a month. In February, Mount Sinaburg in Indonesia blew. In June, the volcano in Guatemala blew. There are 10-20 eruptions in any month at any one time. In 2018, the Ring of Fire was so strong, that four of the eruptions and last five earthquakes occurred there. Volcanic eruptions and earthquakes are often clustered together. In 2019 there have been over 50 significant earthquakes from all around the world.

Some scientists believe that there is an 'influencer' in our galaxy that is causing a disturbance not only on our planet, but several of the planets in our solar system. Speculation of a large comet-planet with an elliptical orbit that comes in contact with our part of the Milky Way every 3,600 years is due in the next 3-7 years depending on whose doing the math. There are many good DVD's and video's on the subject. My all-time favorite was the one I mentioned earlier in this book in the story titled, *"An Attack of a Different Order"* Paul Begley's *"Heavens Are Shaking."*

Supernaturally. As the fight between good and evil escalates toward the imminent return of Jesus Christ to this planet as described all through the Book of Revelation, we see all around us evidence of the supernatural.

I can't talk with anyone anymore who find out I am an author of books on miracles, that they don't share their numerous experiences with me. Dreams and visions are on the rise not only with Christians from all over the world, but also with Jews in Israel and Muslims in the Middle East. Conversions are on the rise. I personally believe that the last Great Revival will be led not only here in Southern America (Tennessee) but in Israel too.

As a personal example, this past spring (of 2019) Katie Yocum and I were travelling home from a conference and were hit at 65mph passenger side. A hit and run. We were both checked out at the hospital and walked away from a crash that buckled the car frame in two places totaling it. I don't believe in coincidence. I believe we're not done here in these last days so there but for the Grace of God, we go.

I will tell you one last thing. I believe as the heavens unfold, our generation will see the Rapture of the Church and the Second Coming of our Lord and Savior, Jesus Christ.

My timeline, as I see it:

In a telling dream in 2017, I heard Obama say, "I'm not finished with America yet." I believe what I heard.

Nathan of Israel was told in 2015 by the Christ Himself, that Obama was Gog. And a great war was coming. The Pharisees at the time, thought the time line was around two years as Nathan heard. That would have made it 2017. What could have happened in 2017 that changed the time line? My personal opinion? Donald John Trump and the Lord God.

What if this really is one last reprieve? What if revivals are really going on right now?

I saw, in an early 5:30 a.m. vision on Easter 2018, a Great Light that reached to the Third Heaven from a tiny town on the south eastern side of Tennessee. In physical seconds, it scattered to the whole earth.

The Catholic Charismatics have been told through prophets and seers (Catherine Emmerich, Padre Pio, Fr. Michel') different parts of the time line just before Jesus return:

Catherine, "There will be two popes at the end times, one is a black pope."

Pio, "There will be three days of darkness."

Fr. Michel, told by Jesus Himself, "I am coming back soon. Prepare the world."

Others such as William Branham from Jeffersonville, Indiana in the 1930's to the 1960's, saw <u>just</u> before the return of Christ, there would be self-driving cars. This my friends, is not three years away as of this writing. Scientists have been testing them for the last two years.

I myself, woke one morning to hearing, **"Prepare to Rapture Up."** August of 2017. It is coming to a head. **"Time is coming to a close."**

At the Heavens Conference this past May 2019, Katie and I found out the rest of the planetary story. The dates given there were anywhere from 2022 to 2029. And the gentleman from the CIA in the audience, thinks it closer to the earlier date. The governments of the world are planning for the earlier date.

And do you think it a coincidence that the only real wreck I have ever been in, that could take our lives, was right after that conference on our way home? A conference where I had purposed in my heart to tell everyone I knew what is about to happen? I don't see where he could have survived hitting us at 65 mph, why he didn't go through the windshield or have an engine in his lap. He should've died in my opinion. *Unless*, he was already dead. You can't kill what is already dead. You think I'm kidding? Look up the books on Real Documented accounts of Zombies by Paul Begley.

And at the end of the conference, the person from the CIA came up to John, one of the presenters, and said, "I'm the CIA, and I want to tell you something. Your time line is off. Since you retired, they have changed it up. Sped it up. It is no longer 2023. Tell your people they better be prepared before then."

The great physicist I spoke of from the same conference, mentioned the year 2023, but could be pushed back to 2025.

And we personally have friends in West Virginia who were told by an angel that sat with them, that Donald John Trump would be elected again in 2020, but he will not finish his term in 2024.

When you put all the visions and peoples that are coming forward now in numeric order, **be ready** anywhere from between the end of 2022 to the year 2025. Do you understand what this means? Do you have any idea? *It means we are now in the last seven years.*

One of the last conferences we went to in 2016 was in Tennessee. The pastor hosting it asked the audience what year they thought we were in, prophetically speaking. He asked all that agreed with each of his years to stand when he said them. He started with 50 years and went down to the last one he said.

"Under ten years?" (As of 2016)

Mark and I and about 100 people out of over 5,000 stood.

He said, "See those people? Find them after the conference and ask them what they know, what they see."

In 2019, I was told in the Spirit, loud and clear, "Prepare your body, but save your soul." And bring as many with you as possible!

If you walk the numbers back from 2025 itself, minus seven years, 2025, 2024, 2023, 2022, 2021, 2020, 2019. The seven years started this year. The Fall of 2019, this Fall, the Jewish Fall Feasts.

Mid-trib is when things get rocky according to scripture. Beginning of 2023. Just like the angel told our friends, President Trump won't finish his second term.

What if the reason he doesn't finish, is because we all go in a Mid-Trib Rapture? All those who love the Lord, born again believers, we all go when God calls HIS Holy Spirit off the earth, all the believers that were spirit-filled, would have to go up too.

Think about it:

Two popes

Self-driving cars

Line up of the nations

The pole shift coming

The comet-planet coming

The fight between good and evil already taking place in Rome and in the heavens

The Black Pope

Pope Emeritus said last year, "Great ship is in danger of capsizing."

Earthquakes in diverse places

Wars and rumors of wars

Israel in 2019 built an altar waiting for their Third Temple coming in 2020.

In 2016, the evil one's representative asked me if I knew the exact day Jesus Christ would return.

I replied in spirit out loud, "I would be a liar if I told you I knew the exact day Jesus would return."

But what if, embedded in me before I was born, that I would recognize the appointed **season** when it came due, and to tell everyone at that time appointed. "Prepare ye the way of the Lord."

It's time.

So what do we do now?
- Prepare ye the way of the Lord.
- Take care of your family.
- Preach the Good News of the Gospel of Jesus Christ—He's coming back in our lifetime.

And I still know **not** the day nor the hour.
But I watch and pray…*See you in the air!*

Deb's Christmas Cookbook
A Collection of Recipes
from
Four Generations of
Family & Friends
...plus Stories!

Deborah Aubrey-Peyron
With a little help from my friends!

Deb's Christmas Cookbook
A Collection of Recipes
from
Four Generations of
Family & Friends
...plus Stories!

Deborah Aubrey-Peyron
With a little help from my friends!

MAMA
MOMMA
MOMMAH

There is a spirit
that comes upon some,
full of compassion and love
and even a lot of fun.

Though the days flew by
as all life winds down,
for that I did try
to earn a gold crown.

For this reason, I was sent here,
to be there for each and one another.
In joy, laughter, sorrow or tear,
I am simply made,
a mother.

For the ones who counted first—
you taught me to count.

---

* With three little boys, they each decided they would
spell my name differently so I would know which one
had given me a card or note of love.

(Cheesy) Root Soup

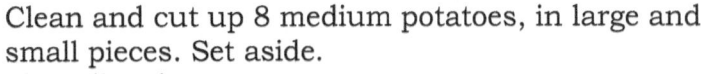

*On a cold winter evening,
   this soup hits the spot!*

4-8 large Potatoes
2 Carrots
1 Onion
2 cloves of Garlic, minced
2-3 quarts of Vegetable broth, or Chicken broth.
Salt and Pepper to taste.

Clean and cut up 8 medium potatoes, in large and
small pieces. Set aside.
Thin slice the carrots.
Thin slice the large onion.
Mince the garlic cloves.

In a large pot, melt half a stick of butter and simmer
the carrots, onion and garlic in it. (Two minutes.)
Add the vegetable or chicken broth.
Add the potatoes. Bring to a boil. Reduce heat then
cook 30 minutes on a medium simmer.
Add: 2 cups of Milk
½ stick of Butter
4-6 ounces of Cheese (whatever kind you like. I used
a processed cheese loaf.) Stir while adding the cheese
until melted.
Salt and Pepper to taste.
Simmer for 5-7 minutes

If it needs to be **thickened**: in a 1 cup container, put
1/4 cup of flour, add hot water and stir until
completely dissolved. Then pour it into the soup.
Cook one minute.

Grab the crackers – you're done!

Grammy Fran's Christmas Ham

(This always told me, it must be Christmas Day!)

Preheat oven to 350 degrees (F)

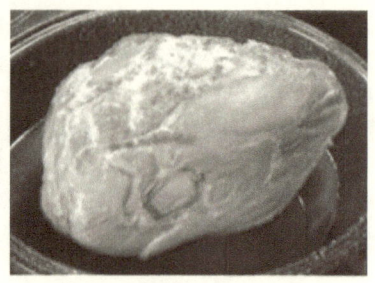

For a precooked 5-7 pound ham cook it 10 minutes per pound. If an 8-10 pound ham, still 10 minutes per pound. If uncooked, it is 20 minutes per pound.

I always use a spiral sliced ham. Sometimes they come with a packet of seasoning. If your ham comes with one, you may want to reduce or take out your allspice. It should already be in the packet. You will still use the rest of the ingredients.

Pierce the ham with whole cloves over the top and sides.
Wrap the ham in foil in a baking pan.

Combine in a bowl:
¼ cup of Brown Sugar
4 ounces of Pineapple Juice
½ teaspoon of Allspice
Mix it together.

Now Momma liked to pour this on about ½ hour towards the end of baking. But I like to put it on at the beginning and baste it every 15-20 minutes. Some people even put the ham in upside down while cooking to promote juiciness.

After it's done, take the foil off and take out the cloves. Cover back up until ready to serve.

Serve with Raisin Sauce (Recipe below)

Raisin Sauce

1 ½ cups Water	2 Tablespoons Butter
1/3 cup Raisins	2 Tablespoons Flour
¼ cup Sugar	1/8 teaspoon Nutmeg
1/8 teaspoon Salt	

Boil these ingredients for 15 minutes-medium boil. Add 2 tablespoons of butter, let melt. Stir 2 tablespoons of flour into 2tablespoons cold water. Add a little of the hot mixture and stir, then stir into the pot. Let it come to a boil for 1 minute.

Turn off and add the nutmeg.

David's Story
(Close in age, close in heart.)

Some of the sweetest stories any of us can tell, are the ones from our children's lives. The same goes for me

My babies were hard fought for. The first three – including a twin – were miscarried – much to my sorrow.

My fourth baby, Paul Benjamin, came out fine and healthy finally! I thought with such a lousy track record, I would be happy with just one live birth.

By the time Ben was two, he and his father started to conspire against me. We would all go to the shopping mall and no soon as we would step through the doors, off they would go to look at baby clothes – little dresses or blue baby onesies, were always the order of the day. I would take off to find them in the same place, holding up their wares and smiling at me. I finally nodded my head, "yes."

What none of us knew, at that time, there was already a "bun in the oven." Baby number two was already growing inside me. My "yes" was rather like agreeing to let the horse out after the stall door had already been opened.

Little David arrived early by three weeks and breech. We brought David home at barely six pounds and 18 inches – almost two pounds and 3 ½ inches shorter than his brother at birth

On the way home from the hospital, my husband, who we agreed could name all the boys and I would name all the girls – spoke, "Thomas Andrew Carlisle Merk."

"Excuse me?"

"Thomas Andrew Carlisle Merk. That's what we will name our next boy." He was all smiles.

I replied, "Well you better write it down some where because we'll forget it in three more years." I smiled.

Sixteen and a half months later, I delivered 8 pounds 4 ounces, 20 ½ inches long – Thomas Andrew. Sigh.

We brought the new baby home on Christmas Eve. The grandparents met us at the house with little David and Ben. Not only did David think Andy was his Christmas present as soon as he saw him, but he thought Andy was "his baby!"

"I want my baby to eat with me!"

"I want my baby to play with me!"

"I want my baby to sit with me!"

After watching so many people come by and hold the new baby, by the time Andy was three months old and almost 18 pounds, little David, at 19 months and 22 pounds, decided he wanted to hold "his baby!"

David crawled up onto the couch, one afternoon, next to me and said, "Mommy, I want to hold my baby!" He held out his arms.

I looked at their father and Ben who nodded their approval. After all, David was sitting right next to me, I could hold both of them if I had to. Neither would be in danger of falling off the couch.

So I gently placed that big baby into little David's lap. Within three seconds David fell back onto the couch cushion with Andy on top of him. All you could see were David's hands and feet waving away! Before I could react, a small cry came out from under Andy.

David cried out, "Get my baby off me!!"

I laughed as I picked up Andy and tried to console our little lamb. David cried because he was not big enough to hold "his baby."

I told the little sweetie that they were all my babies, my little boys, and that I loved them so much. I consoled David with "One day, you will be big enough to hold 'your baby.'"

Footnote: I am the proud owner of a picture of David, at 19 strong years old, picking up and carrying his little brother, Andy. David did it just to prove he was finally big enough to carry "his baby" brother.

Love, in our family, is never lost.

Mark's Mashed Potatoes

Preheat oven to 325 degrees

10 pounds of Potatoes
1 cup of Sour Cream
2 cups of Whole Milk
1 stick of Butter
1 – 8 to 10 oz. bag Sweet Onion Potato Chips

Wash your potatoes, peel them, cut out any bad places, and dice in quarters.
Boil your potatoes 30 minutes, or until soft.
Drain well.

Put the potatoes in a mixing bowl. Add one whole stick of butter. Mix the potatoes and the butter. They will be thick. Put in a cup and a half of milk and mix thoroughly. Then add one cup of sour cream. If the potatoes are still too thick, add more milk until the potatoes are of a whipped consistency. Then add salt and pepper to taste.

Spoon the potatoes into your baking pan. (Ours is an 18 x 15 Pyrex pan.)
Open one corner of the bag of potato chips and let the air out of it.
Crush the potato chips. Empty the crushed chips onto your casserole and spread out to cover the top.

Bake at 325° for 20-30 minutes until the chips are a golden color.

A CHRISTMAS MIRACLE

In the beginning of our third year of marriage, Mark and I had several people, who were not acquainted with each other, come forward to tell us that we were to go look for land, build a home, and even who our builder would be. Since we do not believe in coincidence, we started early in the year of 2002 looking for land. I wrote on a piece of paper "$18,000.00" and "for sale by owner." That is how we would know the land when we saw it. Mark even got the feeling of where we should drive. When we stepped onto the land, the Holy Spirit fell on me from my feet up. This is it. We are home. We did indeed buy the land for $18,000. Everything went well; we built a home and were in before Christmas. We held many Bible studies and prayer groups there.

By the fourth year of our marriage, and two years into our new home, my back broke. It fractured at L5-S1. We had no health insurance. The muscles along the left sciatic nerve, from the Gluteus Medias to the Achilles tendon, froze. I had a charley horse 24 hours/seven days a week. All the doctors could do was immobilize me with medication. From the pain, my temperature would go up to 100 degrees and my hair fell out in clumps. My blood pressure was rising week after week.

After seven weeks of incredible pain, I laid on the floor at 3 a.m. during Thanksgiving week, and cried out to the Lord, "I know you are God. You can do anything! Take me up! Get me out of here! Take me home! I don't want to be here anymore! You can do it!" I even told Him I didn't want to be a wife or a mother anymore. My husband was on the floor next to me rebuking every word out of my mouth.

Our youngest son Andy was hollering in the hallway, "Momma, stop it! You are scaring me!"

As if someone was standing right next to me, I heard a voice. I believe an angel said, "*Hang on! Your Christmas Miracle is coming! Your Christmas Miracle is coming!*" Being in the frame of mind I was in, I cried out again, "Christmas! It's not even Thanksgiving!" With my next breath, I said, "But not my will, but thine be done." My husband rubbed anointed oil on my back and leg and prayed over me for two hours. I was finally able to get back into bed and sleep a little while until my next round of medicine was due.

While this was going on, I played praise music over and over again until I wore out a CD. The doctor scheduled me for an epidural block. It was Christmas time, and my husband Mark was a bench jeweler, so he was pressed for time and was unable to stay and help me afterwards. He took me over to the hospital that morning, and the nurses prepared me for the procedure. The head nurse in charge of me blew the right vein three times trying to put in an IV for medication distribution.

When they finally got me ready and wheeled me back to the operating room, the anesthesiologist ran the medication for the block down the wrong leg two times! By this time, I had inflammation and pain on both sides!

Mark brought me home, and my good friend Margaret stayed with me. She cooked us a lovely beef stew as she waited for the next round of people who came to help. My cousins came and brought us dinner. By that time I was in terrible pain. I was breaking out in a cold sweat and started to moan and yell. Gail told me as she was leaving our home, "Deb, you aren't praying hard enough! I'll be praying for you."

The next day, my dear friend Mary came and stayed the whole weekend with us. She cooked meals and did dishes, made cookies, and brought me wholesome treats. Anything that might cheer me up, she did. We prayed together and cried together. She took wonderful care of me. Mark owes a debt here he can't repay. It took all the stress off of him.

The day Mary had to go back home, our friends Lee and Anne Schwarz called. They wanted to come and see us the next evening. It was soon to be their 25th wedding anniversary, and they wanted Mark to make an opal ring for Anne's present.

The next morning while praise music was playing, I was laying on the floor trying to wrap a few Christmas gifts for our children. All of a sudden, I heard beside me, ***"Be very sorry for everything you have ever done."***

I took off my glasses, put my head on the floor and cried for half an hour before the Lord. I had a repentant heart. I did not understand that I was being prepared for what was to come.

The Schwarz's came over that evening, and I was laying back in the recliner. I was sweating with pain. Anne conducted her business with Mark quickly, then she came over and sat on the couch by her husband and took a good look at me.

She said, "Debbie, you look terrible."

I replied, "I know Anne, but I keep hearing somebody next to me saying over and over that my Christmas miracle is coming. I believe I am going to have a miracle sometime this season!"

She got really excited and grabbed Lee by his arm. She said to him, "Lee, did you hear that? Debbie is going to get a Christmas miracle!" Then she looked at me and said, "We believe in that too! Lee's hands are anointed like the Apostles."

I knew right then and there my time for full healing had come. Lee and Anne looked at each other. She said, "You have to ask him in faith."

I asked Lee, "Would you please allow the Holy Spirit to enter you and heal me?"

He said, "Why sure!" as if I had simply asked him to go get me a glass of milk.

Mark and Lee gently laid me on the floor. All I could see were knees. Mark was on his knees at my feet, Anne was sitting on the couch beside us, and Lee was on his knees at the middle of my back. He said to me, "Debbie, say a prayer in your head. I will know when to start."

In my head I said, "Lord, I come before you humbly. Please find nothing in me that would cause you to turn away." Lee put one hand on my head and the other hand started down my back without touching me. He was inches above me. Immediately I felt heat. It felt hotter and hotter, until he got to the place that was damaged. I was yelling, "Hot! Hot!" Anne was giggling on the couch. She knew what was coming!

The damaged disc area began to tingle, to incite as if it were waking up from a sleep. The nerves were firing up! The left lateral muscle L5-S1 moved back into place. I *felt* the disc heal, wiggle and move. Lastly, the right lateral muscle moved into place as well. At that point, Lee put his hand on my back and it felt like a "surgeon closing from surgery". All the pain ended. Gone.

Lee sat back. In an instant, I jumped up all by myself! I could've flown! I yelled, "Yyyyyiiiipppiieee!" Then I started to cry.

We all started to cry. Mark cried out, "Praise the Lord!" It was an instantaneous miracle of regeneration.

I looked up at Lee and asked, "How can this be?" All of a sudden, it felt like I went back in time to Jesus as Lee replied, "Woman, your faith has saved you."

I asked him again, "What did it feel like when the Holy Spirit entered you and healed me?" He said he felt tremendous joy. He told me that I had no stoppers and that my faith was complete.

Now, I could stand and sit again. We laughed and cried. Like Peter's mother-in-law after she was healed by Jesus, I got up and served people drinks and snacks. It was the least I could do. The fracture was healed, and I knew my sins were forgiven. What a glorious day!

I couldn't speak a whole sentence for three days. I was overwhelmed. My muscles were tired due to the stress of what they had been through, and I did physical therapy in my home with a book we found online as my guide. The next day, I could even dress and drive myself again.

Three weeks after my healing, I was laying on the family room floor doing my daily physical therapy, and I was cold. There was a draft coming in from the patio doors. From my side view, I saw a man in white pick up my blanket off the couch and bring it over and lay it on top of me. I said, "Thank you." No one replied because no one was there. I went down the hall. Andy was in his room doing homework, and Mark was in our bedroom doing bookwork. I tell you, it was an angel sent to comfort me after all I had been through.

If God, being no respecter of persons, will do this for me, what will He do for you?

Evidently, all we have to do is ask... and wait to receive.

Grammy Fran's Chip Dip

As children, we used to fight over this one.

1 eight ounce package of Cream Cheese, softened
1 large tablespoon of Classic, Whipped-Type,
Sandwich Spread
Enough Ketchup to color this pink (several
tablespoons)
1-2 teaspoons of Worcestershire Sauce (to taste)
1 teaspoon of Yellow Mustard
4 teaspoons of Milk

Mix all ingredients together.
Refrigerate for at least one hour before serving.

Store in refrigerator afterwards.

Grammy Fran's Pretzel Salad

Preheat the oven to 400 degrees

1 cup of crushed Butter Pretzels. If you can't find
      butter pretzels, regular pretzels will do.
1/3 cup of Sugar
1 stick of Butter, melted

Mix all ingredients together.
Press this into a baking pan.
Cook for 10 minutes.
Cool.

*After the pretzels, butter and sugar have
cooked for 10 minutes, put in the fridge for
20 minutes to cool. When it's hard, break it
up. I use a meat hammer. Or you can use a
regular hammer if you don't have a meat
hammer.*

303

In a bowl, combine:
1 cup of crushed pineapple, drained
8 ounces of cream cheese, softened
8 ounces of whipped topping
½ cup of sugar
Mix this with a mixer.

Crumble up the pretzel mix into your mixture.
Refrigerate for at least an hour before serving.

Deb's Best Ever Chicken Pot Pie
(A third generation recipe)

Preheat oven to 350 degrees

½ cup Butter
½ cup All-Purpose Flour
1/3 cup chopped Onion
1/3 cup Celery
¼ teaspoon Pepper
2 ½ cups Chicken Broth
1 cup Milk
2 cups of cooked, cut up Chicken
1 package of Peas and Carrots, or you can cook and slice carrots
2 medium sized Potatoes

Cut up your potatoes and boil 25 minutes, drain.

Boil chicken. If whole, about 1 hour, if pieces or breasts, 30 minutes or until done. Set aside and cool. Cut up. Keep the broth.

While it's boiling, take out a 3-quart sauce pan. Put on low-to medium heat. Heat butter until melted.

On low heat, blend into the butter, flour, salt and pepper. Add onion and celery, stirring constantly, until smooth and bubbly. Remove from heat. Stir in milk, and then broth. Heat to boiling, stir

305

constantly. Boil and stir one minute. Take the pan off the heat.

Grammy Fran and I always use prepared crusts from the dairy case in our local store. Or you can make a crust from the dumpling recipe I gave you. Make sure it's rolled out to ¼ inch thick. Line the bottom of your cooking pan with your crust.

In a large bowl combine:
Potatoes, peas, carrots, chicken and broth. Mix well. Pour into your cooking pan lined with crust. Put a second crust on top, making a few small holes with a knife or fork to let out heat.

Cook 1 hour, check. It may need a few minutes more. See if it looks done on top. Filling should be bubbly. Serve. Enjoy!

*This can be made as a **Turkey pot pie** using leftover turkey instead.*
***Beef pot pie:** left overs of a pot roast, using broth from a gravy/mix.*

THE PAPER CROSS

(The first week of December, 2014)

Gifts from the heart can take many forms; but they most always emit an emotional response from the receiver. Be blessed with what you have and your loved ones that surround you.

It had been a rough couple of years for Mark and me. Over the last six years, I had lost my job, we had to sell our land, we were without a home of our own for a whole year, and my mother had passed away. At the end of all that havoc, Mark and I finally settled down into a nice little suburban home in Corydon, Indiana. It was just in time for more good deeds to show up at our new front door....

SUMMER OF 2014

I had just unpacked the last moving box when calls started coming in...

"Yes, son...of course we can help keep your children through the summer. I have a request. You live so far away, on the days you want us to keep Matt and Lily in succession, may they stay with us instead of us driving back and forth between houses? It would help us with the gas cost. We're a little tight money-wise right now."

Lily and Matthew ended up with us four days a week all summer long.

At the same time, our friend Lisa was getting ready to go through a messy divorce. Due to a dream given to me weeks before, I felt her request coming. I spoke with Mark about her predicament. He asked me where we would put five more people along with Matt and Lily. I told him God knew.

By the first week of June, the call came. They, like us the year before, were about to be homeless.

Lisa said, "He laid hands on me. He hurt me." She sounded so sad.

I replied, "Come on. You can't stay there any longer. We'll make it somehow. Come on." Mark came home that evening to a household of nine.

We'd already put all the money we managed to save into our new home. And the garden we planted had only been in for a few weeks. There was not enough food in our home or budget to feed nine people a day.

The first week of June, on a bright sunny morning, I went out to our garden alone for a talk. I sat.

"Okay, listen. Here's the deal. We have nine people in our home that we can't feed. You have to come up quickly and feed us. I will come out every morning and pray over you. I'll even sing praise songs. I will feed and water you. But I need you to keep your end of the deal."

In the meantime, friends gathered around and gave money and groceries to the cause; 'cause we didn't have any yet.

All the timing went perfectly.

By the end of June, just three short weeks after my first prayer, we had food-a-plenty out of our garden. Tomatoes, squash, green peppers, green beans and more were at the ready. It looked like a feast to us!

In the late summer, another friend found Lisa and her children a home for the time being not too far from us. During the fall, we still had many meals together. Later, it was decided that Lisa and her four children would move to Texas with her parents to have family support.

As Thanksgiving approached, Lisa said they would stay long enough for one more celebration together. It was agreed the kids would trim our downstairs' Christmas tree. Lisa's children were very thoughtful and kind, especially for all that they had been through in those last months. Lisa has two older children and two younger children.

We set up for one last Sunday meal together. They arrived on time. I made one of their favorite meals; homemade chicken pot pie. Greetings were given, prayers were said and conversation commenced. Lisa spoke about the coming move and all it would entail. The younger children were excited about decorating our Christmas tree, eating homemade cookies ...and opening presents!

After dinner, while the adults were cleaning up the kitchen, the younger children went downstairs to draw and color while waiting for us to bring in the boxes for tree-trimming. After a bit, young Adam came upstairs.

"Mrs. Peyron, may I have a piece of tape?" he asked.

"Sure, I'll get it for you." I handed him a piece.

Adam went back downstairs. We joined them a few minutes later.

While the children were putting ornaments on the tree, Adam came up to me with something in his hand. He stood shyly before me and spoke softly.

"Mrs. Peyron, I didn't have any money to get you something for Christmas, so I made you something."

From behind his back, Adam brought out his present; two torn slips of paper taped together in the form of a cross. I studied his small token of affection for a minute. I understood the love it represented—just like the love given 2,000 years ago; born in a stable and died on a wooden cross—and the lack in Adam's meager household.

Fighting back tears, I smiled. "Come upstairs Adam. I know the perfect place for it."

We walked up the stairs together and into our living room where the children's Christmas tree stood. The paper cross had nothing to attach itself to the tree, so I laid it on a branch over the nativity set.

"Adam, as long as there is breath in my body, your gift will be placed on the children's tree over our nativity every year in remembrance of this day."

Adam nodded his head soberly then went back downstairs with the other children. I sat with tears running down my face as I pondered my special gift from a homeless child. It will be with me always.

Persimmon Cookies
from a second generation recipe
Pat Merk

2 ½ cups Flour
2 teaspoons of Baking Powder
¼ teaspoon Salt
2½ teaspoons Cinnamon
1 teaspoon ground Ginger
½ teaspoon ground Nutmeg
½ teaspoon Allspice
1½ cups of Sugar
½ cup of Shortening
2 Eggs, beaten
1 teaspoon Baking Soda
1 tablespoon warm Water
1 cup Persimmon Pulp

Sift together:
Flour, baking powder, salt and cinnamon

Cream together:
Sugar and shortening.
Beat in eggs into it.

Mix soda and water, stir it into the
persimmon pulp.

Add dry ingredients and pulp to creamed mixture alternately, beginning and ending with the pulp.

Refrigerate 1 hour.

Preheat oven to 350 degrees

Drop by teaspoonful on greased cookie sheet. Bake for 10 to 12 minutes, or until lightly browned. Make sure they are done with a toothpick.

Cool completely before storing in airtight container.

Chocolate Salted Caramel
Christmas Cakes

(These are pick-your-tongue-up-off-the-floor good!)

Cake portion
1 Devil's Food Cake Mix
      with Pudding
½ cup Butter, melted
½ cup Water
3 Eggs
1 to 2 teaspoons Sea Salt

Filling
1 cup Butter, softened
3 ½ cups Powdered Sugar
1/2 cup of prepared Caramel Sauce*
1 teaspoon of Sea Salt
1 generous teaspoon of Vanilla

Mix the cake mix, butter, water, and eggs
together.
Beat at medium speed until smooth.
Let the batter rest for 30 minutes.

Preheat the oven to 400 degrees

Drop the batter by rounded teaspoons, two
inches apart onto parchment lined or lightly
greased cookie sheets. Sprinkle each cookie with
sea salt. Bake for 5-7 minutes or until toothpick
comes out clean. [Can use a Mini-Cake mold,
such as shown in the picture above, but add 7
more minutes to the baking time.]
Transfer to wire rack to cool.

For Filling:

Place one cup Butter in a medium bowl. Beat at medium speed until creamy. Reduce speed to low and gradually add the powdered sugar. Beat until well blended. Add the caramel. Then add the sea salt and vanilla. Beat until well mixed.

To Assemble:

Pipe or spoon by rounded teaspoonful onto one cookie. Place another cookie on top.

Ready to serve!
If there are any leftover, store in the refrigerator.

* Buy pre-made Caramel Sauce or make your own in a microwave oven. In a microwave-safe container place 12 or so unwrapped caramels. Add 1 Tablespoon Whole Milk. Microwave for 20 seconds at a time, stirring well each time. Done when the sauce is smooth.

Orange-Gingerbread Torte
(I have had pastors fight over this!)

Preheat oven for 350 degrees

¾ cup Butter, softened
¾ cup Sugar
2 Eggs
1 cup Molasses
3 cups All-purpose Flour
2 Tablespoons of ground Ginger
1 teaspoon of Allspice
2 teaspoons Baking Soda
2 teaspoons ground Cinnamon
¾ teaspoon Salt
¾ cup Milk
¼ cup Orange Juice (fresh squeezed is best)

Grease 3 round 9 inch baking pans.
Line with waxed paper, grease and flour the paper.

In a large mixing bowl, Cream butter and sugar.
Add eggs, one at a time, beating well after each.
Beat in molasses.
Combine the flour, ginger, baking soda, spices and salt.
Add it to the creamed mixture alternately with the milk.
Spoon in the prepared pans.
Bake for 20-25 minutes or until a toothpick comes out clean.
Cool for 10 minutes in the pans. Transfer to wire racks to cool.

Cream Cheese Frosting

1 pack of Cream Cheese, 8 ounce, softened
¼ cup Butter, softened
2 teaspoons of grated Orange Peel
3 ¾ cups of Confectioners' Sugar

In a small bowl, beat cream cheese and butter.
Then add the orange peel. Gradually beat in the
confectioners' sugar until smooth.

To assemble:
Place one cake on the serving platter, frost.
Add the next cake and frost.
Add the last cake and frost the top.

Refrigerate for a day before serving so the flavors
will have time to meld together.

Epilogue for Now

Thank you to everyone who helped put this all together. I hope it blesses the generations that are here now, and those to come.

And when I am gone, and my (our) children are raising their children, they will have a little bit of us and the generations before me, to share with their family....
And with your families, dear readers.

If you need to know these last things, it is:

Love God with all your heart, mind and strength.

Salvation comes through Jesus Christ, whom I call Yeshua Ben Elohim.

Love your neighbor as yourself. It will always come back to you greater than you gave out.

Cherish your loved ones, whether they come by birth or by a wonderful happenstance.

Works of mercy were what Jesus was all about—**be kind**.

Use all the gifts and talents God gives you. Let none go to waste.

Learn as much as you can.
Work hard, work smart.

And I love you...so does Mark!
Deb and Mark Peyron

Momma (Poem 2)

It was the week before Christmas
and all through the house,
our momma was scurrying
like a quick little mouse.

"I need more flour, more butter, more broth,"
she cried.
"I have 84 people coming to this trough,"
she sighed.

Quick as a wink,
she grabbed bowls and trays,
for the wonderful goodies
she'd set on displays.

On went her apron,
tied in a neat bow,
as she started her baking,
cookie cutters in tow.

At the height of her cooking,
we heard her give cry,
"Oh, look! I have enough
for one more sweet pie!"

Christmas day came
and everyone was fed,
there were even leftovers,
she'd had nothing to dread.

And as she laid down
at last to sleep,
we told our dear mother,
"We'll hear not a peep."

But in her head,
with her eyes closed tight,
she was reviewing recipes,
for the next special night.

Epiphany was coming
in a few short weeks,
She was sure,
knowing her treasured crew,
all the family would gather
as twilight would peek.
"Maybe, we'll have a nice beef stew…"

No words necessary...

...just dish towels, please...

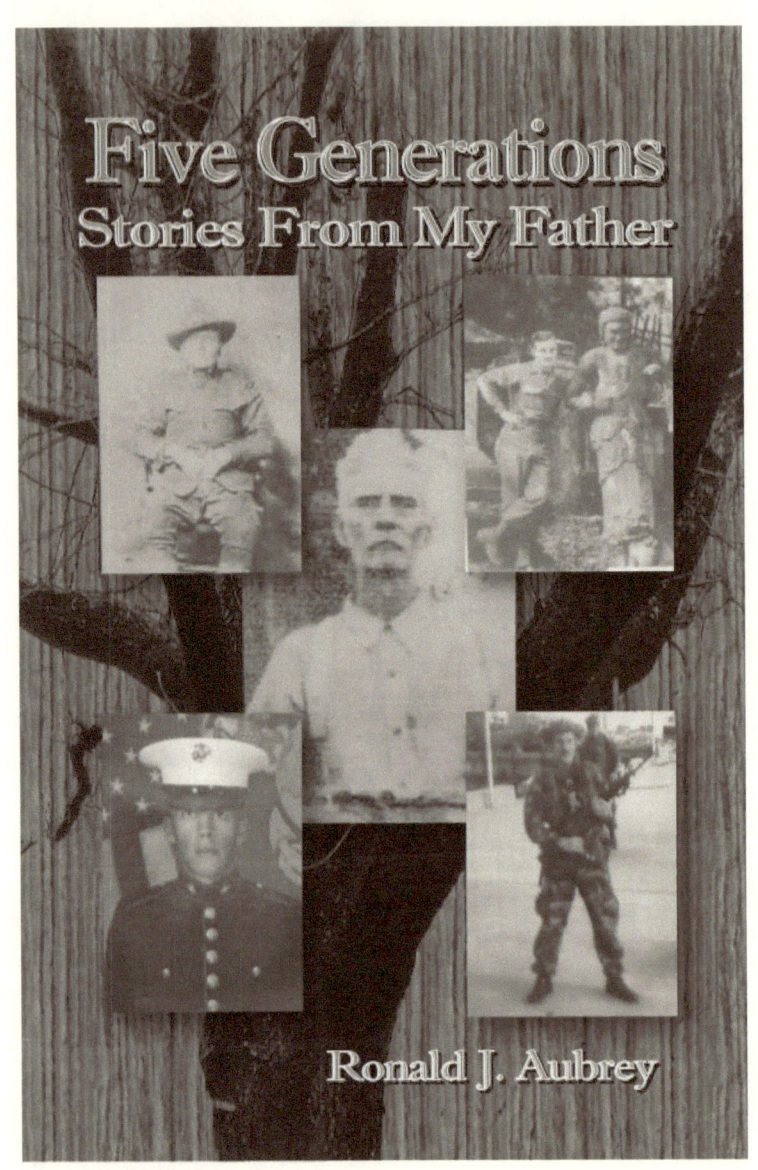

Five Generations
Stories From My Father

Ronald J. Aubrey

Five Generations

Stories from My Father

Ronald J. Aubrey,
Retired US Navy 2003

Introduction

BOOK OVERVIEW

I am not an overly religious man. I do believe that God stands with soldiers, sailors, airmen and Marines. He was with me as I travelled into harm's way; that's the only way I can explain my coming home. It is true; there are no atheists in the foxholes.

Even though most people think of the Navy as large grey ships, there is another part of the Navy I was blessed to serve in. Special Operations (Spec Ops), is a world closed to outsiders. The answer to most questions is, "That's classified."

Where you go, whom you see, what you do is in support of national security and defense mission. If you want to do it, but don't want the world to know it was the United States (U.S.), you send in Spec Ops. No headlines, and the glory is kept in house. See you on the gunline.

Now, ask any family, they all have family stories. Some are funny and some are embarrassing for one or more family members. Some can never be told except in a whisper.

These are the stories of the history of our family that my father told me and to which various other family members contributed. This is only the male line, nothing wrong with the female line, but I don't have those stories.

These stories were told father-to-son for five generations, and counting. They are stories of strength and personal conviction. They are stories of card cheating and loosing army jeeps in poker games. They are stories of good men who chose to stand and protect others when they could have hidden and sought safety. The one connecting factor is that they all teach a lesson about how to be an honorable man. The urge to help others and to do our duty is strong in my family. Some people run into burning houses to save others. Some watch in horror as bad things happen. This is a compilation of stories from a family that has stood up when called upon, whatever the situation required.

Enjoy these stories and the lessons in them. If you don't know your family stories, perhaps this will serve as an inspiration to capturing and building upon them in time.

Robert Whaley

1840-1930

Robert Whaley was an American serviceman
who lived from 1840-1930.

After his service for the Union during the Civil War he headed west to seek his fortune and adventure. In his later years he finally settled in Taylorsville, Kentucky where he met and fell in love with Grandma Whaley. They lived happily until Whaley passed in 1930. He entertained his young grandson Earl, with stories of his travels and adventures. The stories have been passed down through the generations and are retold here.

REVENGE OR JUSTICE

Whaley laid in the desert; he was dying. He had come this far seeking the man who had wiped out the settlers in the wagon train he was leading. A wagon train leader is responsible for the safety of those whom he is guiding. His honor rests on their lives. Whaley meant to reclaim his honor by killing the man who had committed this horrible crime.

He had been out ahead of the wagon train scouting for water when a rifle shot rang out. He had been struck a glancing blow, just enough to knock him out. It was meant to kill him.

When Whaley got back to the wagon train, he was horrified. Men, women, children, all dead. Their supplies were taken; it was a tragedy. Some of the bodies had arrows in them; those persons had also been shot. Whaley looked closely. He could identify most arrows as being made by one particular tribe or the other. These arrows were shoddily made and no self-respecting Indian would have used them.

White men had made these arrows. It was a poor attempt to shift the blame to people who had not committed this crime. Whaley put three of the arrows in his saddle bag and headed for the nearest Army fort.

As he rode, he thought of hatred and vengeance. He thought of killing.

The commander of the fort had seen this work before. He had a name for the man who had committed these crimes, the name was Sidewinder. He agreed to telegraph all forts in the area to be on the lookout. The Army was looking to hang him, or them. Whaley allowed as to how the army could hang the man, if they found him before he did.

Whaley began tracking Sidewinder; murder was on his mind. The trail went into the great desert. Two days into the desert a rifle shot went through his canteen. He continued on. Two days later he let his horse run and started walking. The heat in the desert was murderous. Whaley walked for another day and then he fell.

John Williams, Texas Ranger found a riderless horse just inside the green land west of the great desert. A riderless horse with full saddle and rifle in boot meant only one thing, someone in the desert was in great danger. The Ranger tied the horse's bridal to his own horse's saddle and followed the horses trail into the desert. He found Whaley unconscious, barely alive. He wet the thin man's lips; and when he got a response, he set the man up and got him to drink a little water. Delirious the man mumbled something about a snake. The Ranger checked the man for snake bites but found none. He then threw the poor wretch onto his horse, tied him in place and headed out of the desert. To have any chance to survive, this man had to get out of the heat.

"Easy on that stew," John Williams said to Whaley. "You eat too fast, you'll just bring it back up."

Whaley explained to the Ranger that he needed to kill a man and why. That was when Whaley first learned the philosophy of the Rangers. Justice, not personal animosity was their guiding principle. Rangers stood for the law, protected the weak, and brought wanted men to justice. Rangers worked mostly alone, sometimes, but not very often with other Rangers. The pay was poor, but they got to keep the bounties. If they died in the line of duty, other Rangers would be at the funeral and they would be remembered forever.

Whaley thought for a while and said quietly, "The law, sounds easier on the soul than revenge."

John interjected an important point. "You go where headquarters sends you. If you get lucky, they'll send you after this man you want. If not, eventually they'll send someone else."

"What do I have to do to join up?" Whaley asked.

Whaley was sworn in on the spot. He was given a Rangers star and the turmoil in his soul settled down, slightly.

Whaley would be sent many places over the years; he would bring many outlaws to justice; some would even make it to court. But the prospect of hanging led most to go for their guns and trust their luck. None of them turned out to be that lucky. The next part of Whaley's life had begun.

SIDEWINDER

It was a nasty hot day, in a nasty little town, just south of the border. The town was so nasty, it didn't even have a church. The mayor had quit, the sheriff had been shot and killed months ago, and nobody else wanted the job. Seeing's as how they were actually in Mexico, Whaley had no jurisdiction as a Ranger there; but he did have reports of the man he was seeking. Wanted in six western states for robbery, horse thievery, kidnapping, murder and various other crimes, but mostly and most personally, Whaley wanted him for shooting up a wagon train of settlers, which Whaley was leading, to what they hoped, would be their new home in Arizona. The Texas Rangers wanted him, and Whaley wanted him, too.

Jim, calm as always agreed to go across the poorly marked border with Whaley. Whaley had saved his life on more than one occasion. They had gotten into and out of various scrapes, often by the skin of their teeth. If Whaley wanted to go, Jim's opinion was that he would go with him.

Jim had built up a little savings from the rewards he and Whaley always split evenly. He intended to settle down one day, but that day had not yet arrived. So as always he rode by Whaley's side, ever alert for trouble.

They tied the horses to the rail just down the street from the saloon. Whaley said, "Watch the horses please; I won't be but a minute." Jim had finally taken to carrying a six shooter. And through practice, had become somewhat proficient in its use. But he never went anywhere without his trusty shotgun.

Jim watched Whaley walk into the town's only saloon, and began his own walk in that direction. He had heard about Sidewinder from more than one Ranger. He understood that this man was the most dangerous they had ever hunted.

From just outside the swinging doors, Jim saw the bartender bring up a shotgun. Jim quietly walked in and laid his own shotgun across the bar with his left hand. The barkeep put his hands up and took a step back. In Jim's right hand was his revolver, which he trained to the right, in order to cover the rest of the bar. Jim surveyed the bar.

Whaley approached a table where several men sat playing cards. "Sidewinder!" Whaley called in a firm loud voice. "My name is Whaley, Texas Ranger. You are wanted for horse stealing, cattle thievery, and all manner of vile and despicable crimes; including killing every man, woman and child in my wagon train. Lay down your guns, come along peaceable like and I promise you'll get a fair trial after which we'll hang you with a new rope."

The large fat man that Whaley had addressed this to, stood and stepped away from the table. "Can't say as I favor getting hung, new rope or old."

Whaley's eyes narrowed as he watched Sidewinder for any telltale signs of gunplay. Without moving his hand at all, Whaley quietly said, "I was kinda hoping you would say that. Slap leather you son of a buck!"

Since this was personal for Whaley, it was important that the other man draw first, and so he did. The men watching the scene, would be unable to say witch man started moving first. And even though, both pistols were fired, they heard only one gunshot.

For a few seconds, both men just stared at each other, then Sidewinder smiled. He smiled an evil, greasy, gap-toothed smile. Whaley twirled his gun once and placed it in its holster. He then turned and began walking towards the saloon's door. As he walked, he nodded to Jim, and then he heard a large dead weight hit the floor. Jim holstered his pistol and threw some coins on the bar. He said, "You might wanna bury him before he starts smelling too bad." Shotgun training across the bar as he backed out of the room, Jim said, "Ya'll gentlemen have a nice day."

As the two friends walked down the middle of the street, looking neither left nor right, Jim said, "That's it, we just saunter on out of town?"

"Well," Whaley said, "You might check behind us."

Jim glanced to their rear and brought up his shotgun. He fired once to the left, and once back at the bar. In both cases, men with guns in their hands dropped. Jim cracked open his shotgun, extracted the spent shells, and put in fresh ones before closing the weapon; ready once again for instant use.

"Always a good idea to check the roof lines for shooters." Whaley said as he drew his pistol and shot the man leaning out from behind a chimney with a rifle in his hand. He fell slumped over the peak of the roof. Shifting aim to the left, Whaley fired once, shooting through the dry goods store sign, killing the man whose hat had been just showing above it.

A man with a shovel in his hands walked out of the doctor's office. Both guns trained on him and he put his arms out away from his sides to show that he was unarmed. He got to live.

The two men mounted their horses and paused. Jim waited on Whaley, as Whaley looked around and spat on the ground. "We're done here." The tall man kicked his horse into a walk along the death-strewn street. Jim thought it wise to keep shotgun in-hand, and look back once in while the way they had come.

They left the town in silence and stopped at the first town back across the border. Whaley sent his telegram to Ranger Headquarters. It read, "Sidewinder resisted stop. Headed west stop. Whaley." In his reports, Whaley didn't like to use the words shot or dead. Headquarters knew what he meant. As he left the telegraph office, Whaley ripped down the wanted poster for Sidewinder and left it on the ground. Once a man died, he was no longer wanted.

OLD RANGERS NEVER DIE

As it comes for all men, king or commoner, hero or coward, the day came for Whaley when the Lord called him home. If you're lucky, you go out with drama and flare, saving a baby from a fire, or in a gunfight with a bad man who has to be stopped. If you're not so lucky, painful disease takes you young, or an unlucky accident hits you when you're not looking. If you're really, really lucky, you get to pass quietly in your own bed in the night.

Whaley, at the end, was really, really lucky. After a lifetime of adventure, he met a good woman to love and a good family. He had no regrets, and no complaints. He'd had a life that was full; he had done some good in the world. And his conscience was clear.

May we all be so blessed.

Folk came from all around to pay their last respects. The Widow Whaley, as she would be referred to, for the remainder of her life, was busy. She was busy with her mourning, she was busy worrying about the food she hadn't cooked, because the rest of the family insisted she needn't be bothered. But most of all, she was busy with all the people who kept coming. Folks she had never heard of came to offer condolences. So, perhaps she can be forgiven for one thoughtless comment, to a young boy who worshipped the ground that Whaley once had trod. Whaley, generous as always, would surely have forgiven. But the young Earl was crushed. When he was going on about one of Whaley's tales she interrupted him with a dismissive, "Boy, don't you know he just told tales out his head of things that surely never happened?"

The thought that the old man that he loved best, was not all that he said, was such a horrible thought for the boy that he went off to a corner and cried inconsolably. About that time, an old, distinguished-looking, black gentleman arrived. Smooth shaven with graying hair, he carried himself with quiet, assured confidence. Well dressed in a suit, Stetson Hat, and well-shined boots, he walked up to the casket and spoke quietly to Whaley. No one heard his words, but when his goodbyes' were said, he turned and inquired of the nearest person as to whom he should direct his condolences.

Walking up to the Widow Whaley, he introduced

himself as Jim White, retired Texas Ranger, and longtime friend of the deceased. The first name Jim struck the widow, and slowly, she came to realize that all of the stories that she had suffered in silence for years, just might be true. Then, she realized the terrible wrong she had done to young Earl. She asked Jim if he would have a few words with the boy, to ease his pain. Jim smiled widely as he agreed.

Jim found Earl crying on a couch alone. "Hello, young man," He said. "My name in Jim. I rode with Whaley for many years. He was a good man and I was proud to call him friend."

The boy's eyes widened, his crying ceased. The past and the stories came back to life in his mind. In short order, Jim was telling the same stories that Whaley had told. Finally, the boy worked the courage up to ask the old, black man, "Were you really raised by Indians?"

Jim laughed and said, "When you refer to Indians, it's polite to go by the tribe's name. Yes, the Cherokee raised me. Good people, strong moral character. Then, the time came for me to go out on my own. I thought I was searching for my fortune, but I found something much more valuable. I found a friend, your grandfather. "

The next day was the funeral. Young Earl saw Jim

arrive and the elderly, black man came to stand by the boys' side. Jim removed his hat as the minister said his prayers. After the graveside ceremonies ended, Earl asked Jim if he was coming by the house afterwards. Jim said he had other business to attend to, but promised to see the young man before he left town.

Late that night, Earl was awakened by a shaking. He barely had his eyes opened before Jim said, "Get your clothes on boy. There is something you need to see."

They left the house quietly so as to not awaken anyone, and made their way to the cemetery. Jim stopped in the bushes just a little ways from Whaley's' grave, and put his finger to his lips. He whispered to the boy, "What you are about to see, tell no man until you are my age." Earl nodded his agreement.

Three men on horseback, in dusters and Stetsons, came out of the fog. One of the men led a riderless horse. Earl could see silver stars on their chests. He understood, these men must be Texas Rangers. They stopped a short distance from where Earl and Jim were crouched in the bushes. The men faced Whaley's resting place, and the lead rider called out loudly, "Ranger! Ranger! There's cattle rustlers, horse thieves and the like at large. Ranger! Dying's no excuse to just lay there; we still got work to do."

The boy watched in confusion. He did not know what the men were doing.

"Ranger!" The lead rider called. "Mount up!"

From Earl's left, someone stepped out of the fog. He was dressed as the Rangers were. Duster billowing out behind him. Moving quickly, the man got on the fourth horse the Rangers had brought. As the horse reared up, the man turned and looked right at Earl. The man touched the brim of his hat and called, "Rangers ride!" The fourth Ranger bore an uncanny resemblance to a young Whaley.

As Earl watched the Rangers disappear into the night, he heard Jim whisper, "Old Rangers never die. They just go on to help someone else."

The next morning, Earl woke up, not sure if the events of the night before had been a dream, or had actually happened. That evening, as suppertime came and went; his mother was upset that Earls' father was late. Joe arrived finally and apologized. He explained his tardiness by saying that the cemetery owner had needed him, and several other men, to resod a portion of the cemetery grounds where some men had ridden horses the night before. Earl bent his head down and smiled. He also did not give voice to what he was thinking. He knew who the riders were, but could not say, until he was an old man.

Clarence "Joe" Aubrey, U.S. Army

(1896–1981)

Clarence "Joe" Aubrey, born 1896 and served
Active duty for the U.S. Army in World War I.

Clarence was from a large, Irish family who had a history of land hopping. Back in the 1400's, the *Aubrie's* were originally from Wales. They had titles and land... and an itch to travel. Over a couple of centuries, the family moved to Scotland, Ireland and finally, in the 1800's, to the "land of the free and the home of the brave", America—just in time for the Civil War. When they arrived on America's shores, they changed the spelling to *Aubrey* — to them, it must have sounded more "American."

BRASH ACTS OF BRAVERY

The year was 1918. It was a typical late fall day in Fontaines, France—cold and grey. The Great War was raging on for all of Europe. And America has entered into the fray to try and bring an end to the carnage that has enveloped the land for the last four years. On this seventh day of November, courage under fire was the order of the day.

The war had been stalled for months. Thousands of men died in futile charges, which led to advances which could be measured in yards. Trench foot, disease and trauma were common. The advent of industrial warfare had outstripped the tactics of the generals who were still fighting the last generation's war. Until these tactics were changed, the war would continue to be a long drawn out slog of blood and death.

No one had bothered to tell the newly arrived Americans that brash acts of bravery, and personal sacrifice were not only out of style, but also very likely suicidal. It was under these circumstances, that Private Clarence "Joe" Aubrey, along with three other brave soldiers, volunteered to attempt a rescue of several wounded soldiers in no mans' land. They exited their trench and ran across no mans' land, enduring murderous artillery and withering machine gun fire, to try and reach the fallen soldiers. They were driven back by the hail of bullets and shrapnel to the somewhat safe confines of their trench again.

Undeterred, these brave men took up this perilous gauntlet yet another time, facing certain death to reach the stricken soldiers. Forced to the ground to avoid the murderous machinegun fire, Private Aubrey pulled his last grenade from his belt, and heaved it with all his considerable strength at the machine gun nest. The grenade fell short, but did attract the attention of the machine gun crew. The Germans now knew they were being targeted and sought their attacker.

In the smoke and carnage, they missed the big country boy. He yelled at his friends for a fresh grenade. Before the war, Private Aubrey just happened to be the best baseball pitcher in three counties. Using his previous experience, and totally disregarding his personal safety, the big farm boy pulled the pin on his grenade, and came to his full height of six foot three inches. That is one heck of a target. He gave it his best fastball pitch. The Germans manning the machinegun saw the suicidal American, and tracked their fire in his direction. He dropped back to the ground before the bullets found him. The Germans cursed because they missed him, and then saw the grenade land in their nest. They didn't have time to curse again before the grenade exploded. The machine gun nest silenced; the big farm boy from Elk Creek, Kentucky and his friends, advanced and brought the wounded soldiers to safety.

For this action of heroism, Private Clarence Aubrey, along with the three other soldiers, received the Distinguished Service Cross. Clarence also received the French Croix de guerre. The Croix Daguerre was a French medal, which was awarded to foreign soldiers who distinguished themselves by acts of heroism involving conflict with the enemy.

That was my grandfather.

Ronald Aubrey,

U.S. Navy, Retired

(1960 – present)

"Damn the torpedoes, Full speed ahead!"

--Admiral David Glasgow Farragut (1801-1870)

I was born in answer to a promise Mom made God after my sister, Debbie, was born. You see, she was 11 weeks early, very tiny and blue. The nuns came in and told Mom she wouldn't make it.

So Mom prayed.

She told God, if He would save that little baby girl, she would dedicate not only her life back to him, but she would also dedicate the life of her next baby back to the Lord, too, in thanks.

That was where I came in. I was the next baby; and the last. After all, she had only promised to dedicate two children back to God.

It explains a lot.

DANCING IN THE STRAITS

It was the fall of 1987. Four months earlier, three United States Aircraft Carrier Battle Groups attacked the country of Libya for its government's poor decision to provide personnel and logistical support for a terror attack on a nightclub in Italy that was popular with Americans. The politicians had all kind of fancy reasons for the retaliatory bombing; for me, it was simple. "You hurt us, we hurt you worse. Oh yeah, don't try that crap again, or we'll be back and make this look like a Sunday school picnic."

After the initial raid, each Battle Group went on to some really wonderful liberty ports in the Mediterranean. After some great liberty, the Battle Groups came from three directions in the middle of the night at high speed. We went charging across the so-called Libyan Line of Death, back to our initial launch points, and then, we turned around and went to another great liberty port.

We did this three times. It's called psychological warfare. It is designed to scare the hell out of the bad guys, and to dig the previous message in even deeper. It worked. After being included in the "Axis of Evil" speech, and watching what happened to Iraq—after the attacks on 911— the Libyan government openly declared its nuclear weapons development program. They also requested international assistance in the disassembly and destruction of that program. That was one less country we had to go to war with.

As the USS America approached the Straits of Gibraltar, it was my job as a Master Helmsman, to take the wheel. A helmsman steers the ship during open ocean transits or during flight operations. A Master Helmsman steers the ship during more complex maneuvering. The time for this training is measured in months; it can only be done on the job while closely supervised by an already qualified helmsman.

The transit is rarely easy and the traffic is never light. All of the shipping going into and out of the Mediterranean (East and West), and from Spain to Morocco (North and South), all come together at this one spot. That spot is only ten miles wide. International treaties define lanes for East/West and North/South traffic but when you put real people in real shipping out there, it can get messy.

The whole Navigation Team for our ship was on station. The Captain, also called the Commanding Officer,

(CO) was on the Bridge. He was in overall command and ready to take charge, just in case absolutely everything went straight to hell. The Officer of the Deck, (OOD) in overall charge of the transit stood proudly center stage. He had just finished his qualification as OOD, and it was his first time in charge of a transit by himself. The Conning Officer, or The Conn, stood just to the right of the OOD, and was in charge of relaying engine and rudder orders to the throttle man and the helmsman. The Navigation officer, in charge of the Enlisted Navigation Team, was responsible for relaying the ships position, speed made good, and nearest hazard to navigation, in addition to recommended course to steer to the OOD. The Master Helmsman is responsible for rapidly and accurately responding to orders from the Conning officer or if the Conning Officer was relieved, by the OOD, The Conn will then go to his corner and pout until the OOD tells him to assume the Conn again. The Master Helmsman will then respond to the orders of the OOD.

Finally, if the OOD can't handle the job, the CO will relieve the OOD, who will then call his relief and go to his state room to right his letter of resignation. If the CO can't handle it, the ship is on the rocks and the same Helicopter that brings the new CO, will also take away the old CO, who will then be Court Martialed. In short, if you can't handle the stress of the job, stay home.

I love driving ships. On my duty days I would spend much of my free time reading every ship handling book in the Navigator's library. This greatly enhanced my skills as a Master Helmsman so that on the night that everything had to be perfect, I was ready.

It was the dark of the moon with a stiff wind from the North East as eighty-six thousand tons of aircraft carrier lined up to enter the channel through the Straits. Traffic was extremely heavy, and multiple civilian vessels were ignoring the traffic scheme, causing a hazard to all of the shipping. Once you're in the channel, you're committed. You can't turn around and you can't stop. Sometimes, you just have to dance with the devil and pray.

The situation on the bridge deteriorated steadily. I watched it happen and understood that the Conning Officer was in beyond his experience. The OOD relieved him, and as additional traffic started crossing in front of us, I saw the OOD loose his situational awareness.

It's not that those two fine officers were incompetent,

the amount of traffic and the general disregard of the rules that night would stress and overload any but the finest ship driver. Orders to the helm came fast and furious as we changed course to avoid one contact only to line up on another.

I watched the sail of a sailboat disappear from my line of sight beneath the flight deck at the same time as the CO barked, "This is the Captain! I have the conn! Right thirty degrees rudder."

"Now," I thought to myself. "Now, we're gonna dance."

In order to avoid the shipping in front of us, it would be necessary to turn the ship to the right. Unfortunately, this would send the stern of the ship to the left and sink the sailboat. Ships aren't like cars. The directional force in a car is applied from the front. On a ship, the directional force comes from the rear, or the stern. In order to turn the ship to the right, the stern swings to the left.

The CO had just ordered the ship to turn right. The resultant swing of the stern to the left would sink the sailboat, "Unless," I thought to myself, "the Skipper is going to pivot the ship around the sailboat." A ship when handled properly, will turn around a point at the middle of the ship lengthwise. It's not hard to get right, but when the lives of a smaller vessels crew depend on it, the sweat factor is unbelievable. I knew what he was going to do.

I answered up smartly "Right thirty degrees. Aye Sir!" It takes an incredibly long time for the rudders on an aircraft carrier to transit thirty degrees. At least it does when lives are at stake. I nailed that thirty degrees. It wasn't twenty-nine and a half, it wasn't thirty one, the rudders stopped at exactly thirty degrees. "Sir, my rudders are right thirty degrees." The next step I knew was to shift the rudder to left thirty degrees. I waited what seemed like forever for the next order. The Captain is responsible for his ship. He is also responsible for anyone killed or injured by the ships maneuvering. It was the Captain's responsibility. It was the Captain's call.

Finally, "Left thirty degrees rudder!"

As soon as the CO said left I turned that wheel as fast as I could, while answering up "Left thirty degrees. Aye Sir!"

The OOD barked to Boatswains Mate of the Watch, "Boats, I want to know when the aft lookout has that sailboat in sight. I want to know its condition!"

Another snappy, "Aye Aye, Sir." Boats sent the information over the sound powered phones.

Another eternity passed and Boats reported, "OOD. Aft lookout reports sailboat in sight to port. No apparent damage."

"Right fifteen degrees rudder." The CO ordered.

"Right fifteen degrees rudder, Aye sir." I said as calmly as I could.

There were no other close calls that night. And when the ship got into open waters in the Atlantic, I was relieved by the scheduled Helmsman. I took the chance to step into the chart room and light a cigarette. My best friend on the ship, Kevin, a fellow Master Helmsman, came into the chart house, very excited, and said, "Dude! I've never seen anybody drive like that! How did you do it?"

I took a drag on my cigarette and said calmly, "I just followed the Skippers lead." I hoped he didn't notice that my hand was still shaking ever-so-slightly. The Captain may be responsible, but my hands were on the wheel. And yes, I did take a second to silently thank God that no one got hurt. At that point, the CO's orderly, a young Marine, burst into the Chart House and said, "Man! You just got a Navy Achievement Medal! (NAM) The Skipper said he never saw anyone drive like that!"

I looked at Kevin and said, "Is there an echo in here?"

The Marine explained that the Captain had told the

OOD to write me up for a NAM. Some sailors take years to get a NAM. I just got one in one night.

Not a bad night's work.

DEPARTMENT OF THE NAVY
USS AMERICA (CV 66)
FPO NEW YORK 09531-2790

The Secretary of the Navy takes pleasure in presenting the NAVY ACHIEVEMENT MEDAL to

QUARTERMASTER SECOND CLASS
RONALD JUDE AUBREY
UNITED STATES NAVY

for service as set forth in the following

CITATION:

"For professional achievement in the superior performance of his duties while serving as Senior Master Helmsman, Navigation Department, in USS AMERICA (CV 66) on 28 August 1986. Petty Officer Aubrey's alert response and execution of a series of rapid helm commands were instrumental in averting a potential collision with a group of poorly lit and illegally placed fishing vessels while the USS AMERICA transited the restrictive waters of the Straits of Gibraltar. His cool, flawless, and precise application of difficult rudder movements were indicative of his superior helmsman ability and avoided a possible catastrophe. Petty Officer Aubrey's superior performance, attention to duty, and professional ability reflect great credit upon himself and the United States Naval Service."

For the Secretary of the Navy,

R. C. ALLEN
Captain, U.S. Navy

LIBYAN LINE OF DEATH

I started out on the Flight Deck of the USS America launching warplanes. A dangerous job but you get some fresh air. On the down side, you work long hours. If it's hot outside, you're hot, if it's cold outside, you're cold. In addition, it is greasy, dirty, nasty work. I felt like I could provide more to the Navy than just being a wrench turner on a catapult. Not saying anything bad about the guys who do this work, my hat is off to them. I worked my way up to the bridge by studying for, and passing the test for Quarter Master third class. I had eight hours every other day all to myself. My first love was being on the helm. After a while, you can feel the ship through your feet. The ship talks to you, and you talk back by tweaking the rudder just a little, or a lot, left or right. You can be told this, but it's not real till you drive that way.

There are two modes of ship driving. One is Open Ocean with no one around. The second mode of ship driving is close in to another ship, or in a restricted narrow body of water. To drive under more exacting conditions requires months of experience and training. This is where the Master Helmsman comes in. As the senior Master Helmsman, I was the most experienced and the most nuanced in my driving skills.

Coming alongside another ship for refueling, or resupply, is a touchy business. Two ships, one hundred twenty feet apart, doesn't leave a lot of room for error. Once while alongside an oiler taking on fuel, we found an offshoot of the gulfstream, (a powerful ocean current) that had not yet been charted. We managed an emergency break away without damage or injuries. We spent most of the rest of the night crossing and crossing again to chart this dangerous current, which information we sent to the National Oceanic and Atmospheric Administration, (NOAA) for inclusion in warnings and updates.

So we found ourselves off the Libyan coastline some two weeks after the Libyan dictator had taken credit for a bombing at a club which was known to be frequented by American service members. Three aircraft carrier battle groups had assembled in the Mediterranean for an Alpha Strike on the Libyan coastal cities.

My watch station was Quarter Master of the Watch. I was responsible for tracking the ships position. Upon being relieved that night, I quickly went to the ships store. I was low on smokes, and then returned to the bridge in order to watch the ordnance loading and launching of the strike aircraft. My friend and fellow Master Helmsman, Karl, was on watch as Quarter Master of the Watch. As the first A-6 bomber launched Karl looked at me and asked, "Dude, why aren't you driving? This is history!"

I pointed to the young seaman on the helm and said, "You see that guy driving? It's his moment in the spot light. Years from now he can tell his grandkids he drove for the bombing of Benghazi. Maybe he won't care. Either way, who am I to take that away from him?"

Kevin thought deeply for a moment and said, "I didn't think of it that way."

It was afternoon when the word came down; an Iranian launching platform deck (LPD) had been caught laying mines just outside of the Bahrain channel. Our mission was to intercept the lifeboat that the crew had jumped into when the shooting started and turn them over to a U.S. Navy ship for transport to the Red Crescent. The Red Crescent is the Muslim equivalent of the Red Cross. I was in the pilothouse navigating while the prisoner handling detail got briefed out on deck. The Commanding Officer of the detachment was Paul Evancoe, a Navy Seal; he was on our boat PB-758. Before we got to the life boat, Commander Evanco had us come alongside the Iran Ijar and he jumped over to the boarding ladder. We had no secure communications; we hadn't even been issued our crypto keys yet. But we did know there was a seal team onboard taking down the ship. It seemed incredibly dangerous to approach an armed and active seal team without prior warning, but that was the way the skipper lived—just grab it and go.

The prisoners we took turned out to be regular Navy, and did not seem to have an overwhelming desire to die for Allah. We would meet the Iranian Revolutionary Guard (IRG) later. The IRG is where they put the fanatics, and they were willing to die.

The Captain of the Iran Ajar turned out to be on our boat. He protested that we could not treat an officer of the Iranian Navy in such a fashion. The Boat Captain had someone put a sock in his mouth. No disrespect intended, just standard procedure.

OPERATIONS OFF THE SOMALI COAST

I saw fireworks and thought, "The last time I saw something like that, was off the coast of Somalia." For just a minute, I was there again, driving a landing craft off a hostile coast. I was in my element and quite happy.

The U.N. peace-keepers needed to evacuate from Mogadishu, Somalia. The U.N. had given up on that Godforsaken part of the world. The Marines went ashore to cover the peace-keeper's withdrawal. The Marines could cover their own withdrawal. We had everything for that op: Amphibious Assault Vehicles, Landing craft, attack helicopters and an Amphibious Ready Group to back it up.

My claim to fame was that the landing craft utility's (LCU) Quarter Master had broken his leg and they needed a replacement. My Chief, not much of a combat type, but he was great with the paper work, made it very clear that I didn't have to go. In my mind, I had small boat and weapons experience. I had an obligation to go. There was a bit of conflict between the LCU chief and my shipboard chief. The LCU chief finally told my chief, that I was with the LCU crew getting ready to go into harm's way, and that my chief should go back to the bridge and do some paper work— which was all he was good for. In the world of men, that is one heck of an insult.

Amphibious craft, full of Marines, hit the beach at the airport. This would be the security detail and last to leave. Marines then fanned out to the port and strategic positions to cover the retreating peace-keepers.

The LCU's crew and I spent the day readying weapons, loading magazines, and checking for proper operation. I pulled the speed loader out of the belt of M-16 ammo and fitted it to an empty magazine. M-16 ammo comes five rounds to a clip, the clip inserts into the speed loader. Then you just push all five rounds into the magazine at once. The LCU's gunner looked at me and said in awe, "What did you just do?" I explained the mechanics of the operation to him, thinking in my mind that he was testing me. It turned out, that I had more small arms experience that he did. After that, he just called me shooter. I have a coffee mug with that name on it. I consider it quite the compliment.

We pulled into Mogadishu harbor to load up with our

Marines. After several hours, and one sniper alert, yes I grabbed my M-16, we took the Marines back to the ship and got underway for further taskings.

The General in charge of the whole shooting match had been adamant about being in the last amphibious vehicle to leave the beach. When the general wants something, he gets it. Unfortunately for him, his amphibious craft took on water and sank. The General and crew got off the craft. All of this took place against the background of tracer fire going into and coming from the beach. At this point, we were out of range of the small arms the insurgents had. We found the General and crew and took them onboard. He did a very meaningful thing.

The first words out of his mouth were, "Do you have someplace my crew can get warm?" When the General asks, you answer quickly. We put the crew below decks in the galley. We gave them our extra blankets and all the coffee they could handle. That impressed me greatly. A General should take care of the men under him, but to see it happen, is beautiful.

The second thing the General asked was, if we had secure communications. I stepped out of the way so the General could get to the radios. For a few precious minutes, we were the General's flag ship; which was pretty cool. Then, we made the well deck of the amphibious ship we were attached to, and the General and his crew did a MacArthur and walked through the knee-high water to go back to work. We got back underway, and followed the battle group up the coastline.

SOMETHING IN THE WATER

Just another boring mid-afternoon on the Barge Hercules; do a little maintenance, throw a little football, duck as the two fighters blow by overhead at low altitude at high speed. The lead aircraft punched off his spare fuel tank to grab more speed.

What the heck!!

Iran and Iraq were at war: An Iranian fighter was chasing an Iraqi who had wandered into the wrong airspace. The barge had been at the same spot for so long, the Iraqi's had started using us as a turning point. The Barge was moved shortly after this and the Iraqis bombed their own Island by mistake.

We ate dinner early because the skipper wanted us to recover the fuel tank that the Iraqi had dropped. The Sun was low on the horizon when we got underway. We approached slowly and Vito called "All stop!" I was confused. Hooks were on deck attached to lines, everything was ready. Vito said, "I see something in the water near the

367

fuel tank."

I looked with the binoculars, "I got nothing." I reported.

Vito grabbed my arm and said, "Look closer. There is something in the water, and it looks just like a mine."

I smiled and said "Logging it!"

I knew the game now. Proper procedure for a mine at that time was to blow it out of the water. That was later changed to send EOD in with explosives to detonate it properly. It seemed that some of the mines fired on simply sank a few feet and exploded later. We backed off to six hundred meters—that was right out of the play book. I was on the radio and got permission to open fire on the "mine like object" The sun had set; we needed light.

"Lume!" Vito called. The guys fired the sixty mm mortar right up.

We had illumination flares hanging from their parachutes. Heck, I even fired a few from my M-79. The MK=19 grenade launcher and a couple of fifty cal's got in on the act. I even saw somebody grab an M-60 and start popping off bursts. It was great; we relieved a lot of stress. Finally, we reported area clear. The Barge inquired as to whether we had retrieved the fuel tank. We reported that it had taken collateral damage and was sunk.

All was nice and calm until we got alongside the Barge. We heard a familiar voice bellow, "Vitigliano!"

Vito quickly said, "Wheels. You and your log, with me."

I got to wait in the passageway outside the skipper's stateroom, while Vito went inside with the log. It was pretty muffled, but just at the end, I did hear the skipper yell, "Get out!"

Vito came out smiling.

It was a good day.

Paul Benjamin Earl Merk
US Army
SOLDIER UP!

If you are headed for Army boot camp, I strongly advise you not to go in the summertime. For one thing, it's hot, and for another you could die, like my nephew almost did.

This is Ben's story:

Soldier Up!

(Written by Ben Merk)

Well, let's see if I can remember the details…

I shipped out for Ft. Sill, Oklahoma just a couple months after my 20th birthday. I can't remember my exact MOS, but I think it was 25 Sierra. I had wanted to be in satellite communications, and thought, with an 85 or 87, whichever I got on the ASVAB, but alas, my engineering score on the test was just under par. Or so my recruiter told me. 25 Sierra was the next best thing; setting up satellite relay stations. Seemed like an exciting enough career, and was linked with SatCom, so I was sold on it. I think I shipped out around June 20th. I was headed to the armpit of hell for the summer.

My drill sergeants were Drill SGT Kempen, and Drill SGT Mills. My head Drill SGT was Drill SGT Kempen; he was about my height and Caucasian. Despite his physical size, his intensity always made him seem more imposing. He took nothing; and smoked us more than any drill sergeant smoked the other platoons, hands down. We were the 4th platoon Young Guns of the Delta Dogs Battery. And we were also the only platoon to get smoked the morning of BRM qualifications at the range in front of everyone else. Drill SGT Kempen definitely kept us humble and tired. Especially, considering the fact that if we tee'd him off on bivouac, he had no problem putting on on 50-50 fireguard rotations. He was perennially tee'd about having been pulled from teaching sniper school in Alaska, to teach a bunch of newbies how to stay alive.

Drill SGT Mills, on the other hand, was a much more physically-imposing man, but had a surprisingly gentle demeanor—until pushed. He was the good cop to Drill SGT Kempens bad cop. Standing about 6"2, or 6"3, and weighing in at what I would have had to figure at 240-260 pounds, of mean-looking black man. But, like I said, he was the nicer of the two; looks can be deceiving.

Both were excellent at what they did. I distinctly believe they held us to a higher standard than any of the other platoons in our battery.

As for memorable individuals, I'll start with the best and work down to the worst. If I'm starting with the best, I better reference my battle buddy, Trosclare. I remember little about him other than his goofy big-eared appearance—and his constant hilarity. He was lined up in the bunk across from me and that made him my battle buddy, according to the drill sergeants. He was the guy who had a lot of heart and a really hard head. He had no problem embarrassing himself, or in some cases, others, but mostly himself. He was never in peak fitness, but he, like me, tried to stay in the very middle of the pack; especially when it came to attracting the drill sergeant's attention. When it came to getting the platoon's attention, though, that was his specialty. He was the guy who took the $15.00 bet to smear icy-hot all over his privates. And that was just the kind of stuff he'd do; whether to get a laugh, get a buck, or just to get attention.

Then there was Baley. He was probably in his early 30's; had a wife and a couple of kids at home. He was a little more timid, but took things very seriously. Probably as he should have being the family-man he was. He was never the best, but he had a certain quality that made you begrudgingly accept that he was somehow in charge. It was that leadership-by-default thing, I think. By filling that role naturally, he stood out to the drill sergeants. Since he seemed to want to take the weight, they did make it official for some time, giving him temporary titile of platoon leader. He got some of the credit for our good behavior and caught the brunt of it when we were out of line. I hate to say it, but there were probably more than one occasion he rubbed the group the wrong way, and our behavior sank simply to see him forced to weather the storm of responsibility. Had we known who would eventually replace him as platoon leader, we probably would have acted right for him.

Which leads me to Private Bush. He was the worst of the best. An Arena League football player in his mid-20's, 26 if I remember correctly. He was chunky around the middle, but he was conditioned to keep up with just about any physical activity we were presented with. He was the jerk jock that most people hated in high school. He was more than happy to proclaim his greatness and his right to leadership, but very infrequently helped those in the platoon who needed a hand up. He was more of a push-you-down, kind of guy. Fourth Platoon was also the only platoon who, after a certain point in basic training, weren't allowed to have any of the sweets from the mess hall.

For most platoons, that started between two to four, needless to say, our drill sergeants were the no-frills kind of guys, so that wasn't the case for us. Eating any of the good stuff equaled one serious post-meal smoking. I mention that to reference that Bush was also the guy who ate three cakes every day after week three, for the simple sake of being a self-serving person. On another note, he had the highest pitched voice and was absolutely hilarious to listen to him holler, "Yes, Drill sergeant!" It was a tiny, little chipmunk voice. It was almost impossible to take him seriously. He also had a short-run as platoon leader, but his ego and arrogance lost him the position rather quickly.

There was a really good guy whose first name was Mark. I think he was the only person whose first name I actually knew. He didn't talk much; he was strong and had been a golden-gloves boxer in New York before joining the army. He did his thing and mostly kept to himself. We had a few conversations; some funny, some serious, but always good. I respected the fact that he could have bested almost anyone there, but he kept his ego in check. He took no stuff from anyone, and dealt none to anyone if he could help it. He also helped to encourage our weaker men in the platoon. He was just a really standup kind of guy. I was 20, and he was about 28. And he was the one guy I looked up to in the platoon. He had a short run as platoon leader, but saw it end quickly because he never had the desire to be the center of attention. No fault that I remember, simply no desire to be in charge.

Now we start the worst list: Of course all names are changed to protect everybody involved.

There was one, fat, egotistical, self-centered, brain-dead, ugly rat-of-a-man, who had come into training with a civilian nick-name of "Bull". This guy was a less-talented, less-gifted, less-capable version of Bush. Those two actually got into a fist fight once. My theory was there could only be one ignorant, self-absorbed, egotistical, incompetent rat-of-a-man at a time, trying to claim the reigns of leadership. Well, this same punching bag started to pick a fight with me. Or perhaps, I started to pick a fight with his whiny-loser self one night when we were making it back late from a bivouac.

We all had sand in our butts, and were pretty chaffed and tired. I remember the situation. He was griping and picking on one of our weaker privates, as he regularly did, being the bully that he was. It's always been my nature to stand up for those who have been picked on, so I started to insert myself into the confrontation. He wasn't exactly thrilled with that because I wasn't the type of guy you could bully. It led to a bit of a standoff. Finally, after a bit of verbal prodding, he pushed me.

I was about to raise him off the pavement when the aforementioned Mark, grabbed me from behind (I didn't know who had grabbed me at the time). As I was grabbed from behind, the spineless rat-of-a-man, sucker punched me in the face; and then stepped away as several people wrestled me to the ground. I fought until I found out it was Mark who had grabbed me.

After I calmed down, he explained that he grabbed me to keep me from injuring Bull; and in the process, hurting myself—and the platoon. Mark was wise, and I think he knew what I was capable of; which at the time, I truly didn't know myself. At the end of the day, Bull got the sucker punch, but I kept blood off my hands.

Let's see, our physically weakest private was Private Bells. I always felt so bad for him. He was just a weird guy who had no strength coming into bootcamp. I remember seeing him at the unit where they prepped us before sending us on to real basic training. He couldn't seem to stand still. They were always making him do pushups; which he wasn't capable of doing. And he was always misplacing his Army handbook; which was supposed to be on us at all times— which led to more pushups that he was incapable of doing. He wasn't a bad guy. He was just ill-prepared for the task at hand. He was the guy that bully-types flocked to; and the guy I always felt compelled to defend. He taught me a lesson though.

One time, the final time I tried to defend him, he actually turned on me in anger, because he had decided he wanted to fight his own battles—even if he knew he was going to lose them. He may have been the weirdest and the physically weakest, but whether he had it when he started, or developed it while he was there, he had strength of character. After that one instance, I respected him and let him alone to fight his own battles.

Last, but not least of our very worst, was the private I only remember as Craige. He was that guy that immediately struck a nerve with the drill sergeants; and he kept on their worst side throughout. He didn't do himself any favors by not shaving on a daily basis. He got smoked and pointed out more than anyone else, but mostly with good cause. I think it was two weeks into training before they took his rank. I think he was somehow coming in as PFC, and by the end of training, he was forced to start at the beginning of training with a rank of E1. He was the guy who would sneak down to the PX and purchase cigarettes, and dip logs to sell for quadruple the price to the other platoons. When Drill SGT Kempen found out, we all wanted to beat him to death; because we got smoked from midnight till 3:30 a.m. He was just a waste of space while there.

That's pretty much it for all the characters I found

memorable enough to be of mention.

As for me, I did my best to stay really middle of the pack. Although I was always the loudest when I came to yelling "Sir, Yes, Sir!" I guess despite everything I did manage to stand out, some. I was notorious for working with our weakest links to help pull them up. Some weak links liked being weak, and others genuinely appreciated the support.

I remember on our 5k march out to the BRM range, being at the very back of the pack in formation with Private Westley. He was another guy who just didn't have a lot of physical conditioning. And other than this instance, wasn't profoundly memorable.

Just behind us, were the 1st Lt. and a cadet recently out of West Point there for training. Behind them, was a transport vehicle; which I eventually figured out, was there for picking up all the privates who fell out on the march. It wasn't half-way into the trip when others started lagging behing. Westley included. Every time anyone would fall behing, I would run back to give words of encouragement; or tell them to hold onto my gear and I'd help drag them back to the pack. My being vocal about it, did lead to some of my other platoon mates to insist that I shut up. But I explained that no one in Delta Dogs battery should fall out on a 5k. And at the very least, 4th platoon Young Guns was gonna finish with every man that started.

They still weren't happy about it but I never shut up. And neither the CO, nor cadet ever said a word to me about shutting my mouth. I figured I was in good shape. Needless to say, you can't save everyone. People I tried to drag along fell out. But Private Westley dug deep within himself and found the courage and the will to continue.

4th Platoon Young Guns was the only platoon to finish with the same number as we started with; much to our drill sargeant's surprise. Weastley tried to thank me, but my only response was that I was simply the motivation and he was the motion. He had done all the hard work, and was much stronger than he had ever known. That was a really good day, and we got to start playing with M-16's, which made it even better.

There were a lot of fun times in basic training. There was our first big group activity; an obstacle course. Not everyone completed it; most caught up and fell during the rope crawl at the start. I remember being so nervous for this thing. Heights have never been my favorite by any means. I remember having difficulty, but making it through each and every obstacle until I finally reached the repelling station. Man, my confidence had been climbing and climbing with each obstacle, until, of course, I looked down that wall….

Well, drill sergeants have a great way of getting you motivated to do things you might otherwise avoid. Drill SGT Kempen said something like, "Merk, if you don't go now, I'm cutting this friggin rope!" –while I was hanging straight out over the ground. Yes. That got me moving with quickness.

I remember Drill SGT Mills passing out mail and laughing as he cracked jokes on different people; and how everyone couldn't wait to do the 25 pushups required per piece of mail you received. I also remember the deep sorrow when you seemed to go weeks without seeing a single bit of news from family or friends.

The gas chamber was one of those experiences you have to love the build-up for. I remember them having us all seated on the bleachers giving us all the warnings. They pulled an awesome joke that is probably done at every boot camp. It went something like this:

"Now privates, close your eyes because this next question is very important." He made an off-color remark that made everyone laugh, and broke tension. Everyone cracked up, and then the drill sergeants quieted us down, and he got really, really serious again.

"It is important you do well here, or this gas chamber could cause serious injury, or in some cases, even fatal."

I remember the burn of trying to scream "I want to be an Airborn Ranger, I want to lead a life of danger!" – ten times before our drill sergeant would let us try to start out of the room. I say try because as we were walking down the side wall, two drill sergeants kept jamming us against the walls and holding us back from getting to the door.

At about that point, I thought my throat was closing up from the gas, and I was so happy when we finally got outside. But my breathing didn't get any better in the seconds after I hit the door. It felt like I was being asphyxiated. I saw a drill sergeant and tried to explain I couldn't breathe at all. He started to examine me and then cracked up laughing as he pried the hands of the battle buddy behind me, off my collar, which he had grabbed instead of my shoulder. He had twisted it so tightly, I was actually being asphyxiated. Once he let go, oxygen came back; and the only pain I had left was my eyes, which stayed that way until long into the night.

I was there through the fourth of July. Because of that, we got a unique privilege not many others got; a chance to be a part of the crowd. Montgomery Gentry was playing that night on base. Those of us who were willing to lose the sleep, were allowed to take a long march to the concert. We ate and drank as we wished; as much soda and pizza as we could afford. I went, enjoyed myself, and had a mighty good time.

What most of us didn't think about, was that the next day was our Pre-PT test, to evaluate where we were at about week six. When we got in that night, rather late, they smoked us out in the commom area to the viewing pleasure of all the smart privates who'd stayed in that evening to be properly prepared for their PT tests.

I'm not gonna lie, it was worth every painful minute of that punishment to have that short period of freedom again. The next morning, I got up and kicked butt. I didn't score a 300 or anything, but I was pretty close to my personal best at pushups and situps; despite the late night and two tons of junk food I had eaten the night before. What I was really excited about was, that I did a two mile run in 14:28. A personal best for single mile time, let alone to be able to have paced a 7:14 mile for two in a row! I was proud and rather excited. Little did I know, that around a week and a half later, I would be finding out—I had a bad heart.

It was towards the end of basic training, probably week seven--or the middle of week seven—when we were coming back from a three-day bivouac. I was worn down, exhausted, my body was probably still recovering from a really bad case of laryngitis I had a few weeks before. Needless to say, I had been ground into dust at that point.

That night, we didn't get much sleep, or maybe it was just me. I don't remember getting smoked or having any problems, but I remember wearily pulling my fireguard shift and praying for my last hour of sleep to be very restful and regenerative.

That morning, we woke up for regular PT, and our ability group runs. I started the run and felt funny but kept on going.

On the return portion of the run, I thought it was funny that my left side was going numb. I was having real difficulty keeping my arm pumping in rhythm. Eventually I slowed down.

It's funny, but I kind of laughed to myself, about how I was probably having a heart attack. The idea of it seemed so absurd, considering everything I had done physically in training.

Well, it was the only run I ever fell out of and I think I had set an expectation for myself. I half-hobbled, half-jogged into the finish. The captain called me out for having fallen out. I tried to explain I had gone numb, and was still numb and having trouble breathing.

They weren't buying it and said, "Sprints, NOW!"

I'm kinda hard headed, so I started hobble-sprinting with my left arm limply flopping around back and forth until they said they's seen enough. Not long after that I explained to my drill sergeant what was going on, and they put me on a special solo trip to the medical center.

When I was finally seen, my blood pressure was still ridiculously high. I didn't know that at the time, because I had no idea what my blood pressure was supposed to be. I don't remember the exact numbers, but Mama could give them to you. I'm pretty sure she remembers. (220/120, heart rate 220—courtesy of Ben's Mama, typist).

That led to several days of continued testing at the actual hospital facility. I wore a heart monitor and some other fun stuff like that.

It was like three days after the initial heart trouble, we were waiting in lines to get our dress uniforms. I was going through line wondering if there was any point in my waiting in line at all. Apparently, Drill SGT Kempen was thinking the same thing. He was at the very end station and asked me why I looked so sad, and if I had been wasting his time.

I looked at him, and in my sadness, simply said what my blood pressure had been, and that I didn't know what it even meant. He pressed on and asked me if that was bad. I responded that I didn't know, but the doctors seemed to think it was. Apparently, he asked someone what that meant because he didn't say another thing to criticize me.

The last time I saw him, was just before I was going to

be sent to the injured unit. I waited outside the office, and when he walked out, I told him that I was sorry for having wasted his time.

It meant the world to me when he looked me in the eyes and said, "You didn't waste my time, private." He turned and walked away, and I went to begin packing my belongings; feeling just a little better about having failed everyone in the world.

The last time I saw Drill SGT Mills, was when he was transferring me to the injured unit itself. He took me up to the closet where we put all of our civilian belongings, eight weeks earlier. As we made the short journey, I explained that I was sorry for failing. But, that I was going to go home and get my health sorted out, go to college for a few years, and come back as an E4 specialist. I think he appreciated my enthusiasm because he smiled as I spoke about my desire to come back.

It was at that time he said something I never expected anyone to say to me, let alone an enlisted officer.

"Son, you did a good job. And if you ever come back, I strongly suggest you apply for officer candidacy school."

I was more than a little shocked, and even thinking about it now, I still can't believe he thought I had leadership quality. Those two small comments from both of my drill

386

sergeants helped soften the blow of failure.

It has taken years, and lots of love from family and friends to really dull the pain of bottoming out of basic training. But I know now, that God has had a plan all along. And now I'm working to bring those same skills to light in myself to brighten the lives of others.

I will never forget the things I learned, and the experiences I had in training. There are still times in my life today, when I am in the right mental condition, I tell myself to "Soldier Up!" – to accomplish things I have trouble believing I'm capable of.

Uncle Ron, thank you for having me write my story. I'm sure this is more than you were hoping for or expecting. But I wanted to share the mostly whole of my memorable experience at basic training. Feel free to use and discard as much as you see fit. This was the first time since training, I've put these thoughts and emotions down on paper. It was nice to pull them out of my brain and give them a tangible space in reality.

I love you very much and I appreciate your support for me after basic training. I'm proud of you for writing this book. I am much honored to think that you would want to put my story in as well. Sorry it took me so long to get it to you. And it was a little longer than I thought it was going to be. I look forward to seeing you again, soon.

Sincerely,
Your nephew,
Paul Benjamin Earl Merk

.Joshua Aubrey,
U.S. Marine Corps.

"For over 221 years our Corps has done two things for this great Nation. We make Marines, and we win battles."

General Charles C. Krulak, USMC (CMC)
5 May 1997

Joshua Daniel was born in Portsmith, Virginia.

So was his sister. The day she was born, he picked her up and held her in his arms. After all, no one had told him he couldn't. He has always been a very protective son; whether it's his sister, or his family, or his country. And he still is.

STORIES FROM HIS FATHER

When my son Joshua, left for Parris Island, we anxiously awaited for the first piece of mail from him so that we could begin sending letters. It is part of the Boot Camp program, that as soon as you class up, you are instructed to write your family and let them know you arrived safely. My experience at Great Lakes, Navy Boot Camp was a little odd. One of my fellow recruits had left home as a result of some problem and no one knew where he was. He had a private chat with the Company Commander, and was assigned other duties while the rest of us wrote home. Joshua's letter arrived about a week later. We were pleased to learn that Devin and I could send a small picture of the two of us. We quickly got that in the mail.

During Joshua's time at Parris Island, we had a little weather problem (first hurricane to visit Louisville, Kentucky, in fact, the region.) A wind storm had taken out the entire citie's electricity; and a month later, an ice storm—which did the same thing all over again. If everything else fails, the mail will get through. I had to hand write some, but kept the mail going.

Getting mail is a very big deal in Boot Camp. It helps to keep your spirits up, and reminds you that someone in the world still loves you. Along with each letter I wrote to Josh, I included a short story or poem with a military theme. He shared these writings with some of his fellow recruits; whom I had a chance to meet on graduation day. We had gone to the barracks to pick up Joshua's sea bag and hanging clothes bag, when I heard one of them ask, "Is this the story guy?" I was in shock that someone would refer to me in such a way. But also deeply gratified that I had made such an impression on people I didn't even know.

Josh said yes and introduced us. The two young freshly minted Marines, who happened to be African Americans, wanted to shake my hand and tell me how much they had enjoyed reading my writings. It seemed they approached Josh one day, had heard of the stories and poems, and wanted to read them. In boot camp, anything from the outside is a God send. I thanked them for their service. Devin and Ceara were with us at the time, and they were very impressed with the young Marine's manners.

Following Josh's successful graduation from Marine Corps boot camp, the prayer above was enscribed.

If my end should come tonight

Let it not be in coward's flight

But just like in an old time story

Cover me in blood and glory

HUH RAH!

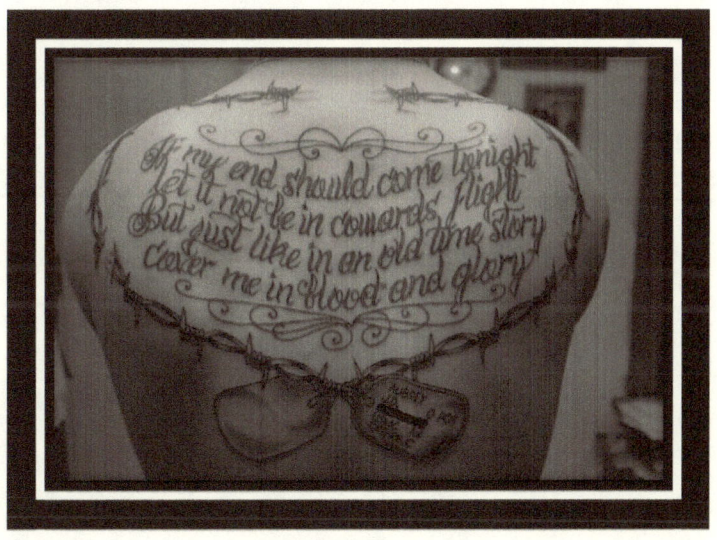

Bootcamp Stories

INTRODUCTION

The following stories are a compilation of short essays drafted and sent to Joshua Aubrey during his time in Marine Corps boot camp on Paris Island.

These stories were symbolic to help improve his morale and spiritual strength—coming through as a fifth generation warrior.

Understand your mission:

Don't die for your country-
Make the other poor bastard die for his!

WE SAVED THE WORLD

She was a world-class physicist. Weapons weren't even her specialty. She took the job at the weapon's research facility because it paid well. It turned out, she had a natural ability with firing sequence codes. The pinnacle of her career, was the night she broke the Russian nuclear weapons firing sequence codes. Actually, it was worthless information by itself, unless of course, you had a stolen Russian nuclear warhead that was already armed in front of you, which she had. It was going to go to Washington D.C., it was going to Tel Aviv. It didn't matter where it was going to go—all that mattered was that if it went off here, it would be seen as the U.S. government using a nuclear weapon against a peaceful people; and that would start a war that would never end.

They were a half-mile underground in an Islamic terrorist hide out. The way in was littered with dead bodies and empty M-16 magazines. She should be at the mall, shopping. The weapon was armed and counting down. There were dead Marines all along the route they had taken in. There were an even greater number of dead terrorists in various side tunnels.

She was in great shape. That was one of the reasons she was asked to go on this mission. She'd had her hair done last week; it needed to be done again, soon. There might not be a soon, if she couldn't stop the firing sequence, there might not be tomorrow for anyone.

Anywhere.

It wasn't her fault; she just went to work one day and this man was there. He lied about his name. She knew that now. Not that it did her any good in her current circumstances. He had talked about lives. He had talked about obligations, he had talked about country. If he had talked about duty and honor, she would have said no. She didn't know about such things then, but she did now. She had seen good men die for duty and honor, and it was all for nothing, because she couldn't stop the countdown. Someone better than her had found the code and changed it. In five minutes they would all be dead, because she couldn't do what they had died to bring her here for. The CIA agent, she, and a Marine were all that were left. She turned to the Marine and, said, "I can't stop it. I can't stop it."

The Marine was a man of few words. He simply said, "You really need to stop it now."

"I can't!" She screamed. "They changed the damn code! I could do it in a year. I could do it in a month, but I can't do it in five minutes!"

Then I'll do it in four minutes." The Marine said, as he slapped a device onto the warhead and flipped a switch.

"What the hell did you just do?" The CIA agent asked.

"That's five pounds of C-4. It goes off in four minutes." The Marine said. "If we're lucky it will blast the bomb apart and it won't go off. In any event, this whole cave system will come down on top of it. We should start running now."

A half-mile in four minutes, she could do. She had done it many times. Not after a forced march of twenty miles in two days. She hadn't done it after a death filled fire fight into a terrorist stronghold. She hadn't done it after the greatest single failure of her life.

"I can't," It was all she could say.

The Marine grabbed her by the shoulder and threw her towards the exit. "Move now!" He barked.

Something inside her responded to the tone of

command in his voice and she started to move, just not fast enough. The Marine butt-stroked her with the M-16. "Faster!" He yelled. She got a lot faster after that, because that is when the gunfire started.

Every cross tunnel they came to, gunfire erupted out of. She ran faster. The Marine and the CIA agent came behind her, firing as they ran.

On the best day of your life, you can run a half a mile in four minutes. On the worst day, you can do it in three-and-a-half. She ran faster. They shot more. The good part was, she forgot about the nuclear warhead behind her counting down to Armageddon. She forgot about the five pound of C-4. She forgot about anything but running for her life.

The detonation, when it came, dropped the mountain on top of the tunnels. It buried the radioactivity for ten thousand years. It erased any trace of the terrorist stronghold It erased any trace of their operation; but it didn't erase them. They made it out by a hundred yards.

"We did it!" She yelled, slightly delirious. "We did it! We did it!"

She looked at the Marine, "Now what do we do?"

"We walk back to the pick up point." He answered.

"I'm not walking back." She said calmly. The Marine had already started walking. She ran to catch up with him. "I want a helicopter." He didn't respond.

"I want an SUV or armored personnel thingy! I walked in, I am not walking out!"

The Marine stopped and looked at her, "Okay," He said. "Then you die out here. Nobody is coming here to get anybody."

It only took the government agents a couple of weeks to get her to agree to never talk about the operation. That, and a few million dollars they offered to put in her bank. Then of course, the threat of her spending the rest of her life at a safe, secure, undisclosed location, for the good of the country.

Funny thing, she thought, those government agents, the ones in the suits, the ones who had never worn camouflage, they never talked about duty or honor. Those were the reasons she finally agreed to stay silent. She learned those concepts from the Marines who fought and died that day. She learned that from the men she had looked down on when she first met them. She learned that from the men who died to save the world. She learned that from the men she would love for the rest of her life.

Every year after that, a black limousine pulled up to the gates at Arlington National Cemetery, and a woman walked the grounds, and prayed and wept.

Happy Veterans Day.

Happy Veterans Day to all of us who, at one time or another, saved the world.

OPERATION HERO FLIGHT

As a general rule, the cooler the operation's name, the more difficult the actual accomplishment of it would be. Some genius back at headquarters, had decided to call this one, "Operation Hero Flight." The Marines in the back of the C-130 had never done anything like this before, and they hoped to never have to do it again.

The aircraft hit the runway hard and fast. It was going to be a short landing. The co-pilot looked out the windshield, "There's a crowd just off the runway." He told the pilot.

"There's always a crowd." The pilot said as he clicked on the intercom to talk to the Marines in the back of the aircraft. "We've got company up here people. You might want to get your "A" game on."

As the C-130 approached the end of the tarmac, very close to the crowd of people, the two men in the cockpit could see many in the crowd had their fists in the air, and they were chanting. As the aircraft stopped just across from the crowd, separated only by a gate manned by two unarmed guards, the pilot began to turn the aircraft. "Ahead on Starboard engine, back on port, drop the cargo bay ramp. They want Marines, let's give them some."

In the back of the aircraft, the Gunnery Sergeant walked out onto the cargo ramp before it even hit the ground. He held onto a strap with his right hand and looked out at the crowd. He smiled. He looked back at his men. They had come a long way for this. As the engines throttled down, he raised his left hand, and just as the cargo ramp hit the ground he called, "Marines!" He brought his left hand straight out towards the crowd and watched as the men hit the deck at a jog.

The two guards suddenly opened the gates and ran for their lives. As the crowd surged forward, with the roar of the engines dying down, the Marines could hear the crowd chanting.

They were chanting, "USA! USA! USA!"

Then the Marines had something happen that hadn't happened during their entire year long mission. They were overrun.

They were hugged. They were back slapped. They were kissed.

They were home.

Still on the cargo ramp, the Gunnery Sergeant said quietly to himself, "Welcome home, men. Welcome home."